# Escaping into Nature

*For Carrie and Chris,*

*who have always made me proud to be their Dad.*

# Escaping into Nature

*The Making of a
Sportsman-Conservationist
and Environmental Historian*

JOHN F. REIGER

OREGON STATE UNIVERSITY PRESS • CORVALLIS

*Front cover photograph:* At three-and-a-half years old, the author fishing with a hand line from the stern of his father's boat along the South Shore of Long Island.
*Back cover photograph:* The author sitting on Miley Bull's duck boat in December 1976 after a hunt at the mouth of the Housatonic River.

The paper in this book meets the guidelines for permanence and durability of the Committee on Production Guidelines for Book Longevity of the Council on Library Resources and the minimum requirements of the American National Standard for Permanence of Paper for Printed Library Materials Z39.48-1984.

**Library of Congress Cataloging-in-Publication Data**
Reiger, John F.
  Escaping into nature : the making of a sportsman-conservationist and environmental historian / John F. Reiger.
      pages cm
  Includes bibliographical references and index.
  ISBN 978-0-87071-710-9 (alk. paper) -- ISBN 978-0-87071-711-6 (e-book)
1. Reiger, John F. 2. Wildlife conservationists--United States--Biography. 3. Fishers--United States--Biography. 4. Hunters--United States--Biography. I. Title.
  QL31.R44A3 2013
  639.9--dc23
                                                                        2012044613

First published in 2013 by Oregon State University Press
Printed in the United States of America

Oregon State University Press
121 The Valley Library
Corvallis OR 97331-4501
541-737-3166 • fax 541-737-3170
http://osupress.oregonstate.edu

# Contents

# Introduction

This is the story of how one person's love of the natural world evolved into a career as an active conservationist and environmental historian. The individual relating the narrative is probably not what many today would consider a typical "nature lover," for as an angler and hunter, I have been a hands-on, direct participant in the natural world my whole life. The traditions of the rod and the gun and the models of what I call "sportsmen-conservationists," like George Bird Grinnell, Theodore Roosevelt, and Aldo Leopold, have had a greater influence on me than those who demand that we humans, omnivorous predators though we may be, give up any desire we might possess to pursue and eat "game" wildlife, and remain instead simply onlookers of the nature around us.

What I had learned as a sport (recreational) fisherman and hunter in a series of "special places," retreats where I could escape the stresses of my life, *prepared* me intellectually for the ethical teachings of Aldo Leopold, the ecologist and philosopher whose writings I discovered as a college student in 1963. I have described some of my adventures in detail, because if I had not had my fishing and hunting experiences, I do not believe I would have been able to understand fully the meaning of Leopold's "land ethic," particularly that part of it that states: "A thing is right when it tends to preserve the integrity, stability, and beauty of the biotic community. It is wrong when it tends otherwise."

Unlike many others who have read this famous passage from *A Sand County Almanac* (1949), I understood immediately that unless the target species is a threatened one, hunting did not conflict with Leopold's prescribed code of behavior. In the case of some species, like invasive Eurasian starlings, or native white-tailed deer that have exceeded the carrying capacity of their habitat, the removal of individual animals

1

can actually improve "the integrity, stability, and beauty of the biotic community." In any event, it is not the individuals that should concern us, but the preservation, and restoration when possible, of whole ecosystems.

While Aldo Leopold's philosophy was pivotal in forming my worldview, it was the activism of George Bird Grinnell and Theodore Roosevelt, who I discovered while researching my doctoral dissertation, that inspired me to leave the security of a tenured professorship and engage in full-time conservation work as executive director of the Connecticut Audubon Society. How my commitment to the conservation of wildlife—the preservation and management of both game and nongame, and the habitats upon which it depends—evolved over time represents a large portion of this autobiography.

Along with nature, a love of history has also been at the center of my life from early childhood. The two in fact are interrelated, because I have always felt cheated that I was not able to see the natural world in America before it had been transformed by Europeans and their descendants. I am aware, of course, that it was never "virginal," because Native peoples had made their mark on the land long before Columbus arrived in the New World. Still, their destructive impact paled in comparison to what came later, particularly in the nineteenth century when the forces of unfettered capitalism and industrialization combined to wipe out perhaps the most abundant avian form of life ever to have lived on the planet, the passenger pigeon, and came precariously close to doing the same thing to the bison, whose numbers in 1492 may have been in the tens of millions.

My desire to understand why and how this destruction of the continent's wildlife took place, and who it was that began the movement to stop it, played a large role in my choice of a subject for a history doctoral dissertation, as well as in my later scholarship as an academic. My experiences on the way to becoming a teacher-scholar and environmental historian represent another large part of this book.

Perhaps the biggest challenge I faced in recording my memories was deciding what to include and what to leave out. As the reader will discover, I have given a great deal of coverage to my childhood, probably more than is found in most autobiographies. More common, I think, is the approach of explorer Roy Chapman Andrews, who, at the beginning of his *Under a Lucky Star: A Lifetime of Adventure* (1943), wrote: "Of my early days there will be just enough to give a background for what follows ... As a rule, nothing of much interest happens to a young man until he is out of college." Unlike Andrews and other authors of autobiographies I have read, I know that a detailed analysis of childhood experiences is key to understanding who and what we become. In my own case, this basic tenet of the discipline of psychology may be even more true, since it was in my boyhood that I developed my love for nature and history, the two central components of my orientation to the world.

In relating my memories, at whatever age, I have been surprised by how vivid many of them are, even after the passage of decades. Some, in fact, were difficult to record, because they affected me emotionally, even bringing tears to my eyes. Human memory is an amazing power, but it is always a two-edged sword, for we remember the bad just as intensely, and maybe more so, than the good.

This unfortunate reality seemed to be particularly true when recalling my interactions with the male members of my original family. Though I made peace with my abusive father before he died, I have never been able to build a close bond with either of my two older brothers. Even after Tony, the oldest, achieved success as a high-school teacher and guidance counselor and my middle brother George became nationally known for publishing books on fishing and hunting and writing an op-ed column for *Field & Stream* magazine on conservation issues, my relationship with them never improved, remaining today just as fraught with tension and the determination to dominate and disparage as it had been when we were children.

My response to the continuous stress caused by this unhappy situation is an undercurrent theme of this autobiography. I had to discover my own path away from the family, and it was only by escaping into nature that I could obtain the peace and harmony I sought.

Before starting into this book, the reader should know that everything in it I believe to be the truth. I am not claiming, of course, that I am infallible in my ability to remember the details of events from many years in the past, but only that I have made an honest effort to present them just as I recall them; there has been no embellishment of my memories to make them more dramatic or exciting. To do otherwise would be to break what I consider to be the sacred contract I have with all readers of my work that what is contained here is historically factual and not fiction masquerading as nonfiction.

Finally, I should say something about how the project of writing my autobiography began. The idea did not originate with me, but with Mary Elizabeth Braun, the acquisitions editor of Oregon State University Press, who approached me with the proposal in 2007. As Mary knows, I was hesitant at first, but at last decided that my experiences might, after all, be worth recording. What I thought would be a relatively easy task, taking no more than a couple of years, has turned out to be far harder than I imagined, and it was 2012 before I finally finished the book. After reading it, I hope that most people will think Mary's idea was a good one.

# CHAPTER ONE

# Discovering Nature:
## *New York City, 1950-1951*

First, there was the insect world. Almost from the time I could walk, I found these tiny beings fascinating. Perhaps it was the variety of their forms and often brilliant colors, and the ability of many of them to fly away, or maybe it was the possibility of hunting and capturing them for close examination, two urges that I have always possessed and which I have never tried to suppress. To have done otherwise would have made me feel like a mere spectator looking in at nature rather than being a "player" on the field.

Insects seemed to occupy a parallel universe, one that I could enter at will by walking, or even crawling, through the thick, high weeds in a vacant lot near our home at 135 Puritan Avenue in Forest Hills Gardens, in the borough of Queens, New York City. That vacant lot was my first special place, where I could escape the many anxieties of my young life.

Almost eyeball to eyeball with grasshoppers, katydids, stink bugs, and a host of others, I quickly learned that some species could be caught easily, while others were more elusive, and that when I was sitting perfectly still at the edge of an opening near flowering plants, even wary butterflies treated me as just another part of the landscape. Although I didn't know it then, I was already learning to be a hunter, and after I acquired this ability to "freeze" at a moment's notice until the prey was in range, I used it in the coming years to bag countless "game," like a butterfly winging its way toward me along a line of bushes, a duck circling over my decoys, or an old gobbler moving slowly up a hillside in my direction, warily searching for the hen my friend's calling has told him should be somewhere nearby. In such circumstances, the best camouflage clothing in the world will not hide you if you move.

Even though the vacant lot that became my first special place was officially part of New York City, a human-made environment that would seem to be a hostile and dangerous place for a child of seven, the lot was part of a green oasis in the middle of that rapidly growing metropolis. The Forest Hills Gardens suburb had been the creation, in the early twentieth century, of the son of famed landscape architect, Frederick Law Olmsted, who had designed, among many great projects, Manhattan Island's Central Park. The son, Frederick Law Olmsted, Jr., was an eminent landscape architect in his own right. It was he who used many of the same techniques his father had perfected to lay out a "garden suburb" of 142 acres, modeled on a traditional English village, that seemed to embrace the natural world instead of dominating it. Unlike so many suburban developments today that are devoid of sidewalks, forcing pedestrians out into the street, "the Gardens" has sidewalks everywhere. By 1950, when I was seven years old, pathways had large oaks or elms extending out over them, and as the seasons changed, I never lost my enthusiasm for exploring, and re-exploring, every corner of my neighborhood. In the warmer months, particularly inviting were the side streets and cul-de-sacs that had European-style courtyards and individual gardens with flowers so luxuriant, colorful, and pungent that they often attracted large numbers of butterflies. The sight of these insects often compelled me to trespass by going through a wooden gate or even climbing over a low brick wall to get a closer look.

My family had moved to the Gardens in October 1945, after my father, a medical doctor, had left the army. He had been stationed in Georgia and Florida during World War II, where he probably did the best work of his career treating returning soldiers who had lost limbs in combat, which is the reason I was born in Augusta in an army hospital on June 10, 1943.

The view that many parents had in that period after World War II that children, even very young ones, should "go outside and play" was one that my mother accepted without question. After all, she had been told by her own mother to do the very same thing when she was a child.

Before my grandfather, George Washington Dance, a tobacco farmer in south-central Virginia, contracted tuberculosis, my mother, Sally, had many happy hours playing outdoors by herself, as she didn't seem to get along well with her older brother and sister. But after her father could no longer work, and the family fell on hard times, the tensions between her and her siblings, particularly her sister, intensified. Finally, the financial situation became so dire that her mother felt that she could no longer afford to care for all three children, and she decided to "farm out" Sally, as she later put it, to a wealthy relative. His children never let my mother forget that she was the "poor relation," and they picked on her unmercifully. Near the end of her life, she once told me how they would often hide her shoes so that she had to walk to the one-room schoolhouse in bare feet, and always far behind them on the dirt road, in order to show off their superior social status.

Mother spent a lifetime trying to get that status back. She began by leaving the little town of South Boston behind and going to the capital, Richmond, where she successfully completed a registered nurse program. Then, with what was probably a conscious desire to escape the bad memories of her Southern childhood, she boarded a train for New York City to begin life over again in the great metropolis. There, she fell in love with another highly ambitious individual, my father, Anthony Cutte Reiger.

But while my mother's chief goal in life seems to have been the acquisition of the high social standing she never had as a child or young woman, my father's goal was less complicated. He wanted "success," defined in the usual American way as the accumulation of wealth. In the late 1920s and early '30s, apparently one did not need a bachelor of science degree before going on to become a physician, and after attending Columbia University for only two years, Dad entered medical school and "became a doctor at the age of twenty-one." I never asked him exactly what that meant. Was he only twenty-one when he graduated from medical school, or when he passed the licensing examination, or when he actually started his general practice? In any case, he never tired of citing this impressive accomplishment, especially when any of his three sons had an accomplishment of their own. Until the end of his life, even after he had mellowed considerably, my father enjoyed competing with us, and nothing we could do could ever match his success, either as a brilliant physician, able to diagnose maladies that had baffled other doctors, or as a money-maker, who was so successful that he was able to retire in his late forties and travel the world.

My parents constantly fought with each other and often seemed to regard their children as if they were burdensome responsibilities, to be ignored when possible or to be handed over at a young age to strangers and institutions for upbringing and guidance (i.e., summer camps and boarding school). What I interpreted as their unloving behavior made me feel rejected and anxious from very early in life and led me to seek my own way outside the family. But, ironically, their poor parenting, at least by today's standards, had a profound and beneficial result, one that would last a lifetime. By escaping into nature in a series of special places, beginning with that vacant lot near our home, I found the constancy, peace, beauty, and spirituality that I never experienced within the family.

The stresses that fueled my need to find special places did not simply spring from my poor relationship with my parents. Some of them were the result of having two older, domineering brothers, Anthony ("Tony") Elton, the oldest, and George Wesley. With just the right spread of years between them and me, seven and four respectively, I would forever be the "little brother," to be dominated when necessary and taken advantage of when possible. Because Tony was so much older, there was far less interaction between the two of us than between George and myself. But even with George, the interaction occurred mainly during school vacations, for he had already been packed off to Lawrenceville, a boarding school in Lawrenceville, New Jersey, for nine months of the year by the time I was seven.

George, then, was a much larger part of my life than Tony, and from the beginning, I have always felt that he has had the need to be in complete control of every situation in which we were both involved. Although he had no real curiosity about insects, he soon became concerned that here was an interest that I might be able to develop on my own, without his direction. Of course, the more he wanted to exercise power over me, the more I wanted to be free to pursue my avocation on my own. Whether my father knew what was going on or not I'm not sure, but he decided to support me in my desire to learn everything I could about the insect world. It turns out that Dad had collected butterflies and moths as a child, and, perhaps, he felt as if he could relive some of those childhood experiences through his youngest son. Whatever the reason, he began now to encourage me to move beyond my primitive approach to insect study. It was one of the few times in my life when he expressed genuine enthusiasm for an interest of mine, without any need to compete with me.

On my earliest expeditions to the vacant lot, I had gone with no collecting equipment at all. Instead, I simply caught in my hands whatever I could catch, and after examining them at close range, without squeezing them, I let them go. Even after all these years, I can remember the sight of the brown fluid grasshoppers often expelled into my hand and on my fingers in an effort to escape. Later, I learned that this "tobacco juice," as I called it, was from the grasshopper's crop and that it was a defensive regurgitation of undigested food.

In order to study insects systematically, I needed to collect them, and my father suggested that I bring a large glass jar with me to the vacant lot in which to put my "little friends," as he humorously called them. I don't remember him actually going with me to the lot, but I do recall the importance he placed on my punching holes in the metal, screw-on top on the jar to let in air for my captives, which continued mainly to be grasshoppers. I also learned that I had to provide some plant food for them, as well as sprinkle a few drops of water into the jar, if I expected the insects to live for even a few days.

Soon, Dad decided that it was time for me to move into the big leagues of collecting and to become an accomplished butterfly hunter. It was then that I received one of the great presents of my boyhood, a large, wide-mouthed butterfly net. It had a strong handle made of hickory or ash, about four feet long, that could be detached from the circular metal net ring, and a deep, green, soft, nylon mesh "bag" extending far enough back from the mouth of the net to keep butterflies trapped in the back of the bag once the net quickly closed over them. My father purchased this beautiful object for me at a biological supply store just on the other side of the East River in Manhattan.

What a fascinating place it was. Everywhere I looked were sights that drew me closer, like mounted birds and animals and glass display cases filled with exotic butterflies and moths. The store was like a tiny natural history museum. High on the wall to my right as we entered the store, I noticed a giant moth mounted in a small, glass-topped, black Riker display case that the store's owner said was an *Attacus atlas* from India, one of the biggest insects in the world. It was the larger female of the species, with a wingspan of over eight and one-half inches and a length, top to bottom, of almost six inches. He also told us that the "natives" of India considered its body to be a delicacy and that it belonged to the same family of "giant night fliers" as the North American cecropia (*Hyalophora cecropia*), polyphemus (*Antheraea polyphemus*), and luna (*Actias luna*) moths.[1] If we purchased it, he warned, we should make sure to keep it out of direct sunlight to preserve its beautiful soft colors of yellow and brown.

As if we wouldn't purchase it! My pleading became too much for my father, and I brought it home, to be treasured to this day. Unlike the butterflies and moths in the display case my father had collected about 1920 when he was a boy growing up in Brooklyn, my atlas moth never had direct sunlight on it, and is probably almost as bright and beautiful now as the first moment I saw it all those decades ago.

The impact this magnificent insect had on me is hard to exaggerate. First, it made me feel as if nothing in the world could be any more resplendent than some butterflies and moths, a sentiment I still hold today. Second, it inspired me to go out with my new butterfly net and start collecting butterflies and moths equal in beauty, if not in size, to the atlas. Unlike those in Dad's exhibit case, I wanted to obtain insects that were fresh and which I could preserve in their full loveliness for all time.

The third sentiment the atlas moth engendered in me was a desire to travel to distant lands like India and see, in the wild, exquisite large moths and butterflies for myself. Though I have never gotten to southern Asia, I have seen the giants of the butterfly world, the dazzling blue morphos and owl butterflies (*Caligo*) as they flew in and out of the sunlight along the heavily wooded banks of a stream near the Pacific coast of Costa Rica and along a tributary of the Amazon River in Ecuador. On both occasions, their appearance thrilled me and made me think of my atlas moth, which still hangs in a secluded corner of my house.

After getting the new butterfly net back home that evening, I could hardly wait to visit my vacant lot and see what beauties I could catch. That night I barely slept, so filled was I with anticipation of the chance to capture a host of butterfly species. The next morning was a Saturday, and without even waiting for breakfast, I sallied forth, walking as fast as I could toward my special place. As I got close to it, I saw trucks and some kind of heavy equipment, probably a bulldozer, sitting on the sidewalk where I entered the lot. Because there were no people around, I at first thought that the presence of these machines posed no particular problem for me. My only concern was that if their owners were there, they might ask me to leave. Then, as I made my way between and past the trucks, I saw what had been done to my special place. That lot, with all its thick jungle of beautiful weeds, bushes, and small trees, had been completely cleared, and my little world and all its ecological interconnections were gone forever.

In the weeks to come, I returned to the lot many times and stood on the sidewalk, dejected and resentful, as the house went up. Somehow, I seemed to think that a miracle might take place, and that the owner might change his or her mind and return the lot to what we would later call "open space." But, of course, no such miracle occurred, and I watched helplessly as landscapers put in a token tree or two and a lawn that seemed to attract neither insects nor birds, with robins the only exception.

It was probably at that time that I first came to hate lawns. All they do is to replace ecological complexity with a sterile monoculture. What I learned later was that they are, in fact, barren wastelands that only support a handful of insects that the "lawn-care" industry will tell you must be killed at all costs. With all the chemicals that people dump on their lawns, much of which runs off into streams or percolates down into groundwater, we have created a monster in this country that seemingly can't be controlled. Though most Americans think of fertilizer as being nontoxic, it is a major contributing factor to "red tides" in coastal areas, which cause massive die-offs of marine life.

Even though it took many years to develop my philosophy regarding lawns, I know that my strong negative opinions about them began to form with the loss of my first special place. After a period of mourning for the vacant lot, I finally came to accept the fact that it was gone, and never coming back. I had to find a new special place, or maybe more than one, because I could never be sure again that another of my precious natural spaces would be safe from the same impersonal, all-powerful forces that had destroyed the first one. In the years to come, many such retreats would be taken from me by an economic system that encourages Americans to view nature as nothing more than a commodity that can be bought and sold as a way to achieve personal wealth, what we invariably mean by "success."

It was at this time, when I was eager to find a new special place rich in butterfly-collecting opportunities, that I heard the frightening news that the family was going to South Florida and that I should get ready for the move. We first relocated to a cramped apartment out of the Gardens along busy Queens Boulevard, several miles closer to Manhattan. There we waited to hear that the house in Forest Hills had been sold and that the new one being built in Florida was habitable. Though I lived in the apartment for an unremembered number of months, I was kept inside most of the time because my mother deemed the area unsafe, and I was, therefore, unable to look for new special places. I remained in a state of suspended animation, waiting for the great change. It seemed that my life was about to be turned upside down, and I was right.

# CHAPTER TWO

# Entering a Saltwater Universe:
## *South Florida, 1951-1952*

In May 1951, when I was not quite eight years old, we left New York City, presumably for good, and moved into our nearly completed home on East Broadview Drive in the Bay Harbor Islands near North Miami, on the southeastern coast of Florida. The community had been the brainchild of Belarusian immigrant Shepard Broad, who came to America in 1920 at the age of fourteen. After becoming a wealthy attorney in New York City, he moved to South Florida in 1940, and five years later, he acquired the two undeveloped, mangrove "swamp islands" that would become the Bay Harbor Islands. With no environmental laws to control him, he had the mangrove forests cut down and mud flats filled in, and the biologically rich shoreline, with thousands of arching prop roots of mangrove trees, replaced with sterile, concrete sea walls.

In the 1970s, when I was a history professor at the University of Miami in Coral Gables, I became fascinated with the pre-Columbian Indians, whose village sites were, or had been, in the area, and I wondered what irreplaceable archaeological information had been destroyed with Broad's huge dredge-and-fill operation. Of course, I also wondered if our house had been near, or even on top of, one of those sites.

In 1947 the town of Bay Harbor Islands was incorporated, with 103 acres on West Island and 150 acres on East Island. During the next four years, the community would grow to over five hundred people, including the Reiger family. Our house was on the water on West Island, in the northeastern corner, near the mouth of where our canal opened out into Biscayne Bay.

My new world of subtropical nature couldn't have been more different from the one I left behind in New York City. After crossing the bridge over our canal for the first time, and driving up East Broadview Drive toward our house, what I noticed immediately were all the strange trees and bushes growing along the road in the many vacant lots and on the front lawns of the houses that had already been completed. This was my first experience with native cabbage palms, saw-palmettos, seagrape trees, and slash pines, as well as introduced Australian pines (*Casuarina equisitifolia*), which are not pines at all but true flowering plants.

Because my first "special place" had been a vacant lot and because the only "natural" areas on my new island were these, as yet, undeveloped house sites, I was eager to explore them. The day after we moved in, I received permission to venture out of the house, and immediately went to the nearest lot and penetrated the saw-palmetto thicket that covered most of it. The movement that first caught my eye was a green anole lizard (*Anolis carolinensis*) about six inches long running along a branch. There was nothing like this back in New York City! I soon discovered that these small green, but sometimes brown, reptiles were ubiquitous on my island. Sometimes, one would manage to get inside our house, and I remember the first one we discovered after switching on a light. It was clinging sideways to a wall, after having turned a ghostly white that made my mother gasp in horror. Like African chameleons, anoles change color in response to changes in light and temperature, and perhaps even whether they are frightened or at ease.

Penetrating deeper into the saw-palmettos that covered most of the vacant lot, I flushed a bobwhite quail, the first one I had ever seen. When we first came to the island in the spring of 1951, we found these fast-flying little game birds to be quite common. Walking or driving around the neighborhood, we would often see a pair or even an entire covey run out of a thicket on one side of the road and duck into cover on the other side. Often, when I spied bobwhites crossing a road, I followed them into a saw-palmetto thicket to see if I could flush them. Sometimes I did, but it was surprising how many times they seemed to disappear into thin air, apparently running ahead of me and then circling back. When I was successful in getting them to fly, I enjoyed hearing the whirring of their wings as they sped away. After a little practice, I also became proficient at imitating their *bob-bob-white* whistle, and it was always fun to receive an answer back.

But very quickly, the quail population on our island began to decline as one vacant lot after another had its vegetation cleared away, to be replaced by a house and the sterile lawn. It was my first real experience with what habitat loss on a large scale meant for the wildlife that depended on it. This was not the clearing of a single vacant lot like my first special place back in Forest Hills, but rather the ecological degradation of an entire 103-acre island. As the months went by, I saw fewer and fewer quail. By the time my family moved back to Forest Hills in November of 1952, I saw none at all, and my *bob-bob-white* whistles received no replies. Because the sight and sound of "my" quail delighted me, I mourned their loss and never forgot the lesson they taught me—that nothing will make wildlife disappear quicker than the destruction of their homes, their habitats, and we should do everything we can to stop, or at least mitigate, that process.

When I first arrived in South Florida, I not only discovered exotic-looking subtropical trees, interesting anoles, and endearing bobwhite quail, but new, strikingly beautiful, butterflies like the orange barred sulphur (*Phoebis philea*) and the zebra (*Heliconius charitonius*). And while I originally intended to do the butterfly collecting that was interrupted by our move to the Sunshine State, I quickly found myself pushing this interest aside in favor of another pursuit, one as old as our species. For the chief lure of my new island home was not the land, but the water, more specifically the canal that ran behind our house, and the bay and ocean beyond. I became a fisherman, or more accurately a fisherboy, and my new special place was the concrete sea wall that kept our large backyard lawn from washing away when storms drove high waves against it, as well as the small adjoining dock where we tied up our boats.

Before coming to Florida, I had gone fishing many times with my father and brothers on the bays of Long Island's South Shore and even in the ocean. But because my father didn't trust me with a rod and reel, which I guess he thought I might drop overboard, I often just watched the proceedings and didn't fish myself. An exception might occur when we were after relatively small bottom-feeding species like flounder (*Pseudopleuronectes americanus*) and fluke (*Paralichthys lethostigma*) that could be taken on a hand line. Though this type of angling could be enjoyable, it would not compare to the excitement and personal satisfaction I was to experience in my fishing along our sea wall. I would now be able to go after the denizens of the saltwater universe at my doorstep without supervision or interference from the older male family members, and every success or failure in that pursuit would be mine, and mine alone.

Every incoming tide brought clean ocean water through nearby Baker's Haulover Inlet into the bay and then into our canal. And when the tidal flow reversed course and began to drop away, the many fishes that had come in with the high water now began hurrying out again, often right past our sea wall. Because the Bay Harbor Islands and surrounding area had not yet been completely developed, there was little pollution run-off from streets, and the water in our canal remained quite clean the whole time we lived on the island. But what was most striking about it was how clear it was much of the time, especially on an incoming tide. I never tired of "walking the wall," as Mother called it, peering down into the water and seeing all the way to the marl and mud bottom. The excitement of walking the wall and around the edges of our dock came from the knowledge that I never knew what fish species I would see—and perhaps capture.

Early in my time on the island, I managed to persuade my mother to take me to a fishing-tackle store and buy a gig for me. Because my brothers were away at boarding school or summer camp for most of the year and my father was back in New York trying to sell his medical practice in order to reestablish himself in Florida, and only in "the Islands" on occasional weekends, it was just my mother and me most of the time. I'm not sure how I learned about these fish spears, but I seemed to understand quickly that unless I had one, and learned how to use it, I would have little chance of capturing any of the many fishes that swam below me as I stood above them on the wall. As in the case of the insects in my first special place, the vacant lot, I wasn't interested in simply being a spectator *to* nature—I wanted to be *in* nature. Passively looking at the many varieties of fishes as they swam below me was hardly enough. I needed to catch them to identify the various species, to see their often brilliant colors up close, and to examine the differences in teeth, fins, etc.

Going to that fishing-tackle store in downtown Miami was an experience something akin to the earlier trip I had taken with my father into Manhattan to buy my butterfly net. Like the large biological supply store, the tackle emporium also had mounted specimens on the walls, only these were various species of game fish instead of cases of insects. It was the first time I had seen a big tarpon and sailfish up close, and their beauty dazzled me. The tarpon was probably about six feet long, with a dark blue back and bright silver sides and belly. With its long, slender spear jutting out from its head, the sailfish was probably about a foot longer than the tarpon, and it also had a dark blue back, but with amber sides fading to white on the belly. What struck me, of course, was its gigantic, deep blue dorsal fin that rose above the fish like a sail and which gave it an appearance like nothing else that swims in the ocean. I remember hoping that I would have a chance one day to catch a magnificent tarpon and sailfish like those staring down on me.

16

Though I could have spent much more time looking at the many game fish mounts in the tackle store, I was eager to get my hands on a gig and try it out. I don't recall anything about our conversation with the sales clerk, but whatever we said, it did the trick, for I brought home exactly what I wanted. Unlike the smaller and narrower gigs with three relatively thin barbed prongs used in South Florida at that time for spearing bullfrogs for their tasty legs, my gig had four, heavy steel, widely spaced, barbed prongs coming off a thick main shaft. Into its deep, hollowed-out base fit one end of the wooden gig pole, cut and smoothed in such a way that it fit snugly into the shaft, and held in place with a large, stainless steel screw. Near the other end of the stout hickory or ash pole, about seven feet in length, was a hole through which I tied one end of a long length of super-strong, nylon parachute cord. The other end of the line I tied around my left wrist while I threw the gig with my right hand.

After I got it home, I experienced the same kind of excitement I had felt earlier when I could hardly wait for the dawn to break so that I could try out my new butterfly net. Now, it would be my challenge to see if I could hurl this new collecting tool with enough force and accuracy to hit and hold even the largest fishes as they swam, often with great speed, below me. I soon discovered that throwing a gig with precision was difficult. But as in any test of skill, practice makes perfect, or at least pretty good.

That practice took place almost every morning, even on school days. By far, the most common fish species I met on my walks up and down our sea wall were mullet (*Mugilidae*). Torpedo-shaped, with silvery sides, and usually not much over a foot in length, these bottom feeders would grub on the bottom for algae and detritus.

Sometimes, however, they would come closer to the surface and gather together in great schools extending almost across the width of the canal. But the largest congregation I ever saw was so awe-inspiring that it seems almost like a dream today. One day, as Mother was driving back home over the high Baker's Haulover Inlet bridge, we came to a traffic jam in the middle of the span caused by people who had stopped their cars and gotten out, and were looking down into the water. Naturally, we joined the crowd to see what was so interesting that it had stopped traffic in both directions.

What a sight! Up Biscayne Bay to the west, as far as I could see, there was one tightly packed, seemingly endless school of mullet, perhaps a football field in width, up on the surface approaching the bridge. It was as if every mullet in every creek, river, and canal leading into the upper bay had come together to form this throng that contained so many individuals that I remember thinking at the time I must be looking at a million fish. Whatever the real number, it was one of those occasions in my life when I have seen such a multitude of a particular wildlife species—other examples are greater scaup ducks on Long Island and wildebeest in Kenya—that I felt spiritually uplifted and very lucky that their lives intersected with mine at that precise moment in time. While I hoped to stay and watch the mullet, my mother wanted to get home, and the police soon arrived to force us back into our cars and unjam the traffic on the bridge.

Because of the relatively narrow width of our canal, the schools of mullet that came within reach of my gig were, of course, much smaller than the throng I had seen from the inlet bridge, but on a few occasions, their masses did stretch almost all the way across to the opposite sea wall. At such times, they would be pursued by predatory game fish like snook and tarpon and especially the jack crevalle (*Caranx hippos*). While the first two species were present off my sea wall, I had no direct contact with them in my year and a half on West Island. Jack crevalles, however, were a different story, for I had many encounters with them that developed into a respect for their energy, speed, and power. Whether gigged or hooked on a fishing line, they displayed a bull-dogged determination to fight to the very end.

To me, the crevalle's appearance seemed to reveal its disposition as an aggressive predator. Bluish-black above and silvery or yellowish below, it has an extra-large forked tail that exudes power, a high, blunt head, with intelligent, but somewhat mean-looking eyes, and a determined jaw that gives it an almost sinister look. Countless mullet that came into our canal discovered that the jack's threatening appearance was more than skin deep. Indeed, the most dramatic events I witnessed in my early morning walks on the wall were the crevalles' attacks on schools of mullet. Even before I saw the crevalles, I knew they were there. Suddenly, mullet would start racing here and there just below the surface, and, then, whole groups of them would leap into the air to escape the oncoming jacks beneath them.

If, instead of my sea wall, the original mangrove shoreline had been there, with a bottom that sloped gently upward into the mangrove prop roots and the muddy floor of the forest beyond, many of the mullet might have won their race for life. They could have gotten up into the shallows where the much bigger predators couldn't follow, but the destruction of that habitat and the construction of the sea wall changed everything. Now there was nowhere to go to escape. Even at low tide, the water next to the wall was at least two or three feet deep, and the crevalles took advantage of that fact by driving the mullet up against the wall and then grabbing them as they tried to flee out along its side. In their frantic efforts to escape, mullet sometimes even struck the rough, barnacle-encrusted surface of the wall, crippling them for an easy kill and dispersing their tiny scales through the water.

But what surprised me most about this drama of life and death in front of me, and sometimes right below me, were the sounds accompanying it. Though it is very hard to describe those sounds, probably no one has done a better job than the famous conservationist and avid angler, Gifford Pinchot. Several decades before my adventures on the sea wall with mullet and jacks, he had his own "great show," as he called it, where schools of countless thousands of mullet were attacked by large predators, probably mainly tarpon, right before his ears. With vast expanses of water all around them, Pinchot and his fishing companions camped one dark night on a narrow strip of land sticking out into Florida Bay, a body of water indenting the shore line between the southwestern end of the Florida peninsula and the upper Keys. While what he heard lasted far longer than anything I experienced and was much louder because it involved an infinitely greater number of predators and prey, the sounds he describes are very close to what I remember when, on several occasions, schools of mullet and crevalle collided in a tumult that extended almost across the entire width of my canal. As Pinchot recalled:

> The water all about us was crowded with great schools of mullet. Every instant, on one side or the other, or on both, some big fish would smash into these schools, hundreds of thousands of mullet would spring into the air in a wild effort to escape, and the roar as they tore out of the water and broke in again was like the growl of all the lions in forty circuses, or the rumble of a heavy train over a trestle, or the thunder of a hundred drums. I wish I could make you hear it as I heard it through the darkness of that interminable night— the long drum roll of the mullet as they left the water, the crash of the big fish that drove them into the air, and then the louder roll again as the multitudes fell back. The intermittent sound of it was more like Niagara with the hiccups than anything else I can think of. The thunder of one school of mullet had no sooner died away than the thunder of another began. Roar! Crash! Roar! For hours the diapason of life and death was almost continuous. It came from every direction, at every moment. How many millions of living creatures there were within reach of our ears that night, no man could tell.[2]

When my own, much smaller version of Pinchot's "great show" played out beside my sea wall, I knew it was a golden opportunity for me to share in the feeding frenzy; only I was after the jacks, not the mullet. With so many targets churning up the water, I often hit a fish when I threw my gig, but sometimes the prongs only glanced it, or penetrated too close to the tail to hold it. Early on, I learned that I had to lead a fast-swimming fish. If I hurled the gig right at it, the distance it traveled by the time the spear arrived would invariably put the gig behind the fish. When I did strike a jack solidly, especially one that was over say seven or eight pounds, it was always exciting, because the gig pole jerked around violently, and, then, when the crevalle sped away, the line would run out so quickly that it would have been yanked out of my hands if it had not been tied to my left wrist. But the truth is that I missed more jacks than I struck, and because predator and prey were so mixed up together, I sometimes hit a mullet instead of the crevalle I had targeted.

Over time, I developed other techniques for catching jacks in addition to my beloved gig. For about half the time we lived in the Bay Harbor Islands, all I had to fish with, other than my gig, was a long hand line, a few plain hooks, leaders, and sinkers, and some shiny metal "spoons" several inches long. Named for the oval-shaped bowl of a spoon without a handle, these lures imitated silver-sided "baitfish" like small mullet as they wobbled through the water. When a feeding frenzy was on, I quickly unwrapped my hand line from the piece of wood that kept it from becoming tangled, and coiled it on the top of the sea wall. Then, swinging the spoon in a circle once or twice over my head, I hurled it out as far as I could into the melee and retrieved it with a rapid, overhand jerking motion. The crevalle loved it, inhaling the lure with such force that the line instantly pulled tight, and I knew I had a strike. Even when a fish struck and escaped when I yanked back to set the hook, I would often only have to retrieve the lure a few more feet before another jack took it and was solidly hooked.

I caught many of these wonderful game fish, including what I considered to be big ones that may have approached ten pounds in weight. Their tenacious fighting spirit always delighted me, for they never accepted defeat, even when being pulled from the water. Because I admired them as the "boss fish" of my canal, I always released those caught on a line.

While it was fun to catch a big crevalle on a hand line, I knew that it would be a greater challenge and more exciting to take one on a rod and reel. As I have said, I had often accompanied my father and brothers on their saltwater fishing trips in the bays of Long Island's South Shore, and sometimes in the ocean as well, before coming to Florida, and I had learned the basics of how to use a rod and reel from watching them. Though I now wanted to move up to a more advanced approach to fish-capture, I never forgot the joy I had experienced when I used my hand line in the early '50s in South Florida. Twenty years later, when I was teaching at the University of Miami, those happy memories would return whenever I saw a recent Cuban immigrant throwing his baited hook at the end of a hand line off of a bridge or sea wall as I passed by in my car. Silently, I always wished him luck.

My goal, then, became the acquisition of a rod and reel, a fishing "outfit" of my own, for my brothers had given me orders not to use theirs while they were away at boarding school. Because Dad would come down from New York City only on the occasional weekend, when all he wanted to do was to lounge around in the swimming pool and not be pestered with the trivial concerns of his youngest son, I had to rely on Mother to get me the rod and reel I craved so much. Finally, after several weeks of pleading, I convinced her to take me back to the fishing tackle emporium in Miami and buy me a basic outfit, along with the necessary accompaniments of line, hooks, swivels, and sinkers, as well as a new group of lures that included wooden "plugs" which, like my spoons, imitated the small baitfish often pursued by jacks and other predators.

With my new fiberglass rod and conventional "bay" reel with a revolving cylindrical spool, I could now cast out into the canal, or simply fish straight down next to our dock's piles when the tide was high, and use an assortment of enticements for many different species depending on their feeding habits. These allurements included the "artificials," the spoons and plugs, as well as natural baits, mainly pieces of frozen shrimp and cut strips of mullet.

Because our sea wall was near the mouth of a canal that opened out into the upper, as yet unspoiled, Biscayne Bay, and because Baker's Haulover Inlet to the open sea was not far off, many species of fishes swam by my special place. Some even lingered in their travels, pursuing small marine life like shrimp and crabs that used our sea wall and dock piles as home base. I wanted to catch them all, whether by gig, hand line, or rod and reel. Virtually every nonrainy morning, school day or not, I was out on the wall and dock at first light looking for species I had not encountered before, trying a novel method of fishing, or simply peering down into the water, which was sometimes very clear, to see what I could see. It was as if I had a giant, continually replenished and ever-changing aquarium in my back yard, a fascinating new universe just beyond the patio, swimming pool, and sterile lawn.

It was on one of those early morning walks that I had my big adventure with a spotted eagle ray (*Aetobatus narinari*). Though I had seen one before, leaping from the water, it was out in the middle of the canal, and I only glimpsed it for an instant. Because I was continually concerned about spooking a fish before I could hurl my gig at it, or tripping and falling into the canal, I always moved along the wall softly, slowly, and carefully; the art of gigging is, after all, much more like hunting than what we usually think of as fishing. As I proceeded along on that memorable day, just after sunup, I noticed something huge and strange on the surface up ahead against the sea wall that seemed to be moving slowly in my direction. Backing up and circling around on the lawn, I tried to come up on the wall right over whatever this thing was, for I still had no idea what I had seen. As I slowly crept out onto the wall and looked over, I found myself on top of a gigantic eagle ray, perhaps six or seven feet wide. Though I didn't think about its weight at the time, it may have gone over two hundred pounds.

What a beautiful creature it was, with regularly arranged white, yellow, and greenish spots all over its back and wings and a black whiplike tail that seemed to be longer than the ray was wide. Though it had beauty, it also seemed to possess an ominous, even sinister quality, the wings and tail reminding me of a huge bat. This was the 1950s, and I had been taught certain unassailable natural history truths. Among these were that bats were vile creatures that sucked human blood, carried disease, and lacked any value whatever. Surely anything that reminded me of bats must be just as worthless, and I knew that rays could be dangerous because of the barbed spine at the base of their tails. I had already gigged some small stingrays (*Dasyatis americana*) to use for bait in my crab traps and had made sure to avoid their nasty "stingers." But those rays were tiny compared to the monster below me. I think I spent a minute or two watching it push its shovel-shaped snout up against the sea wall, just below the surface, apparently trying to trap small crabs that lived there.

In that short time, I weighed my options. Should I let this prize, the biggest fish I'd ever seen, simply go on its way, or should I become a fisherboy without equal? One question, I think, that immediately came to mind was how could I ever make anyone believe I had seen such a marvel in my own backyard if I didn't have the trophy to prove it? Whether these were all the questions I asked myself as I watched the ray work its way slowly along the sea wall, I can't remember. But I do know that I hesitated before acting, because I was actually scared of the great fish.

Finally, I decided to go for it despite my fears. After all, I was safely up on the lawn, and it was down in the water. Perhaps I thought that after gigging it, I would simply dig my heels into the back of the sea wall, in the space between it and the edge of the lawn, and hold on until my prize tired out. Then, I could tie the end of the gig cord around a nearby sprinkler head and run to wake up my mother, so that she could get some men to haul it in. I may have considered some of these possibilities, but it is more likely that I thought about none of them. At that moment, all I knew was that I couldn't pass up this opportunity to capture the ultimate trophy.

Once again, I moved very slowly back from the wall and on to the lawn, and then circled around a short distance to where I thought the ray had moved while I was watching it. When I crept up to the wall and peered over the edge, it was positioned perfectly below me, still focused on its feeding. The tide was very high, and the fish was up near the surface, so that I didn't have to hurl the gig any distance, but instead could jab it straight down. After knotting the cord tightly around my left wrist so that the line wouldn't jerk out of my hand at the end of the ray's first run, I took the gig pole in both hands and lifting it up as high as I could, I thrust it straight down with all my strength into the middle of the great fish's back. As the four barbed tines went in, the ray turned on a dime and with a mighty thrust of its wings shot out toward the middle of the canal.

Everything was fine for about three seconds, or whatever time it took for the line loosely coiled at my feet to run out to the end. All at once, my left arm jerked out in front of me, and I was being pulled through the air. I hit the water and, dazed, I found myself being towed behind this behemoth that I had been stupid enough to think I could conquer. In telling this story, it would be tempting to claim that I was taken all the way out into Biscayne Bay, but the truth is, my unexpected water trip ended somewhere in the middle of our canal. After probably no more than a minute or two, the gig worked loose, and, suddenly, I was free.

But I still had to get back to the wooden ladder that went up the side of our dock. Somewhere along the line, I had learned how to swim, if dogpaddling counts as swimming, and I now dogpaddled as fast as I could back to the dock. I was terrified the whole way, because I thought the creature might turn around and attack me for the hurt I had caused it, and I can still vividly remember the relief I felt when both feet were planted firmly on the last step of the ladder above the surface of the water. After climbing up over the sea wall, I collapsed on the lawn and vomited up the salt water I had swallowed. The next thing I clearly remember was standing outside Mother's bedroom, strangely cold and shivering, while I called repeatedly for her to come to the window. It took her awhile to wake up, but finally I saw the venetian blind rise up and the welcome sight of her surprised face behind the glass.

What happened after that is mainly a blur. I don't even recall my mother coming out to get me, but I know that she did, and that she was concerned. I know, too, that it took me some time to recover emotionally from my adventure and that I was kept out of school for a day or two.

My meeting with the great fish was not only a shock to me physically and emotionally, because I correctly believed that I had been in danger, but intellectually as well. From that time forward, even as my love for the natural world continued to grow, I understood that nature could be harmful as well as beautiful and fascinating. A second lesson I learned from the encounter with the eagle ray was that the peril I had found myself in was of my own making. In the coming years, I would have other brushes with physical harm while escaping into nature, and the danger I experienced invariably sprang from my own bad judgment. The reality began to sink in, even at this early age, that if I was going to be a player in the world of nature—as distinct from being a mere spectator watching from the sidelines—I had better learn the rules of engagement. And the number one rule was to be cautious when encountering new animal species, like those powerful enough to yank me off a sea wall!

For a time after the eagle ray incident, Mother tried to discourage me from returning to the wall in the early morning hours, but she knew that I would sneak out anyway if she tried to stop my gig hunting. Finally, she even stopped warning me about the need to be careful. She knew that I had learned my lesson and would never again try to gig anything alive that was bigger than I was.

One bright morning, not long after the great adventure and when the water in the canal was particularly clear, I approached that portion of the sea wall where it intersected our dock. Looking down and ahead, I saw a truly amazing sight. There, resting on the bottom under our small dock was another spotted eagle ray, much bigger it seemed than the one I had gigged. My memory is probably exaggerating its size, but it was so large that it took up a significant portion of the space between the piles. Cautiously moving down the sea wall toward the ray, with the canal to my left, I could see that as it lay on the bottom facing in my direction, its right wing tip curled up against the side of one of the outer piles!

Even if I had been stupid enough to try and gig it, I couldn't have done so because of its position under the dock. There would have been no way to throw the spear in at that angle. But hurling the gig at this beautiful but menacing giant was the last thing on my mind. Just seeing it filled me with the same fear I had experienced in my dogpaddle back to the ladder after the gig had pulled out of the earlier, *smaller* ray. After watching my dock visitor for a minute or two, I remember giving it a little salute of respect, and good-bye, and turning around, I walked back across the lawn to the house. After school, I returned to see if the ray was still there, but it was gone.

A few months after my meeting with this second huge ray, I was to discover that danger did not always have to come in large sizes. Sometimes, it arrived in the form of an iridescent, pale, blue and pink, balloon-like float, no more than eight inches long and about half that in width and height.

My father was down from New York City for one of his weekend visits, and my mother was busy making his, and my, favorite dinner, Southern fried chicken and honey biscuits. Though I usually didn't go gigging in the late afternoon, this was a special occasion, and I was probably anxious to show him my prowess with a gig by spearing a good-sized fish like a jack crevalle. He could see me on the wall, as he was ensconced in his usual place in the shallow end of our pool.

As I proceeded slowly down the sea wall in my usual semi-crouching stance that made me less visible, I hoped, to potential targets in the water, I noticed that there were a number of the little floating balloons pushed up against the wall by onshore winds. I must have seen Portuguese man-of-wars (*Physalia physalis*) before, but if I had, I paid them no mind, and no one had told me to avoid them at all costs.

Finally, I saw a worthy target, though I don't remember what fish species it was, and threw my gig. As was true more often than not, I missed, and I hurriedly retrieved the spear up on the wall in the hope of getting another opportunity to impress my father before dinner. As I pulled the cord in hand over hand, it and the gig passed through a tightly packed group of man-of-wars, and some of their long blue tentacles broke off and got wrapped around the line where it was tied to the gig pole. I often cleared floating seaweed off the cord after bringing in the gig, and because I was in a rush to get back into action, I jammed my right hand into the widest, thickest clump of tentacles to pull them off. Like an electric shock, the pain that instantly shot through my fingers and hand was like nothing I've ever felt, before or since. Yanking the loop at the end of the line off my left wrist—after the gigged eagle ray incident I no longer knotted the cord tightly around my wrist—I ran crying over to Dad.

Instead of rushing to my side, he rose up rather casually, I remember thinking, from the steps in the shallow end of the pool where he was sitting and walked over to where I was jumping around hysterical with pain. The toxin of the man-of-war is one of the most potent in the natural world. Welts began to rise on the fingers of my right hand, and on the hand itself, and looked like burns. What my father, the medical doctor, did next was to take me into my bedroom and tell me that I had to buck up, because the pain would soon subside. Of course, it did not.

Mother at least tried to do something by rubbing butter all over the welts. We now know this is an ill-advised treatment because it can cause infection, but in the early '50s it was considered the first thing to do for any type of sting or burnlike wound. She may even have suggested the obvious, which was to rush me to the emergency room of the nearest hospital, where the staff was, undoubtedly, prepared to deal with man-of-war stings, a medical emergency they had seen many times before. Whatever she may or may not have urged, Dad was calling the shots, and he had determined that the simultaneous stings from multiple man-of-wars were not worthy of a visit to the hospital. Instead, I was left alone on my bed, with stomach cramps and nausea, writhing in excruciating pain, crying and whimpering, while my parents calmly sat chatting at the dinner table just outside my room eating my favorite meal of chicken and biscuits. At one point, my loud crying must have disturbed my father, for I distinctly recall him getting up from the table and pulling hard on the doorknob of my bedroom door to make sure it closed completely. Apparently, he required silence when he was eating.

The pain seemed to go on forever, but I eventually fell asleep, and I don't remember how long it took for the welts to heal. I believe that I still experienced at least some discomfort in my hand and fingers for many days afterwards. Because I had no frame of reference for how a parent was supposed to treat an injured child, it was only years later, especially after I had two children of my own, that I fully realized just how unbelievable, and how unacceptable, was Dad's response, or lack of response, to the fear and hurt felt by his youngest son.

Though I may not have understood at the time that I had been the victim of child abuse, I did learn two lessons from the experience. The first was that I couldn't count on my doctor father for help, even in the area of his supposedly greatest expertise, the physical well-being of his fellow human beings. I just never trusted him again in the way I had before. The second lesson was that there was something strange, even sinister, about the indifference he had shown me. Though in the years ahead, he would often psychologically (but never physically) abuse me, this incident with the man-of-war stings was my introduction to this side of his personality, and it changed my relationship with him forever.

*When my two brothers were at home* during that year and a half in South Florida, between May 1951 and November 1952, their presence brought me new opportunities to interact with the saltwater world beyond my special place of the sea wall and adjoining dock. I could now go with them in one of our two boats and fish under the nearby bridges for a greater variety of species. Eventually, I would even accompany them in our bigger boat out through the narrow and dangerous Baker's Haulover Inlet and into the open ocean beyond.

These greater opportunities to escape into nature came, however, at a steep price. While I was still only eight or nine years old, George was twelve or thirteen, and Tony was already a big teenager at fifteen or sixteen. They constantly fought with each other when out on the boat, and Mother would later say that she could often hear us approaching the dock even before she saw us, because the sound of the yelling between my brothers was so loud and carried so well across the water. Invariably, they would try to draw me into the middle of their arguments, which sometimes led to physical blows between them. After making the mistake of taking sides on several occasions, I finally came to understand that I had to remain completely neutral during my brothers' disputes. If I agreed with George, Tony would exert his authority as the oldest and not allow me to come out on the boat on the next trip or two. If I took Tony's side, George would retaliate in his customary fashion, which was to hit me repeatedly.

Despite all the yelling and fighting that went on whenever we were out in the boat, we did manage to get in some serious fishing, and I wanted to be included in the discovery of new fishing hot spots and possible special places. The first of these was the wooden catwalk and the water around it under the bridge over Indian Creek, which separated the Bay Harbor Islands from the community of Bal Harbour and the ocean beaches to the east. We always referred to this high bridge on 96th Street (Route 922) as "Hump Bridge" to differentiate it from "Flat Bridge," the low structure over our own canal to the south of our house, which did not allow large fishing boats to pass under it as did Hump Bridge.

This new special place, where I spent some of the most enjoyable times of my young life, was only a short run by boat from our home. After tying our aluminum boat to the end of the catwalk on the eastern side of the main channel—why we never seemed to fish off the catwalk on the western side I can't recall—we would take up different positions on the creosote-coated wooden walkway. I still vividly remember how the black, tarlike creosote would stick to the bottom of my sneakers and to the seat of my pants, a small price to pay for the joys of fishing in what I envisioned as our own private saltwater aquarium.

Once we arrived at Hump Bridge, I would take up a position at the opposite end of the catwalk from whomever accompanied me (sometimes only one brother would go on the trip). That way, I could be in my special place essentially alone, which I preferred, for I have always felt most at one with the natural world when I can focus on nature without being distracted by the need to interact with others. And when those others happened to be one or both of my older brothers, who have never been able to relate to me except through competition and domination, that desire to escape, alone, into nature was particularly strong. What was best of all was when I would be dropped off at Hump Bridge by myself, with my fishing tackle and frozen shrimp bait, to be picked up later when my brothers returned from exploring other potential fishing hot spots. Then I was in heaven as I sat on the catwalk, legs dangling over the side, fishing straight down between the piles that held up the walkway. Even on the hottest days, it was cool in the shade under the bridge, and I enjoyed listening to the rhythmic thump-thump sound of cars passing overhead.

Since that first time at Hump Bridge, I have loved fishing, or even just sitting on a catwalk or in a boat, under these wonderful intersections of the human-made world and the natural one. Shady and cool, so safe and serene, protected from the sun, rain, and lightning, listening to the pleasant sound of cars passing overhead, and knowing that their occupants have no idea that I am hiding, so to speak, right below them, I feel that there are few experiences in the outdoors that can match being on the water under a bridge.

Of course, in order to be appealing, that water has to have fishes in it; it cannot be a lifeless world because of pollution or some other factor. Luckily, this is rarely the case, for most bridges over most waterways, whether in fresh or salt water, are fish magnets that give many species cover and feeding opportunities that they would have nowhere else in their area. These structures are, in fact, one of those cases when human "improvements" can actually enhance the natural world by providing a richer environment for a myriad of wildlife. This is another reason why I love being under them.

The water around Hump Bridge was always alive with many species of fishes, particularly at the tail end of a high, incoming tide. Some were residents, and some were temporary visitors, having come in through the nearby inlet, Baker's Haulover, from the open ocean. All of them found something attractive about this structure across deep Indian Creek. Some came for the barnacles, tiny crabs, and other sea life found on the piles, while others came to hunt the small "baitfish" that used those same piles for cover. Whatever their mission, it was exciting to realize that these many species of fishes were swimming right below me, because I never knew what I might catch next.

Even though most of the time I could not see my quarry until I brought it up to the surface, there were some occasions when I could make out the form of a fish moving slowly around one of the piles a foot or two down in the greenish, translucent water. These were mostly sheepshead (*Archosargus probatocephalus*), but there were others as well, like mangrove (*Lutjanus griseus*) and lane (*Lutjanus synagris*) snappers, one of the filefish species (*Monacanthidae*), porkfish (*Anisotremus virginicus*), and what would become my all-time favorite "bottom fish" in Florida, the spadefish (*Chaetodipterus faber*). What a wonderfully elegant-looking fish! I remember well the first one I ever saw up close after fighting it to the surface, and I use the word "fighting" advisedly, for a hooked spadefish is a stubborn battler that sometimes broke my line by taking it around a pile encrusted with sharp barnacles.

Deep bodied and disc shaped, the spadefish has a bronze or silvery gray background color with four to six dark bars running vertically down its sides. These bands, starting with the first one on the head that passes through the eye, fade away to some degree in large, older adults, but the ones I caught at Hump Bridge were younger fish, and the bars were a striking feature of this splendid species. Its overall shape, the vertical bands, and the two, large backswept fins at the rear of its body, both top and bottom, made it look like a huge version of the tropical freshwater angelfish I had seen in pet store aquariums, and supported my fantasy that I was angling in a great fish tank under Hump Bridge.

The spadefish would be one of those species of wildlife to which I would grow particularly attached. Other examples would be tarpon, flounders, fluke; eider, black (*Anas rubripes*), wood, and greater scaup ducks; and brant geese (*Branta bernicla*). In pursuing these fishes and birds, I discovered one or more characteristics about them that especially appealed to me. Whether it was their beauty, wariness, fighting ability, or the natural surroundings in which they lived, or a combination of all of these things, I developed an affection for these species that time cannot erase. I know, for example, that even though I have not landed a spadefish since 1952, if I were to catch one today, and hold it in my hands out in front of me, I would be just as thrilled as I was when I saw my first one sixty years ago.

Though I loved fishing alone off the catwalk under Hump Bridge, I faced a dilemma that became increasingly frustrating. By this time, I had given up my hand line, or so I thought, and was using my rod and reel exclusively. This meant that even though I was fishing right next to piles covered with sharp barnacles, I had to "play" a good-sized fish after it was hooked and not simply haul it up to the surface. In recent decades, with the

*Tony, George, and John on the dock behind our house in the Bay Harbor Islands after a spearfishing trip to the bridge over Baker's Haulover Inlet. Two different types of spear guns are lying on the dock in front of us. I have what looks like a flounder in my hand, and Tony is holding up a spadefish, a favorite species of mine that I regretted them killing.*

development of very strong rods and lines, the latter with surprisingly thin diameters, anglers like those in largemouth bass tournaments can "horse" even big bass right to the boat without needing to let the fish take line off the reel, even on the first, usually most powerful, run. If anglers in the '50s had tried to horse a really large fish with the rods and lines then available, one or the other would have probably broken. And if one went to heavier line, one quickly discovered that its wide diameter would interfere with the smooth turning of the spools on the small and medium-sized reels used in bay fishing. More importantly, the number of "bites" or "hits" one received trailed off to nothing. As I quickly learned with sheepshead and mangrove snappers, many species of fishes are simply too suspicious by nature to take a baited hook coming off a thick, rather stiff, line, even one made of low-visibility monofilament.

So how could I solve the problem of enticing the fishes of Hump Bridge to take my bait and get those I hooked to the surface before they ran my line around a barnacle-encrusted pile, thus cutting it off and escaping? One way, I decided, was to revert to using my hand line. Because its cord was so much heavier and stronger than the line on my reel, I could tie a baited hook on a relatively light monofilament leader coming off the cord. Then, with the bait on bottom and the cord in my right hand, I would yank sharply up when I felt a bite, hook the fish, and pull it in hand over hand so quickly that it had no chance of cutting me off on a nearby pile. By going back to my hand line when fishing off the catwalk, I could continue to fish and not feel guilty about all the break-offs that I had experienced earlier when I used my rod and reel. Even though, presumably, the hooks would eventually rust out or work loose, I didn't like the idea of my favorites, the spadefish, or any others for that matter, having to swim around with hooks in their mouths and a foot or two of line trailing behind.

However paradoxical this may seem to those who neither fish nor hunt, I have always tried to avoid unnecessary distress to the wildlife I pursued. For me, the point of sport fishing and hunting on any particular outing was to win the game by solving the problem at hand and outwitting the target species. It was never to torture fishes or birds. In order to be successful a large percentage of the time in these pursuits, I found that I had to study the habits and habitats, and even the personalities, of my quarry. This requirement invariably led to a kind of intimacy with them that sometimes developed into respect, and even reverence, as it did with spadefish. And the more I learned about my prey, the more I wanted to treat them fairly. Although I didn't know it then, I was already becoming both a budding naturalist and a sportsman, and adopting what I would later call the code of the sportsman, which has had such a powerful impact on the rise of wildlife conservation in America. Fishes, I believed then and still believe now, should be pursued only by means of sporting methods that test my knowledge and skill before I make a catch.

It was this requirement of my evolving code of ethical behavior that began to trouble me when I used a hand line at Hump Bridge to haul up spadefish and other species to the surface without giving them a chance to show their stubborn fighting ability. The way I came to terms with this problem was to accept the unfortunate necessity of fishing with my brothers out of our aluminum boat, and to give up the pleasure of fishing alone directly from the catwalk astride the middle channel under the bridge. Instead, we would anchor halfway between the next two rows of the main bridge piles, in toward shore from the catwalk. I continued to have the pleasures of being in the cool shade of the bridge and hearing the rhythmic thump-thump sound of cars passing overhead, but I now had to endure the ceaseless arguments between my brothers as each one jockeyed for dominance.

Still, I was in, or near, my special place and no longer forced to use my hand line to keep big fish from cutting the line on piles only inches away. When anchored, my brothers and I were close enough to the main bridge supports to find the fishes these piles attracted, but still far enough away from them to use our rods and reels. We could now play a large fish by letting it take line to keep it, or the rod, from breaking, and then work the battler back to the boat and the landing net with a far greater rate of success than when fishing from the catwalk. In this way, we caught many good-sized sheepshead and spadefish, as well as a few other species like gag groupers and black drums (*Pogonias cromis*).

For reasons I can't fully explain, I have never wanted to keep more than a few fish for eating, and often not even these, and have preferred instead to release those not hooked deeply or in the gills, where their chance of survival is small. I was coming to understand that we should not exceed our own built-in limits on the exploitation of these gifts from Nature. Fishing has to have restraints put on it, either personal or legal, or both, in order to keep it ethically sound. I would later discover that the same applies to hunting. But when the catch was a special species, like a spadefish, there was no question about returning it to the water.

Partway through that experience-packed year and a half in South Florida, our father bought us an open sixteen-foot plywood boat with an inboard engine that largely replaced our twelve-foot, outboard engine-driven, aluminum skiff. It was a rare act of generosity on his part, but perhaps he simply tired of hearing about how cramped our boat was with all three of us in it plus our gear. My mother may have also added to the pressure on him because she never felt that the skiff was safe.

As the oldest, Tony was in charge of the big boat, and for the rest of the time we lived in the Bay Harbor Islands, he usually insisted on going "outside," that is, through Baker's Haulover Inlet and out into the open ocean. For a number of reasons, I never enjoyed those trips offshore as much as the earlier ones around the bay. For one thing, they always made me anxious, especially when we were going out or coming in through the inlet, where a vast amount of bay or ocean water is forced through a very narrow channel. When the tide was running hard against our boat, Tony showed real skill in negotiating this treacherous waterway.

The first requirement for a successful negotiation of "the Haulover" was, of course, a boat motor that never quit, which, unfortunately, was not the case with our inboard engine. Once, it stopped while we were in the inlet on the way in, just as the boat was pushing against a great volume of water from an outgoing tide. The plywood craft was turned sideways by the force of the water and nearly smashed against the sea wall on the north side of the inlet before Tony got the motor started again, and was able to steer the boat back out into the middle of the waterway, and home.

Once we were out on the ocean, I could relax and try to enjoy the fishing, though, as always, the bickering between my brothers often made me long to be off somewhere in a special place by myself. Still, these trips could be exciting when the action was hot for species like the "little tunny" or, as we called them, bonito (*Euthynnus alletteratus*) and king mackerel (*Scomberomorus cavalla*). We sometimes trolled with artificial lures and at other times drifted with large live shrimp, especially when fishing for mackerel.

Anglers who have been restricted to fresh water their whole lives and used to catching species like largemouth bass and channel catfish are amazed when they hook one of the great saltwater game fish for the first time. Species like bonito and king mackerel tear the line off the reel and through the water with such speed that the first-time saltwater angler may panic and bear down on the line to stop, or at least turn, the fleeing fish, with the likely result of a broken line or rod.

In addition to the conventional fishing with rod and reel during that year and a half in South Florida, my brothers also tried underwater spearfishing. They used both a conventional spear gun and a primitive device consisting of a hollow piece of wood into which a long spear was inserted, which was then fired by means of elastic, surgical rubber tubing. Tony had charge of the precious spear guns and correctly believed that I was too young to be trusted with them. The only spearfishing I remember them doing with any success was in the protected and relatively shallow water under Baker's Haulover Bridge, just south of the main channel. Here, beside the artificial reef created by the bridge piles and over the rubble on the bottom left behind from its construction, they speared several species, most notably, and from my point of view, most regrettably, the spadefish.

Because at that time I couldn't swim very well, I had only limited experience with diving over reefs, whether natural or human-made. And when I attempted to dive, I had no equipment other than a snorkel, swim fins, and Japanese goggles. While fishing one day along the sea wall on the south side of the inlet, east of the Haulover bridge, I found the ideal spot to explore a reeflike environment without any of the difficulties or fears associated with rough water. The sea wall there had broken through in several places and water had rushed in to form a small pond behind the barrier, probably no more than four or five feet deep. Because the breaks in the sea wall were wide enough to allow small fishes to swim in and out, this giant aquarium contained an ever-changing assortment of beautiful and interesting reef species like sergeant majors (*Abudefduf saxatilis*) and juvenile French angelfish (*Pomacanthus paru*). I spent many happy hours swimming around in this new special place, which I usually had completely to myself, and I remember distinctly how much I appreciated Mother dropping me off on the south side of the Haulover bridge while she went shopping, and how frustrated I was when I heard her car horn and the signal that it was time to go home.

*During that year and a half in the Bay Harbor Islands*, the most traumatic event to occur was the death of "Pop," Anthony Reiger, our father's father. To my mother, he was a wonderful man, greatly loved by her, but not, apparently, by my father. A Hungarian immigrant from the city of Szombathely in the far western part of the country near the Austrian border, he had arrived in New York as one of the multitude of Eastern Europeans coming to the United States at the turn of the twentieth century.

According to his certificate of naturalization, which Dad gave me, Pop was thirty-one years old on March 6, 1911, the date of his naturalization as an American citizen. Assuming that my grandfather applied for citizenship as soon as possible, and because the document states that an individual had to live in the United States for at least five years before applying, Pop probably arrived here in 1905 or 1906, when he was in his mid-twenties. Tall for the times, he was 5 feet 11 inches, with a dark complexion, brown hair, and brown eyes. Already married to another Hungarian immigrant, Roza Kuti, whom he met shortly after arriving in America, Pop lived at 170 Stockholm Street in Brooklyn. The certificate lists their children as Frank (four years), William (two), and Anthony, my father (one).

Something even more significant than his Hungarian origins in understanding this man, who had a great influence—through my father—on my life, came out of a story that Mother told my brother Tony shortly before she died. It seems that there was a skeleton in the closet about which she was embarrassed: Pop was probably Jewish. What other interpretation could one put on the gift of a menorah to my mother on her wedding day?

Even though he was a nonpracticing Jew and seems to have had little or no religious belief, our grandfather obviously cherished something about the culture and traditions of Judaism to give this sacred object to his "favorite daughter-in-law," as Mother proudly called herself. Because of the intense anti-Semitism in both Hungary and the United States at the

*My Hungarian-immigrant grandfather in his later years, standing on the edge of a canal in Mastic Beach, Long Island, getting ready to go out in the boat he built. It was "Pop" who initiated the family's intimate involvement with the natural world.*

time, I wonder if Pop simply chose to reinvent himself on his arrival in America and become an instant Christian. When I asked Dad, who was an in-your-face atheist his entire life, what religion Pop had been in the old country, he snapped, "I think he was a Lutheran, but he had thrown away all of that nonsense before he got here."

What is ironic to me about that wedding gift was that both Mother and Dad found Jewish people socially undesirable, which may be the reason she held back this key fact of our family history to the very end, and why he never acknowledged it at all. Still, she loved Pop dearly, a sentiment not shared by his son, who seemed to be ashamed of my grandfather and sometimes abused him emotionally as a result. One of those instances of abuse finally caused Pop to kill himself.

It was only late in her life, when Mother lived near me in Connecticut, that I heard the whole story. My grandfather was a craftsman, a talented furniture maker and upholsterer, who also designed and built his own fishing boats. From the time he arrived in this country, he seemed to be fascinated with the saltwater environment and never wanted to be far from it. He got his wish, for after living and working in Brooklyn close to Jamaica Bay most of his adult life, he moved to Mastic Beach, a small community farther out on Long Island, wedged between Great South Bay to the west and Moriches Bay to the east. After he and Roza had separated (as a devout Catholic she would not give him a divorce), Pop lived in a tiny bungalow and spent his time fishing, duck hunting, or working on various creative projects for himself and his sons.

One of these had to do with making some kind of canvas top or covering for a portion of my father's big fishing boat, a craft over thirty feet long. Dad picked up the canvas piece from Pop in Mastic Beach and brought it back to the yacht basin in Lawrence, closer to Forest Hills, where he kept his boat. When my father tried putting the piece in place, he found that it didn't fit exactly, causing him to fly into one of his rages. Calling up Pop, Dad berated him as Mother told me he often did, but because my grandfather had spent many days working on the covering and because he wanted it to be perfect, this abuse was more than he could bear. After saying something like, "Don't worry, Tony; you won't have to be concerned about me anymore," Pop hung up the phone.

Incredibly, my father, who considered himself an expert in human psychology, failed to see the meaning of my grandfather's statement, and it wasn't until several hours later, in a long-distance call to my mother in Florida on an unrelated matter, that he happened to mention the argument with Pop. After hearing what Pop had said to my father right before he hung up, Mother immediately feared the worst and demanded that Dad call Pop back, and if there was no answer, call the police. By the time they broke down Pop's door, the pills had done their work, and he was gone.

Though it was sixty years ago, the miracle of human memory makes it seem as if it were only last month, and I am starting to cry as I write these words. There is my mother shaking me out of a deep sleep and telling me to sit on the edge of the bed because "something terrible has happened—Pop is dead." In saying these incomprehensible words, she hugged me so hard it hurt, and it was only then that I was awake enough to see the tears streaming down her face.

It was my first experience with human death. I knew that other life forms, like fishes, could die, because I had killed them, but not people, and certainly not family members.

My mother naturally told me nothing at that time about how Pop died, and when I asked why he died, all she would say was, "That's what happens to people when they get old." But because my grandfather was only in his early seventies when he decided that life was no longer worth living, he might have easily lived another ten years or more. By then, I would have been in my late teens and already keenly interested in history generally and my family's past in particular. I can only imagine all the questions I would have asked Pop, especially in regard to Dad's version of his father's biography. If he had really been an unskilled "baggage handler" on a railroad in Hungary before he came to America, how did he make the seamless transition to skilled craftsman after his arrival here? Was it true that he decided to emigrate after the Hungarian government wanted to force him back into the service after he had already completed his military obligation? And what was most interesting of all: Why did Pop's political ideology include a commitment to the Industrial Workers of the World (the "Wobblies"), as Dad told me on several occasions, and their acceptance of violence, "when necessary," to secure workers' rights? Was there a connection between his radical ideology of class warfare and his Jewish heritage, with its emphasis on social justice?

Even though I was never able to ask those important questions, I do know one thing for sure. It was Pop who instilled in my father his interest in the natural world, saltwater fishing, and boats.

One of the first things my grandfather did after arriving in America, and finding work and a place to live, was to buy a cheap shotgun and go bird hunting along the shores of Brooklyn's Jamaica Bay. He apparently had little concern about which bird species were proper to shoot, and which were not, for he fired at them all. The point of that first outing was to bask in his newfound freedom to go onto public land and hunt with his own gun, a right not open to all people in his native Hungary. On later trips Pop seems to have concentrated on shorebird species like yellowlegs, dowitchers, and sanderlings, but he must have branched out to include waterfowl—ducks and geese—when the changing seasons drove most shorebirds out of the bay. It was probably this proximity of Jamaica Bay and its surrounding marshes and beaches, with the seemingly limitless opportunities for public hunting, fishing, and boating, that made my grandfather an outdoorsman. He would pass on the last two interests to my father, who in turn passed them on to his three sons.

Shortly before Dad died in 1992, I asked him about Pop's hunting and whether my father or his brothers ever accompanied him on these outings. He said that he did on occasion, and one trip stuck out in his mind. There were just the two of them, and Pop was after a big bunch of shorebirds that had landed in a wet field on the edge of the bay. He shot well that day, "much better than usual," according to Dad, and made a "great score" on yellowlegs (*Tringa melanoleuca* or *Tringa flavipes*). Having been interested in collecting and studying old bird decoys, for both shorebirds and waterfowl, since the early 1970s, I wondered how Pop got the yellowlegs into good range, which would have been no farther away than about forty yards; did he use decoys? To my surprise, Dad answered that it was he who had become so adept at imitating the yellowlegs' call that he whistled them in to where he and Pop were hiding in some bushes. Though my father had mellowed toward the end of his life and was much less likely to tell the tall tales he was fond of in earlier years, I found this account of his skills as an imitator of the yellowlegs' wild calls to be highly suspicious. So I decided to test him by asking, "Do you think you can remember today how you made those sounds?" Imagine my amazement when, without hesitation, he pursed his lips and whistled a loud, though musical, slightly descending series of three *whew* notes in a nearly perfect imitation of the greater yellowlegs' whistle that I have heard countless times. This was one story of my father's that I had no problem believing.

While Dad would go bird hunting occasionally in later years—for quail in Georgia and Florida when he was stationed there during World War II and for ducks after the war when he was on vacation in Florida and it was too windy to fish offshore—he never seemed to show much interest in this pursuit until his oldest son got all of us actively involved in waterfowl hunting on Lake Okeechobee, in southern Florida, in the late 1950s. Once again, Pop had been the inspiration for this avocation, which all three of his grandsons have avidly followed in all the decades since.

According to Tony, it was the sight of a pile of wooden duck decoys on the boat dock near Pop's bungalow in Mastic Beach that made him curious about how these interesting objects were used. Dad and Tony had dropped by on that cold, windy day (perfect conditions for waterfowling) without calling first, and Pop was just setting off on a duck hunt in the local marshes. My brother wanted to go along, but his grandfather had one or two friends with him, and in addition to there not being enough room in the boat for another person, Tony had none of the right clothing with him, like a heavy sweater and rubber hip boots or chest waders. Regretfully, Pop had to turn down his grandson's plea to accompany him.

Like so many experiences in life, we really don't understand how important they are until months, or even years, later. We think we'll have another chance, but once that opportunity brushes past, it never comes again. Such was the case here, for it was only a short time later that Pop took his own life, and neither Tony nor either of his brothers would ever have the privilege of hunting with their grandfather. Given the centrality of this activity in our lives, it was a loss beyond calculation. But Pop's legacy did live on, for Tony's curiosity about his grandfather's decoys and how they were used led him to develop a friendship with an experienced and knowledgeable duck hunter who took Tony under his wing and taught him well. Then he in turn passed on the fundamentals of waterfowling to his brothers, who enthusiastically took up the sport.

The death of my grandfather not only removed the man who was the original inspiration for my family's active participation in the natural world, but it also further weakened the bonds of my parents' marriage. Mother had never wanted to leave her friends and active social life in Forest Hills to go to the Bay Harbor Islands, where she knew no one, and where she and I were alone most of the time in that year and a half in the never-ending heat and humidity that she hated so much. And while my parents were apart, the philandering my father had engaged in for years increased dramatically. Pop's suicide, which she blamed on Dad's callous treatment of his father, was the last straw. Before granting him an eventual divorce, Mother now demanded that my father cancel his plans to move his medical practice to South Florida and that they come back to Forest Hills, where they would remain under the same roof only until I reached the age of thirteen, when I could be sent off to boarding school.

# CHAPTER THREE

# Looking for New Special Places:

## *Pre-Prep School Years in New York City, Long Island, and South Florida, 1952-1956*

T**hough** Mother was happy when we returned to Forest Hills Gardens in November 1952, I was sad. Coming back to New York City was hard for me, because I believed that what nature offered in my old neighborhood could not compare with the variety of experiences Biscayne Bay and the Atlantic Ocean had given me on an almost daily basis.

Our new residence, at 57 Continental Avenue, was very different from our old home. Whereas the first house was on a quiet street deep in the Gardens, with lots of greenery around it, the new one was on a busy thoroughfare, with only a tiny front yard and no yard at all in the back or along the side. It was a row house, one of a line of identical houses joined on one or both sides by a common wall. An alley ran behind the homes, with driveways on either end to allow access to Continental Avenue. We had the advantage of being on one end of the row, but the wall between us and our next-door neighbor was not thick enough to keep people on the other side from hearing the many loud arguments between my father and mother or between my brothers and, sometimes, between one of them and me. Mother felt understandable embarrassment over the frequent requests from next door to "keep it down," but the males in the family could not care less about our reputation in the neighborhood as—to use a modern euphemism—"the dysfunctional Reigers."

The best part of nature around our new residence were the large "sycamores," which were actually a hybrid between the American sycamore and the Oriental plane tree called the London plane tree. Quick growing and resistant to disease, drought, root crowding, and air pollution, they have been planted in many cities on both sides of the Atlantic. Three plane trees dominated the mainly concrete alley behind our house, allowing me the fantasy that they were the remnants of a primeval forest. It was only many years later that I learned that they were a hybrid and that they had probably been planted no more than forty or fifty years earlier.

One characteristic of my trees that fascinated me was the flaking off of their brown outer bark in puzzle-like pieces, exposing the yellow and greenish gray wood underneath. This reminded me of how a snake sheds its skin, something I had read about but had not yet seen. The mottled trunks were very attractive to me, as were the fruit balls hanging from the branches like Christmas tree ornaments. From the time our family moved back to Forest Hills in 1952, my three "sycamores" were an all-important connection to the natural world and a symbol of stability in my life while everything else changed, and not always for the better.

They changed too, of course, as the seasons came and went, but they always returned to an earlier state. Every morning after I awoke, I would start the day by going to the window and looking outside from my bedroom at the back of the house, reassuring myself by the sight of these large living things whose branches I could almost touch.

When we returned to a landlocked existence in Forest Hills in 1952 after the joy of almost daily encounters with the inhabitants of our canal, and the bay and ocean beyond, I wondered if I would discover anything in nature as fascinating as what I had left behind. Almost immediately, however, I found myself eager to renew my earlier interaction with the insect world, particularly the butterflies and moths, that I had put on hold because of the allure of unlimited fishing opportunities right outside my back door. I would now hunt these beautiful winged creatures with the same passion I had pursued the often equally beautiful fishes of South Florida.

The first thing I had to do was to reacquaint myself with the butterfly-collecting supplies I had stored in a trunk for the move to Florida and where they had remained during our time in the Bay Harbor Islands. After opening the trunk, I remembered that the folding net for catching winged insects was not the only item Dad had purchased for me at the biological supply store in Manhattan. Another essential part of my collecting equipment that had remained in storage while in Florida was a quantity of triangular-shaped envelopes in various sizes in which to store dead butterflies while in the field.

After the move to the new residence in Forest Hills Gardens in November 1952, and reacquainting myself with the as yet unused butterfly-collecting "tool kit," I could hardly wait for the spring to come to find a new special place and begin my pursuit of these beautiful insects. I'm not sure how I learned the technique, but I would later become proficient at dispatching butterflies while they were still in the net. Waiting until the insect folded its wings back over its body, I would pinch the middle of its body, the thorax, between my thumb and first finger. Then, I would carefully remove the dead butterfly from the net, place it in the envelope with its wings still folded back, and store the envelope in a tin "field-box" that I carried in a rucksack that also contained a glass water jar and a sandwich to fuel me on my mini-safaris.

The largest of the swallowtails, the uncommon "giant swallowtail" (*Papilio cresphontes*), had a special appeal for me. I very much wanted to capture one, but never did. I'm not sure how I knew about this species, but in any case, I would eventually become familiar with most of the species of insects I had a chance to capture from a series of books I acquired. The first two were Ralph B. Swain's *The Insect Guide: Orders and Major Families of North American Insects*, published in 1949, and Herbert S. Zim's and Clarence Cottam's *Insects: A Guide to Familiar American Insects*, which appeared two years later. With its accurate color pictures, range maps, and succinct descriptions, the Zim and Cottam book was perfect for the beginning student of entomology. In later years it would be supplanted by many other works, including the tomes of W. J. Holland, whose *Butterfly Book* and *Moth Book* became my standard references, even though they were first published in 1898 and 1903, respectively.

I discovered these insect books at about the same time I was learning how to read with any kind of comprehension. Though I didn't know it at the time, they marked the beginning of my lifelong love of systematic nature study, especially that part of it that pertains to wildlife, including fishes. I wanted to know everything I could about butterflies and moths and would accept nothing less than the latest, and most accurate, information on their abundance, ranges, breeding habits, etc. Later, as I developed an ever-greater interest in history, I undoubtedly built on this early foundation to become an uncompromising scholar who hates making factual errors in his own work and who is obsessed with getting at the truth of what happened in the past, even if it means stepping on the toes, and interpretations, of other scholars. The new field of environmental history—defined as the interaction, over time, between humans and the natural world—would, as it developed in the 1970s, give me the opportunity to fuse together my fascination with both nature and history in an effort at making a contribution to our understanding of the past.

All of this, of course, lay many years in the future. For now, a boy of nine, all I could do was to wait impatiently for spring to find a new special place in which to begin my butterfly collecting. The frustration accompanying my need to postpone my hunting urges became obvious to my Dad, who, in a rare example of fatherly interest, decided to teach me that it wasn't necessary to wait until warm weather to find the most dramatic American examples of the order *Lepidoptera*, not butterflies but the giant silk moths like the polyphemus and cecropia. Whether they were called "night-flying moths" or "silk moths," the word "giant" always preceded the other descriptive terms and gave these magnificent creatures a romantic allure that no other insect possessed. Furthering that aura were the other terms like "night-flying" and "silk" (a reference to the once widely held belief that these species would one day be commercially valuable like the silk "worms" of China), and the fact that they were named for characters out of Greek mythology. Because of its huge size and the eyespots on the wings, I understood why the polyphemus moth had been named after the one-eyed giant, Polyphemus, when I saw my first one in a glass case in Manhattan's American Museum of Natural History. Only the cecropia is larger. Also called the "emperor," this gorgeous species was named after the mythical Cecrops, the first king of Attica and founder of Athens, represented as half man and half dragon.

One last reason why I came to love this glorious family of insects was that they reminded me of the huge Atlas moth from India that my father had purchased for me shortly before we left for Florida, and which I treasure to this day. Though not as big as the Atlas, these moths were just as beautiful and fascinating, and I felt fortunate to have them to pursue practically in my own backyard. The place my father took me to hunt for their cocoons was Forest Park, 538 acres of mainly trees and fields just to the south of Forest Hills Gardens. While the western side of the park had an eighteen-hole golf course, carousels, and some other human "improvements," the eastern section, closest to the Gardens, was, and still is, largely undeveloped forest land, and had many species like the black cherry and sassafras that provided food for the caterpillars of the large moths. Though it was a long walk, I could enter Forest Park at two points just outside the boundary of the Gardens, and as I got older and bigger, and could wander farther away from home for longer periods of time, I found myself drawn back again and again to what would always remain one of my most special places in the world.

But during that first winter after our return to Forest Hills, I was still too young and small to venture so far from home, and my father decided to show me, personally, how to look for the well-camouflaged cocoons attached to twigs of shrubs and small trees and among leaves on the ground. It was, undoubtedly, an opportunity for him to relive his own boyhood hunts for cocoons in Brooklyn, and he seemed to enjoy taking me on several walks through Forest Park to instruct me on how to find these small treasures.

The most easily spotted, and most numerous, were the cocoons of the promethea moth (*Callosamia promethea*), named after Prometheus, the Titan who stole fire from heaven for the benefit of humankind. We sometimes found them in groups of three or four hanging from the same branch, or branches close together, of a small tree. Once I learned what to look for, they were easy to see, especially on a windy day, as they dangled from a twig, even though they were usually wrapped in the dull-colored dead leaf in which the caterpillar had originally spun them.

After pulling the cocoon off the branch, Dad would hold it up close to his ear and gently shake it in the hope that he would hear, or feel, the movement of a live, full-bodied pupa inside the cocoon and not the dry rattle of one that had been parasitized by one of the species of ichneumon wasps. This is a slender, small to medium-sized insect with a narrow waist and long antennae and legs. The female has an unusually long ovipositor with which it lays eggs on, or in, the body of a caterpillar shortly before, or after, it spins its cocoon and changes into a pupa. Once the wasp's larvae hatch, they consume the pupa, leaving only an empty shell behind. In my cocoon hunts I would find many that had been visited by ichneumon wasps, and I came to hate these vile creatures that fed on a living pupa while it lay helpless, wrapped inside its silken case.

Those that contained a living pupa are, of course, much heavier than the parasitized ones. Even after all these years, I still remember the thrill of seeing a promethea cocoon hanging from a branch before my father did, discovering that it had some weight to it, and then—after holding it up to my right ear and giving it a gentle shake—feeling the living creature inside twist in protest at this unwarranted disturbance. Those winter trips to Forest Park were the most cherished memories I have of my father.

For most of the winter, it looked as if I would be unsuccessful in finding the one moth I wanted more than any other, the reddish cecropia. At up to six inches in width, it is the largest moth or butterfly in the United States.

My quest for this giant of the insect world was finally rewarded in the most unlikely of places. Since my mother wasn't feeling well one night, my father took me out to dinner. There were just the two of us, because both of my brothers were away at boarding school. We went to the Stratton Restaurant in Forest Hills, just outside the Gardens, on a corner of a side street and busy Queens Boulevard. Because my father hustled me into the restaurant, I took no notice of my surroundings as I entered, but as we were coming out, I saw something in a solitary, leafless bush in front of the restaurant. Growing in a tiny dirt area surrounded by the concrete sidewalk and curb, it was the only vegetation around in that sterile urban world except for perhaps a token shade tree or two down the block. There, to my amazement, and my father's as well, was the large (maybe three inches in length), tough, brown cocoon of a cecropia attached lengthwise to a twig in the center of the bush.

With great excitement, I broke off the twig at both ends of the cocoon and anxiously held it in my hand to see if it had the heavy feel of a cocoon whose pupa had not been parasitized and drained of its bodily fluids. Immediately, I knew I was in luck, for not only did it have some weight, but when I put it up to my ear and gently shook it, I felt, and even believe I heard, the twisting thump of a living pupa. I had my cecropia!

Though this memorable event occurred on a night in late winter, there was enough light, perhaps from the restaurant or a nearby street lamp, to see the bush clearly, and we both wondered how many hundreds of people had walked right beside it, and seen nothing. Even at this early age, I realized that I was developing a "hunter's eye," the ability to spot those anomalies in nature that reveal secrets hidden from the average person. Earlier, I had noticed the inability of visitors to my sea wall, like classmates from school or my mother's friends, to see small groups of mullet swimming slowly along the bottom of the canal right beneath them. Though I had no sunglasses to cut the sun's glare and reflection off the water, and the dark backs of the mullet made them difficult to spot, even when the water was clear, I made a game of finding them among the ever-changing lights and shadows along the bottom.

In the coming years, my hunter's eye continued to sharpen as I learned to identify, even at a great distance, all the species of waterfowl I hoped to bag in my shooting areas. Rather than being two separate activities, hunting and bird-watching, or birding as it was later called, became one and the same, at least during the hunting season. And in the off-season, I discovered that the same skills I had honed as a waterfowl hunter came in handy as a spotter on birding field trips, regardless of whether we were looking for familiar species in this country or new ones in Africa, or Central or South America.

Although Aldo Leopold was writing in the 1940s, before the growth of birding as a popular outdoor activity (birders obviously need to develop an ability to locate even small species in thick brush), his observations on the hunter's eye are worth citing. He described what he thought were the "four categories of outdoorsmen," defined by "four diverse habits of the human eye." His vast experience with others in the field and on the water taught him that "the deer hunter habitually watches the next bend [in the river]; the duck hunter watches the skyline; the [upland] bird hunter watches the dog; the non-hunter does not watch."[3] On many field trips on three continents, I have had the same experience as Leopold, with the exception that birders now join hunters in almost always seeing wildlife before the other people in the group. On safaris in East Africa, for example, I have noticed this phenomenon repeatedly, and it was often those who most loudly proclaimed their love for nature who were the least likely to spot first any aspect of that nature other than the most obvious.

After my father and I arrived home from the restaurant on that wonderful night when I discovered the cecropia cocoon, it joined the others we had found, those of a polyphemus and several promethea, on the bottom of a large cardboard box over which I had placed a screen cover that allowed me to make repeated checks on my prizes, and to add a few drops of water occasionally to simulate rain. Of course, my hope was to see a moth emerge and experience the thrill of witnessing its metamorphosis from a shriveled-up newborn into a giant night-flyer. Every morning I came down the basement stairs with a keen sense of anticipation.

It was nothing short of thrilling to find one of the moths hanging upside down from the bottom of the screen. While I never did see the larger cecropia or polyphemus moths actually emerge, I was fortunate enough to arrive one morning just after a purple male promethea had broken out of its cocoon, and I watched, fascinated, as it developed into a fully formed moth.

While I knew that I had to kill these beautiful creatures in order to preserve them for the future, I didn't like doing it. Because they are thick-bodied, I couldn't use the same technique of pinching them as I did with butterflies. I accomplished the unpleasant task by putting them in a large, wide-mouthed, sealed jar into which I placed a cotton ball saturated with some kind of liquid I obtained from my father, probably ether, that emitted fumes deadly to the moth. After it died, I spread it out on the top of a bed of cotton in my black Riker display case, placed the glass cover back on, and inserted pins through the sides of the cover and into the case itself to hold everything together.

In this way, I have been able to preserve these splendid trophies of the hunt, and the memories that go with them, to the present day. And they are indeed trophies, no less so than the grand head and antlers of a huge white-tailed buck on a wall, or the mount of a gorgeous drake wood duck suspended from the ceiling of a den by means of an almost invisible monofilament fishing line. The beautiful moths, deer, and duck all represent the culmination of an outdoor adventure that the hunter wants to immortalize. Perhaps that's what Aldo Leopold meant when he wrote that "critics write and hunters outwit their game primarily for one and the same reason—to reduce that beauty to possession."[4]

*As the winter of 1952-1953 drew to a close* and the days became progressively warmer, I could hardly wait for the emergence of butterflies and the chance to pursue them. But first I had to find a hunting ground near our home, one that I could visit on my own. As it turned out, it would not take me long to find another special place, and after its discovery, I began to develop certain ideas that are still very much a part of my worldview of nature. My new retreat was a long, narrow park in the Gardens, created by Frederick Law Olmsted, Jr. to hide vehicles passing in opposite directions on either side as their drivers proceeded up or down a gently rolling hill. Though it had the hated lawn in the middle, this public (at least for Gardens' residents) space had trees, bushes, and flower plots around the edges that attracted many species of insects.

It was here that I first used my butterfly net to catch a flying insect, not a butterfly but a moth—and what a moth! It was a dark day, late afternoon, and I was anxious to explore the small park, having noticed its flower plots from the window of my mother's car the day before.

On entering this green island between the roadways, I was happy to see no other people and a small yellow butterfly flying about some flowers, a species that I would later learn was a clouded sulphur (*Colias philodice*). With a kind of "buck fever" that hunters get when they see a trophy deer approaching their tree stand, I worked feverishly to insert the two extension rods of the net's metal rim into the brass ferrule at the end of the wooden handle so that I could begin the stalk on my prey. The sulphur was perhaps fifteen yards away from me when I first saw it, and as I slowly moved in its direction, what looked like a tiny hummingbird suddenly darted in from the left and began to hover over a flower near the sulphur. (Though I had not yet seen a hummingbird in the wild, I knew what they

*A glass case with some of my insect "trophies," including the "humming bird moth" in the third row and the cecropia next to it.*

looked like from descriptions I had read.) What was this bizarre creature; was it, I wondered, a bird or an insect? Once it dawned on me that, indeed, it was some kind of insect, all thoughts of the sulfur disappeared.

Since I wasn't used to swinging the net and had not yet developed my technique for bringing it out and over a target, I missed the insect on the first pass, and it sped away with me in hot pursuit. I'm sure my net missed it at least one more time, but luckily, the insect never left the park area as it flew with dazzling speed from one flower plot to the next with me frantically chasing behind. I'm not sure how I managed to capture it; perhaps, I just wore it out! In any case, I know I did catch it, for it resides on a bed of cotton in my Riker glass case along with the other butterflies and moths.

Although I think I was trying to be precise and "scientific" in my correct labeling of the insects in my case, I must have had trouble in identifying this first catch with my butterfly net. Or maybe I just didn't like the correct name—it happened to be a male sphinx moth of the genus *Amphion, floridensis* to be exact—and wanted one that accurately described its unique characteristics.

Apparently, I decided to come up with a name of my own, and my label under the insect reads "humming bird moth," which is how I first conceptualized it. Hardly more than an inch long, with somewhat pointed forewings that are twice the length of the body, the moth is a rather plain brown color except for two, bright yellow, horizontal lines across its lower abdomen. Its fat fuzzy body and wide feather-like antennae show it to be a moth, and like all the other specimens in the glass case, its colors are probably almost as bright today as they were when I "bagged" it nearly sixty years ago.

The little park where I caught the hummingbird moth would give up a number of butterflies in the weeks ahead, most of which I released after examining them in the net, and it became my new special place. But it wasn't perfect. Often, there would be other people in the park, which destroyed my illusion that this was *my* special place and that I had the exclusive right to enjoy it. And the automobile traffic, though not heavy, on either side of the long, narrow park also bothered me, because I could hear their comings and goings, especially the loud music blaring out of car radios. But even though the little park had "problems" that interfered with my desire to be alone and escape into nature, my time there taught me two valuable environmental lessons that I have carried with me my whole life.

The first of these was that public space was better than private space— that if a parcel of land, a piece of nature, belongs to the public, as distinct from a private person, it could be enjoyed by small boys and adults alike "forever." The second lesson was that even the smallest bits of nature, particularly in an urban or suburban environment, have importance and should be cherished. Because I spent so much of my early life in and around the Forest Hills Gardens community of New York City, I was able to experience, in a first-hand, personal way, the dramatic contrast between the natural world and the one made by humans.

Because my new special place had limited "habitat" and was too close to traffic, I rather quickly outgrew its possibilities and wanted to explore farther afield. But because I was still only ten years old, I was too afraid at first to go very far from our home, even though my parents didn't seem to care where I went. Over the next two years, I gradually grew bolder in the distances I traveled from home. In my quest for a new hunting ground, I discovered several huge vacant lots along Queens Boulevard. This roadway is a main traffic artery from this part of the borough of Queens into Manhattan to the west, and what was once open space along it has long since been paved over and built up with apartment houses and businesses. But in the early 1950s, there was still some open land along the boulevard that had not yet been fully developed, the remnants, I believe, of farms that had once occupied much of Long Island.

This area had been cut up into vacant lots, some the size of city blocks in Manhattan. They were overgrown with high weeds, shrubs, and small trees and had dirt paths used by pedestrians that cut across them diagonally. When I stepped off the paths even a short distance, I found that there was usually enough high vegetation to conceal me from passersby, and to allow me to hunt butterflies alone and in peace. In addition to the butterflies, there were small animals that I came across in my wanderings. If one were to drive along Queens Boulevard today, it would be impossible to imagine that in the early 1950s I discovered a remnant population of garter snakes and box turtles still living in these lots.

Because these large, open fields contained many different species of flowering plants, I found my new special places along Queens Boulevard to be an especially productive hunting ground for butterflies. Of those I managed to catch, the great majority were released unharmed. After examining their delicate forms and beautiful colors as they opened and closed their wings in the back of the net, while holding the net bag shut closer to its mouth, I would then open the net and grant them their freedom. There were, however, some especially appealing individuals that I decided to collect in order to preserve them in my Riker glass specimen case.

Though I would give up collecting butterflies and moths in the future as new interests occupied my time, I never forgot how important these small creatures had been in the development of my love for the natural world. Like the quail in the Bay Harbor Islands, I mourned their rapid decline in later years as they became increasingly unable to survive in the degraded habitat left for them by human beings. During my walks around Forest Hills in the warm months, I saw fewer and fewer butterflies visiting the gardens of neighborhood homes, and on my winter strolls through Forest Park, I looked in vain for the cocoons of the once-common promethea. The blanket use of hardcore insecticides, particularly DDT, wiped out whole populations, and the addition of ever more cars, trucks, and buses to the local roadways meant that a large percentage of butterflies and moths never made it from one side of the road to the other. The male insects that did get across without being hit were often unable to mate because severe air pollution from vehicles interfered with their ability to follow the scent trail of chemical pheromones secreted by the females of their species.

As one who cherishes these beautiful and interesting life forms, I believe that the continued decline of moths and butterflies everywhere has made the outdoor world a far poorer place than it was in my youth. Those who have driven with me on long trips know, perhaps all too well, that I will brake and even swerve to avoid hitting a butterfly crossing the road, and I become upset when I see another driver in the opposite lane strike a large species like a tiger swallowtail or monarch. Indeed, I have often wondered how any individuals of this last species ever complete their southward migration, with most of them going as far as Mexico. Every time I see one in front of me successfully crossing the highway, I silently congratulate it and wish it well on its long journey.

*After we returned to Forest Hills in 1952*, Mother re-enrolled me in Kew-Forest, a highly rated private day school on Union Turnpike, just outside the Gardens, that I had attended before going to Florida. I started walking by myself to Kew-Forest, which was about a mile from our house, almost immediately after coming back north.

When I later had children of my own, it struck me as strange that Mother had been so cavalier in her guardianship of her young son—shouldn't she have been more concerned about these fairly long trips twice a day, especially since they involved leaving the supposed safety of the Gardens and walking alone for a time along Union Turnpike with its many fast-moving automobiles? But the 1950s was a more innocent period in American history, she had been on her own for much of her childhood, and she seemed to be supremely confident that nothing bad would happen to me, and, of course, nothing ever did.

Even in the worst winter weather, I remember trudging along with my book bag, still half asleep, through several inches of snow along the as yet unshoveled sidewalk. Coming home was always better because I could take more time. Often, I would sneak through a hole in a fence and walk along the tracks of the Long Island Railroad, which run parallel to the route I took every day back and forth to school. The area between the tracks and the fence that was supposed to keep boys like me away from the passing trains became one long special place. A variety of plants like milkweed, goldenrod, and thistle grew there, as well as cherry, sumac, and other small trees. On my walks back home from school, I delighted in the change of seasons from late summer to spring and all the wildlife that visited this oasis beside the tracks.

I remember how exciting it was on a seemingly lifeless winter day to flush a cottontail rabbit, many of which lived in this brushy haven, and, in the warm months, to begin making ecological connections between plants and animals. Examples were my realization that the large numbers of monarch butterflies I encountered had probably been drawn there by an abundance of their caterpillars' favorite food plant, the milkweed, and that the small flocks of American goldfinches I startled had come for the seeds in the thistle patches. Male goldfinches, or "wild canaries," as people in southern Ohio like to call them, are beautiful birds, and by the time I found the new special place provided by the Long Island Railroad, I had already added birds to my list of the types of wildlife that fascinated me most. While I had mourned the disappearance of the bobwhite quail on our home island in Florida, I had been, up to this point in my life, generally indifferent to the avian world around me. But my developing interest in birds was natural, I suppose, because they have much in common with butterflies and moths. They all defy gravity through the miracle of flight, and many are brightly colored, while some are so stunning that they make an adequate description of their beauty almost impossible.

Like so many other birders, I can remember the first bird to hook me on this new avocation. It was a male golden-crowned kinglet, not even four inches long, that I spotted flitting about in the top of a conifer tree on a cold winter day just as my father and I were entering Forest Park.

Of the countless birds I had seen up to that moment, why is it that this one would make such a lasting impression on me? Perhaps it was because the sighting took place on one of those rare and cherished walks through the park with my father during the second winter after our return to Forest Hills. Perhaps, too, it was because it was the first time I had looked through a pair of binoculars, and even though they were only low-powered opera glasses that a patient had given Dad, I was amazed by how well I could see the orange crown, bordered in yellow and black, of this animated little life form, the only living thing we could see anywhere around.

We had come to the park looking for cocoons, and I don't remember whether we found any that day. But, of course, it didn't matter, because another part of the natural world had opened up to me, one that would continue to enrich my life right up to the present.

It was at this time that I obtained a copy of Roger Tory Peterson's *A Field Guide to the Birds of Eastern and Central North America*, first published in 1934. Mine was the 1947 edition. Though it is rain damaged, battered, and taped, I still have that marvelous book, which did so much to make birding a popular avocation in the United States. When in the 1980s I became the executive director of the Connecticut Audubon Society, I had the chance to spend some time with Peterson, who also lived in Connecticut. I was happy to be able to share with him the story of the golden-crowned kinglet, my "first bird" (for him it had been a flicker woodpecker), and to tell him in person how much his field guide had meant to me in my evolution as an amateur naturalist.

By the spring of 1954, I had discovered a particularly good spot for my new outdoor activity at Flushing Meadows-Corona Park. It would now join Forest Park and the remaining vacant lots along Queens Boulevard as one of my most cherished special places. The parts of the park that most interested me were the two lakes, Meadow and Willow, on the southeastern end and the short narrow canal that connected them. Exploring the mostly undeveloped shorelines of these large lakes was a great adventure for me, and I visited the area as much as possible. Unlike the mainly dry tracts of woodland in Forest Park, this was a freshwater world, and I have always been drawn to water like a moth to a light.

From my first discovery of these new special places, I felt a compulsion to "know" all the wildlife that lived in, on, or by the lakes and the canal that connected them. Many wonderful afternoons I spent hunting butterflies with my net, stalking turtles that had hauled up on a log at the water's edge (I never caught any), and listening to male red-winged blackbirds sing their liquid, gurgling *konk-la-keee* calls that trail off at the end in a trill. I can see one of these striking birds now, swinging back and forth as he hangs on to a bulrush stalk in a stiff breeze, with the feathers of his red and yellow shoulder patches fluffed up, singing away for all he's worth.

While the blackbirds haunted the lake shore, most of the ducks were farther out in the water, where I could only see their colors in detail with my new pair of binoculars. How interesting I thought it was that the males (drakes) of species like mallards and American widgeons were so beautiful, while the females (hens) were drab, which seemed to be the opposite of how it should be. My field observations of waterfowl naturally made me want to learn not only how to identify every species I was likely to encounter but also everything there was to know about their breeding habits, migration patterns, etc. I sought, and found, books that answered all, or nearly all, of my questions about waterfowl and other species that lived in the habitats provided by Meadow and Willow lakes. Unlike some birders I've met, it wasn't enough for me simply to add a species I had never seen before to my "life list" and then move on to the next "new" variety I encountered. While my copy of Peterson's guide proved crucial for identification, it lacked the extended discussion I needed of each bird's habits.

Of the books I acquired in those early years of my ornithological wanderings, none was as important in giving me the additional information I sought than Richard H. Pough's *Audubon Water Bird Guide*, published in 1951. As in the case of Peterson's work, I virtually memorized every illustration in Pough's guide so that I would know the identity of a bird even before I saw it. Not only did Pough's book support my growing love for wildlife and the habitats that sustain it, but it also made me understand for the first time the role played by human beings in the decline of many species. From his general dedication at the beginning—"To all who find joy and recreation in a better understanding of the many forms of life with which we share the earth"—to his discussion of individual species like the snowy and reddish egrets that were decimated by plume hunters in the late nineteenth century, the conservation message is never far below the surface.

While my new special places of Meadow and Willow lakes, or more precisely their shorelines, were a seemingly unlimited source of outdoor adventure, it was the short canal that connected them that would prove to be most fascinating of all. It didn't take much thought to understand that this waterway, only a feeble stone's toss across, had to be an important route for fishes passing between the lakes and a natural place for this hopeful angler to station himself to intercept them. But casting a hooked night crawler or small angleworm repeatedly out into the canal and letting the bait sit on the bottom produced nothing in the way of fishy interest. I received the same result when I suspended the bait up off the bottom by means of a small bobber attached to the line a foot or so above the worm.

Only after many decades of fishing and hunting have I fully realized how important these pursuits have been in the development of what might be called the "naturalist mind." Here was yet another example of being driven to solve the problem at hand, which was how to catch fish I couldn't see, but which I knew *must* be hiding somewhere in the canal, probably just below the surface. Successful fishing and hunting are, in essence, mental exercises, where the predatory animal (in this case me) learns the habits of its prey in order to outwit it. Isn't this the reason why meat-eating predators, like coyotes and lions, are generally more intelligent than the herbivores, like rabbits and wildebeest, they hunt? They have to solve the problem of catching their next meal, which they often do in cooperation with others of their kind, while herbivores need only to look for the nearest patch of edible vegetation—and grass doesn't run very fast!

That first day at the canal, as I stood for a long time at its edge watching dragonflies and swallows darting over the shining water, I wondered what to do next. However appealing the scene, I was no closer to succeeding in my angling quest until I remembered two of the basic rules for successful fishing. First, keep trying different baits until you finally find what the fish are feeding on, and second, locate the cover your quarry lives in, or around, even when it isn't obvious above the surface of the water.

By following these guidelines, I would finally experience the joy of outwitting my unseen prey. Taking the butterfly net I had with me, I waded out into a shallow area at the Meadow Lake end that was thick with aquatic plants and slowly swept the deep net back and forth under the water. To my surprise, every sweep brought up a dozen or more shrimp about a half inch long. A hooked bundle of these tiny crustaceans would, I reasoned, make a tasty treat for any fish in the area.

I now had to find the cover the fish were using. After walking back and forth along the short length of the canal as I studied its shoreline carefully, it finally dawned on me that the sections of wooden bulkheads that held back the bank on both sides of the waterway might be what I was looking for. Of varying lengths, the sections had been placed horizontally, but they seemed to be uneven in how they fitted together, leaving gaps at the ends that might provide hiding places for shrimp and other small prey species. In some spots, the top bulkhead pieces also looked as if they had slid out over the bottom sections, leaving overhangs that would provide attractive cover for both predator and prey.

There's nothing in fishing and hunting so satisfying as thinking up a scheme for capturing your quarry and having that strategy work out exactly as planned. Hooking together several of the tiny shrimp I had caught, I dropped them free-line (without any sinker or bobber) right next to a particularly uneven part of the wooden bulkhead, and before the bait had sunk very far down into the yellowish green water, the line jerked, I struck, and a scrappy fish was on. After a brief, but exciting, fight on my light rod, I experienced what can only be described as exaltation when I finally brought the tired fish up to the surface, and then hoisted it up and over the bulkhead to the grassy area on the other side.

My prize was a white crappie (*Pomoxis annularis*), about ten inches long. Flattened in appearance, with silvery-olive sides, big eyes, and an underslung jaw, it was the first of many crappies I caught using my special technique. Most of these I released, but a few were taken home to be eaten.

While the canal between the lakes would be my special place near home for freshwater fishing, the mouth of Reynolds Channel, between the communities of Far Rockaway and Atlantic Beach, where that waterway meets the Atlantic Ocean southeast of Idlewild (later John F. Kennedy) International Airport, would prove just as dear to me as a saltwater angling mecca. There, my brothers and I used that remarkably hardy baitfish called "killies" (*Fundulus heteroclitus*) to fish for fluke (summer flounder). Hooking them through both lips so that they would swim naturally, we drifted slowly along in Reynolds Channel with the wind or current, depending on which was stronger at the moment, allowing our weighted lines out the upwind or upcurrent side of the boat, often with a shiny spinner rotating ahead of the killie to attract the attention of a fluke half-buried in the sand or mud on the bottom. When the little fish passed over the voracious predator, the flounder would burst from its hiding place and suck it down. In essence, every time a fluke fell for this ploy, we had ambushed the ambusher.

One must not strike too hard, or too quickly, however, when setting the hook in the mouth of a summer flounder. The bait can be pulled out of the fish's mouth or bitten in half, behind the hook. Like most types of fishing, it takes some experience to develop the finesse to hook fluke consistently, but the skill is well worth developing, for big ones of several pounds are strong fighters and delicious eating.

Even though I have been fortunate enough to have caught many kinds of exotic game fishes like tarpon and sailfish, I think I would almost rather slow-drift with live killies in fluke-rich waters than engage in any other kind of fishing. Perhaps, it is the variety of things to look at, like other anglers in nearby boats fighting fish or the changing nature of the shoreline as I move past. Or more probably, it is the chance to live again in an idealized moment from my childhood. My brothers are no longer in the boat with me, engaged in their ceaseless bickering. I am alone, a young boy once more, drifting silently along in Reynolds Channel with the tip of my fishing rod just starting to bend downwards as a big fluke has inhaled my unlucky killie.

*In the years before I was sent off* to boarding school, the closest contact I had with my father, on a day-to-day basis, was on my Christmas and spring vacations. Though my mother had required him to sell the house in the Bay Harbor Islands and return to Forest Hills before she would grant him a divorce—at the same time I left for Lawrenceville—Dad still wanted to return to Southeast Florida every chance he got. His sons' school vacations gave him that opportunity. So, for two or more weeks a year, he brought us to the Ocean Reef Club on the northern end of Key Largo, where he could immerse himself, and us, in his passion for fishing.

I will always be grateful to Dad for providing these unique opportunities to experience the sea world, even though they came with a heavy price. This was because my father had a never-ending compulsion to abuse me psychologically, especially when he had an audience like my two brothers or our fishing guide, Tommy Gifford. He seemed to enjoy criticizing me for my looks (I had buck teeth), stupidity, clumsiness, or some other deficiency, and would often encourage Tony and George to join in the baiting. Both of them enjoyed this game, the goal of which seemed to be to get me to start crying. Then, if I tried to defend myself verbally, I was so hurt and embarrassed that I would excitedly and loudly stammer my response, a reaction that brought great amusement to all three of them. In fact, on these fishing trips my father often referred to me not as John or Johnny, but as the puppet "Mr. Bluster" from the popular television show for kids, *Howdy Doody*.

Despite this unhappy situation while aboard Captain Gifford's fishing boat, I usually managed to do what I have always done in such circumstances, and that was to separate my involvement with nature from my interactions with my fellow human beings. Whether it was fishing, hunting, birding, or going on safari, I have learned how to experience, and cherish, the joys of engagement in the natural world while being at least partially successful in sloughing off the unpleasantness or ignorance of those around me.

When we first encountered him in the early 1950s, even before we left the Bay Harbor Islands to return to Forest Hills, charter boat captain Tommy Gifford was already a household name wherever big-game anglers gathered. Then in his fifties, he had been guiding since the 1920s, and giant game fishes like swordfish, marlin, and bluefin tuna, many of which weighed hundreds of pounds, were his specialty. He had been instrumental in developing the sport of big-game fishing in Montauk, at the end of New York's Long Island; Wedgeport, Nova Scotia; Havana, Cuba; and Bimini, in the Bahamas. Most of Gifford's friends and wealthy clients were well known only in angling circles, but literary giant Ernest Hemingway was the exception. He and Gifford were friends, who held each other in high esteem for their fishing prowess.

So how was it that my father joined this exclusive club of angling enthusiasts lucky enough to have Tommy (he insisted that everyone call him only by his first name) as their guide? The answer seems to be that in the years before my father's retirement and my parents' final, physical, separation, when Dad was still making lots of money as a doctor, he simply had no limits to what he would spend on his indulgences, two of which were fishing and travel. And there was no question about the quality of the angling when staying at the Ocean Reef Club. Despite the unpleasantness of my father and brothers, I will always remember, with fondness, those sunlit days on the green and blue ocean off of Key Largo.

I clearly recall sitting in a chair in Tommy's 26-foot boat, the *Stormy Petrel*, and intently watching the slender, silvery dead baitfish, about ten inches long, with a hook so perfectly threaded through it as to make it seem alive as it skittered along the surface behind the boat. When the sea was up it took great skill on Tommy's part to run the boat at just the right trolling speed to keep the baitfish lure, usually a ballyhoo (*Hemiramphus balao*), moving realistically on the surface. Sometimes, we could see the end of a sailfish's spear come out of the water behind the bait and slash at the ballyhoo before it was able to gulp it down. Once hooked, the billfish would hurl itself out of the water time after time to escape the strange force that enslaved it. However paradoxical it may seem to the nonangler, these leaps, especially those where the sailfish ran along the surface on its tail, with its body completely out of the water, would fill me with admiration and even empathy for these magnificent creatures.

Because Tommy insisted that we use light tackle when trolling for sailfish, meaning that our rod and reel held nothing stronger than twenty-pound test line (defined as line that will break under the strain of any weight above twenty pounds), we had to exercise a fair amount of angling skill to catch our prize. In other words, we had to "play" the sailfish, allowing it to run when it wanted, and tire itself out before we worked it methodically back to the boat. He constantly reminded us that if we wanted to become real anglers, we had to follow a code of sporting ethics and allow the game fish every chance to show off its power and speed before we were able to capture it.

According to one television documentary I have seen on this exquisite species, sailfish are among the fastest fish in the sea, able to swim at speeds approaching sixty miles an hour. Though that estimate seems incredible, I can personally attest to their power, especially in the initial run. After I hooked my first one, I remember very well my amazement at how fast the line sliced through the water, forcing me quickly to move from one side of the *Stormy Petrel* around the stern to the other side. Holding the rod tightly with both hands, I looked down anxiously at my open-faced reel as the line tore off the revolving spool so rapidly I thought the fish would strip the reel, and it nearly did.

The average-sized sailfish we caught was probably about seven feet in length and looked very large, especially with its enormous, dark blue dorsal fin extended, as it lay exhausted alongside the boat. But appearances are misleading, for most of these fish weighed less than forty pounds. The first one I caught was one of these "average" fish, but its capture was still one of the great thrills of my early life.

Though sailfish are good eating when smoked, I don't recall us keeping any. I'm not sure how the others felt, but I had such admiration for their fighting ability and gratitude for the excitement they had provided me that there was never any question in my mind about whether or not they should be released.

In trolling for sailfish, king mackerel, and other large predatory species, Tommy often took us out beyond the inshore waters and into the Gulf Stream, which at times runs only a few miles off the Florida Keys. First described in 1513 by the Spanish explorer and discoverer of Florida, Juan Ponce de León, this warm ocean current originates in the Gulf of Mexico and flows north along the southern coast of the United States. After passing Cape Hatteras, it moves away from the coast and out into the Atlantic Ocean. About fifty miles wide, and with an average speed of four miles an hour, it is a veritable river in the ocean that plays a major role in regulating climate.

It was always obvious when we crossed into the Gulf Stream, because the color of the ocean changed from a pale bluish-green to a deep, solid blue. It was along the edge of this oceanic river, where the inshore and offshore waters meet, that we found our most productive fishing for species like sailfish, bonito, and dolphin—the fish (*Coryphaena hippurus*), not the mammal! (To make sure that diners don't think they're eating a bottle-nosed dolphin, restaurants usually sell this gourmet's delight under the Hawaiian name of *mahi-mahi*.) Not only are dolphin wonderful eating, they are also great fighters, often jumping clear of the water when hooked, and striking in appearance. With an elongated, compressed body, they are a beautiful blue, with some green along the top, and yellow, with blue spots, along the bottom. The tail is also yellow, and all the colors are iridescent. Unfortunately, after it dies, a dolphin's colors fade away to an overall yellowish or silver cast. Most of those we caught probably weighed no more than fifteen pounds.

In trolling for dolphin I was reminded once again that so much of fishing is like hunting, for both activities require an alertness and active participation in the natural world that no one who is content with merely being a passive spectator at the edge of nature can really appreciate. We were not out on the water just to take a boat ride on a sunny day; we were there to solve the problem at hand, which was finding and catching dolphin. In order to achieve that goal, we kept searching the ocean in all directions for patches of brown sargassum seaweed, any type of floating debris, or seabirds diving on schools of baitfish. Sometimes we would spot the panicked baitfish leaping out of the water even before the birds found them, and we knew that trolling or casting baits or lures in the vicinity would almost always bring strikes from the predators under the schools. The importance of the cover that seaweed patches and all types of floating objects provided for small fishes, which in turn attracted large game fishes like dolphin, always fascinated me. Once, Tommy idled the *Stormy Petrel* near a single wooden orange crate, and casting to it, we caught two small dolphins that had made it their home.

In addition to searching for likely fishing hot spots on the surface of the Gulf Stream, I also enjoyed watching oil tankers and freighters plowing the sea in the distance. We mainly saw the southbound ships, because their captains wanted to hug the inshore edge of the Gulf Stream so that they would not have to fight the full brunt of the four-mile-an-hour current farther out. While I always wondered what was in those tarp-covered containers piled up on the decks of the freighters, and where their captains were going, my chief interest was in the dolphins—the mammals this time—that rode the ships' bow waves. It was delightful to watch them with my binoculars and see them come clear out of the water in horizontal leaps.

In the beginning, when I first started to look for these marine acrobats, I assumed that all the *cetaceans* I was seeing, or would ever see, were common bottle-nosed dolphins. Then one special afternoon, while training my binoculars on a southbound freighter running parallel to us about a half mile farther out in the Gulf Stream, I was amazed to see dolphins repeatedly leaping straight up into the air beside the starboard bow and spinning like a top before falling back into the water again. What an exhibition of sheer exuberance on the part of these appropriately named spinner dolphins (*Stenella longirostris*). The happening is still vivid in my memory, as well as the joy it brought me, and like all such exciting events in nature, I am grateful for having experienced it.

The sea off the Ocean Reef Club was, of course, too vast to be conceived of by me as a specific "special place." The closest I came to having one was an area of ocean surrounding a large red bell buoy. Anchored on the edge of the deep water drop-off, right up against the reef ledge, this metal cagelike structure with the rounded bottom was probably, like its modern equivalent, about twenty feet tall and six feet wide. The motion of the waves caused the bell to ring loudly, so that even in conditions of poor visibility, captains would be able to hear the sound and to orient themselves for a safe return into the channel running back to the club.

Even though the buoy was a big, permanent, human-made structure on the surface of a featureless ocean, with excellent fishing in its vicinity, it could never be the equivalent of earlier special places like Hump Bridge in the Bay Harbor Islands or the canal in Flushing Meadows-Corona Park. The main reason it didn't make the grade was because I could never have the area to myself, even for a short time, and the continuous presence of my unpleasant father and brothers kept me from finding the peace for which I longed. Still, the sight of the buoy in the distance as we headed toward it in the morning was a welcome one. Once we were close and anchored nearby, everyone on board felt excitement, for we knew that we would probably soon have excellent fishing, especially for the many barracuda that used the buoy as their home base.

It was after one day of surprisingly slow fishing at the buoy and a particularly intense period of verbal abuse toward me by my father, with both of my brothers joining in, that Tommy announced quite dramatically that the next day he was going to get me a certificate of recognition, perhaps even a record, for catching a big bar jack (*Caranx ruber*) on very light tackle. Perhaps he thought that if I accomplished this feat, the other males in my family would treat me with greater respect. In fact, he often showed a kindness toward me not possessed by my father and sometimes seemed embarrassed by Dad's constant criticisms of me.

As promised, the next day he anchored the *Stormy Petrel* near a deep hole in the reef where he knew a school of large bar jacks lived. I would not fish from the big boat but from a dinghy that he rowed or paddled over to the spot. I don't remember what kind of craft it was, probably the World War II inflatable life raft he kept on board for emergencies. Although Tommy intended that only he, as my coach, and I would be in the tiny boat, my brother Tony managed to push his way into the stern of the dinghy just as we shoved off. Like George, Tony couldn't stand the idea of my getting special treatment and was present to irritate me and, hopefully, to see me fail in this test of angling skill.

Our quarry that day, the bar jack, is a cousin of the jack crevalle, with which I was already familiar from my fishing experiences in the canal behind our house in the Bay Harbor Islands. It even looks something like the crevalle, except that it is whiter and more elongated, lacking the blunt head and underslung jaw that give the crevalle its pugnacious appearance. But like all members of the jack family, it is a terrific battler that never gives up until completely exhausted.

Using spinning tackle with only six-pound test line on the reel, in order that my opponent could exercise its full potential for demonstrating speed and power, I cast a piece of cut-bait out into the middle of the deep hole, and after sinking only a few inches, it was taken by a strong fish that ran a good seventy-five yards off the reel before turning back toward the dinghy. I held the rod tip up high to put pressure on the fish and reeled furiously to keep slack out of the line that could cause the hook to fall out of its mouth. Because I was using such light line, I didn't care how long the fight would take. Unlike a bottom fish like a grouper or snapper, a jack wouldn't try to duck into a hole in the coral formations, breaking the line. I had the whole open ocean to fight the fish, and my only concern was that if I took too long, the hook might work itself out.

Still, the far greater danger was getting impatient and trying to force a "green" fish back to the boat before it had really given up. Tony knew this was *the* danger, but he sat in the back of the tiny craft, behind Tommy who was in the middle behind me, and continually complained about how he was getting sunburned and why I should hurry things up and get the fish in. Tommy finally got fed up with Tony and told him to be quiet.

With Tommy coaching me, I continued to play the fish for about twenty minutes before I could feel it becoming sufficiently tired for me to be able to tighten the drag and pump it back to the dinghy. When the fish finally broke the surface nearby, Tommy exclaimed, "Rainbow runner!" Bringing it alongside, I felt the pure joy of the successful angler when he reached down and grabbing it by the tail, pulled the beautiful creature into the boat.

The rainbow runner (*Elagatis bipinnulatus*) is long and slender, with a pointed head and a large, deeply forked tail that gives it such power in swimming. As its name indicates, this species has a strikingly beautiful color pattern. The back is bluish green, and the sides have horizontal stripes of blue and yellow, while the lower part of the body is white or yellowish-silver, and the fins are greenish-yellow. Though it was good sized, twelve and one-half pounds, and caught on very light tackle, I would get no certificate or record from the catch. While it swims in every tropical ocean of the world, it is nowhere common, and it is especially rare in the waters off Key Largo. What was a certificate of recognition, "suitable for framing," compared to making such a beautiful and unusual catch?! The

*Holding my twelve-and-a-half-pound rainbow runner, caught with Tommy Gifford off the Ocean Reef Club in Key Largo.*

management of the Ocean Reef Club thought enough of my fish that they had it mounted and displayed in a prominent place.

Like so many of my most memorable experiences in fishing and hunting, the fight with the rainbow runner not only made me a better outdoorsman (or outdoorsboy), but it also taught me about life in general. In order to be successful, I had to have patience and remain focused on solving the problem at hand, ignoring the distractions around me.

The major distraction in this case was, of course, my brother Tony's constant complaining. My history with both my brothers, right up to today, has been replete with such efforts to divert me from a positive course of action into a channel leading to failure. This sibling rivalry, with its unrelenting competitiveness and one-upmanship, has covered everything from catching a trophy fish they could, and should, have caught to writing a book they could, and should, have written. Since I had grown up with this relationship, I had gotten used to it by the time I had the adventure with the rainbow runner. What would surprise me in the coming years, however, was that this unpleasantness never declined with the passage of time. In fact, as we reached middle age and beyond, their insecurities about my successes, and their need to kill any effort on my part to share the joy of accomplishing them, seemed to increase, perhaps because they knew that the chances to outdo their little brother were becoming ever fewer.

After several vacations at the Ocean Reef Club, I never saw Tommy Gifford again. I regret that fact, because he had taught me much about what it meant to be an ethical angler, with respect for one's quarry, what I would later call the code of the sportsman. In addition, he was the only person on the *Stormy Petrel* who treated me with genuine affection.

*The years I spent at the Kew-Forest School* after returning from Key Largo are now only a blur. The exception was the seventh grade, when I was twelve, my last year at home. My parents were getting ready for their permanent separation, and I was both depressed and angry that there seemed to be some intrinsic connection between the finalization of their divorce and my being forced out of my home to begin a five-year exile at an all-male prep school in New Jersey. Besides feeling utterly abandoned by my parents, I seemed to know that I was about to lose any chance for a future life as a normal teenager. All during the seventh grade, I pleaded with Mother to let me stay at Kew-Forest one more year, so that I could complete elementary school in Forest Hills and not be sent away to Lawrenceville until the beginning of high school in the ninth grade. Whether or not she ever seriously entertained my proposition, I'll never know. She could kill several birds with one stone by packing me off to boarding school. Even though Kew-Forest was excellent academically, it was not rated as highly as Lawrenceville. She would gain prestige for herself by sending me away, hopefully prepare me for entry into the social elite, especially if I attended an Ivy League college after graduation, and escape any of the hands-on requirements of motherhood for nine months of the year.

That last summer before the start of my five-year incarceration in what one of my sociology professors at Duke called an "institution of total social control" is one I'd like to forget. Unfortunately, much of it is still vivid in my memory.

One of my concerns was that I would be separated from several friends at Kew-Forest, especially my best friend, Chuck Pucie. Another was that for most of the year I would no longer be able to visit my special places, like Forest Park, Meadow and Willow lakes, and that wonderful canal that connected them. And finally, I would lose my retreat on the upper floor at the back of the house, my own bedroom where I could go and be alone, and escape family unpleasantness.

Some time after my thirteenth birthday, in June 1956, my father finally left the house for the last time. There was no ceremony or even a good-bye. For a long while, he had come back home at night less and less, and finally, one day, I realized that he wasn't coming back at all. I was hurt and confused by his leaving, and because both of my parents had tied this sad event to my own departure for boarding school in September, I was made to feel a certain responsibility for their separation.

The divorce proceedings that were already underway were probably no more acrimonious than most, but divorce in the 1950s had a stigma attached to it that it is hard to conceptualize today. For one thing, it was much rarer and had connotations of character deficiencies and moral failure that largely disappeared in later years. It was not just the Catholic Church but "respectable" society in general that seemed to hold to the position that no matter how miserable two people were, they stayed together, especially if children were involved.

That summer of 1956 was, indeed, a bad one. I think I felt like a convicted felon, barely able to function in the last weeks of freedom before being sent off to begin a five-year prison sentence. My relationship with Mother soured to the point that we barely spoke. But as bad as conditions were, I was still at home, and I would soon discover that all my fears about life in a male-only boarding school were completely justified.

# CHAPTER FOUR

# Finding Solace in the Natural World:

## *Prep-School Years in New Jersey, Maine,*
## *and South Florida, 1956-1961*

The seventy-mile car ride from Forest Hills to Lawrenceville was a study in contrasts. It began in a suburban world, with parks, trees, and bushes, moved westward across the heart of Manhattan, where nature had been all but erased from view, southward into New Jersey along the western edge of the New York metropolitan area and through one of the ugliest, smelliest industrial zones of the United States, and finally out into the bucolic, often beautiful, farmlands around Princeton and Lawrenceville.

I had taken the trip a number of times before, when my parents were visiting one or both of my brothers, or bringing them home for vacation, but this ride was, of course, very different from previous ones. Now it would be my turn to endure the harsh realities of the boarding school experience.

Founded in 1810, Lawrenceville is one of the oldest of the American private academies that correspond to the so-called "public schools" of England like Eton and Harrow. In terms of social prestige and presumed academic excellence, Lawrenceville has often been grouped together with two other elite college-preparatory schools, Andover, founded in Massachusetts in 1778, and Exeter, founded in New Hampshire in 1783.

By the beginning of the 1950s, the leaders of all three institutions came to believe that because of the rigorous demands placed on their students to succeed in what were often college-level studies, graduates of their academies were finding the first year or two of college to be a boring repetition of what they had already learned. As a result, educators from the "big three" prep schools joined together with the "big three" at the top of the Ivy League college hierarchy, Harvard, Princeton, and Yale, and formed a committee to study the problem.

In 1952, this group published a report that would lead to the establishment, in 1955, of the Advanced Placement Program for high-school students. Originally, the purpose of AP courses was to have seniors engage in college-level work, like that already being done at the private academies, to be followed by achievement examinations. Those who scored well on the tests would then be given advanced standing in these subjects after they entered college. Many millions have taken these exams, but over the years, they have become less of an opportunity for advanced standing once a student enters college and more of a tool for being admitted to college in the first place. Thus, they have become another example of how students from wealthy secondary schools, with many AP classes, have a distinct advantage over those from poorer institutions with few, if any, of these courses.

Lawrenceville's key role in the creation of the Advanced Placement Program just as I was matriculating there in September 1956 indicates the intensity of the academic pressure I was about to experience on a daily basis. I soon discovered that if I fell behind by even one class assignment, especially in subjects like math and science, there was little chance of catching up. Compounding my unhappiness over this unrelenting pressure to perform well academically for my "masters" (the British term for teachers used at Lawrenceville), without any encouragement whatsoever from my absent mother and father, was the Spartan, spiritually draining physical environment in which I was forced to live and the culture of aggression that permeated the place.

When Mother and I arrived on campus, I learned that I had been assigned to Perry Ross, one of four "houses" in a huge, brick, two-story building called Lower School. Each house was a barrack-like dormitory with about fifteen cubicles, with thin wooden partitions between them, on either side of a wide hallway. As I recall, my compartment had a shallow built-in closet that extended out from one side, and barely enough room for a small bed, a radiator, a bureau with a little lamp on top, and a hard, straight-back chair. Because the sides of the cubicles didn't go all the way to the ceiling, any boy could hear other boys talking several cubicles away. This structural feature, as well as the fact that there was no door at the entrance of the compartments, meant that there was little privacy possible in my new habitat. That first day, as I stood in the hallway looking in at what would be my tiny home for the "first-form" year at Lawrenceville, I longed to be back in my bedroom at 57 Continental Avenue, getting ready to enter the eighth grade at Kew-Forest School.

After we moved in my few belongings, Mother seemed to be in a hurry to leave. Watching her drive away, I felt as if I had been betrayed and left completely alone to fend for myself. Virtually every night for at least the first week, as I laid in bed wondering if I could cope with my new life, I quietly cried myself to sleep.

I would soon learn that in order to become a well-adjusted member of this new closed world I found myself in, I was supposed to give up any desire for a private life and any thoughts of developing a value system apart from the one dictated to me by those in power. This group included not only the masters but the more aggressive "student leaders" as well, who often controlled what went on in Lower School when the masters weren't present, which was most of the time.

Though my mother and father were hardly model parents, they had, on occasion, acted in ways that seemed to show at least a modicum of affection. And like most children, I had a bond with them that could never be duplicated by the authority figures at Lawrenceville.

When I entered the school it still possessed a tradition of hazing "Rhinies," the name given to new boys by those in the forms above them. In some cases, my fellow first formers, who were particularly aggressive, could, and did, follow the example of those in the upper forms and persecute other first-year students.

For a while, my older brothers attended Lawrenceville at the same time, and according to Tony, George had a particularly difficult experience in Lower School. Another boy forced him to polish his shoes, bring him food treats, and perform other humiliating tasks until Tony, who was called "Big Reigs" because he is three years older than George and was then much larger in size, came down to Lower School and beat up the bully. Rather than being grateful for his older brother's intervention, George was apparently embarrassed by it, and the incident widened the long-standing rift between them.

When I was in the first form I had no older brother to protect me, and I'm not sure I would have wanted the protection even if it had been available. One thing I learned about the place was that each of us was strictly on our own when it came to hazing or any other aspect of social interaction.

As one of the biggest kids in the whole Lower School, I would never suffer the same fate as George, but I did have to defend myself, both verbally and physically, on many occasions. My large size may have saved me from some forms of aggression, but not all. Other big boys wanted to challenge me and impress our peers by making me back down by refusing to fight. One thing I found out quickly was that I should never retreat, even if I got hurt in these stupid contests for status. If a boy didn't defend himself, he invariably became a doormat for others, and I had no intention of letting that happen to me.

The fact that so many of the boys in Lower School came from distant places with different cultural values from my own added to my sense of social isolation. Not only were there kids from all over the United States but a number came from Europe and Latin America as well. Except for a few who lived in the New York City area, I had little in common with any of them. Consequently, I found it difficult to make even casual friendships.

I have always felt cheated that I was never able to have the experience of most teenagers, who could escape to their homes after school and on the weekends and live a normal life including daily socializing with both boys *and* girls. I came to envy Chuck Pucie, with whom I managed to stay in touch through all the five years I was away at Lawrenceville. It was Chuck's decision to leave Kew-Forest at the end of the eighth grade and enroll at a local Catholic high school, where he not only received an excellent education but made friends with a group of boys who are still close fifty years later. I, on the other, never kept in regular contact with a single boy I knew in boarding school.

Since every day but Saturday began with a compulsory church service in the Protestant chapel, which even the few Catholic and Jewish students had to attend, and because classes met six days a week (though Wednesday and Saturday classes ended at noon), the only possible large blocks of time I might have for myself were on Wednesday, Saturday, or Sunday afternoons. But even at those times, I was often expected to be at some scheduled school event. In particular, I remember the pressure put on students to be present, and enthusiastically supportive, when the varsity football team played a rival prep school. My Saturday afternoons were too precious to spend on such pursuits, and I skipped many games, even though I received much criticism from both masters and fellow students for this lack of school spirit.

The faculty at Lawrenceville seemed to feel that every minute of the day must be filled with what they assumed were uplifting activities. One of them, Marshall Chambers, would later recall that "ingrained in us masters was the conviction that boys had to be kept busy. Free time meant trouble."[5] During my entire five years at the school, I found most of these forced time-fillers, like watching athletic contests and attending "teas" conducted by the housemaster and his wife, to be a waste of time. These required activities were all part of the institution's ongoing effort to have us internalize its definition of the personal traits that would get us admitted to a prestigious college or university, preferably in the Ivy League, and ensure our later advancement into the elite of American society.

Chief among those characteristics that we should adopt was a love of competition at an almost ruthless level. Whether in academics or sports, we should learn to excel, which usually meant outdoing our fellow students even if they were made to look foolish or weak in the process. If a boy failed to measure up in this macho world, he could be accused of being effeminate, or worse. Because no girls of our own age were present, I think that many of us, myself included, were unsure about whether our sexuality was developing "appropriately."

Given my feelings of social isolation and the stress caused by the unrelenting pressure on me to compete in the classroom and on the playing field, I think I would have experienced an emotional breakdown if I had not been able to escape into nature. My retreat was the rich farmland that bordered the campus along its eastern side. For an unhappy teenager who rejected just about every institutional value Lawrenceville seemed to espouse, this world was my wonderland. When, on an outgoing trip, I climbed over the first barbed-wire fence on the boundary line between the campus and the private farmland, I always felt a tingling of excitement and anticipation, for I had regained my freedom, at least for a time. Just as I felt joy sneaking off the campus, I never failed to experience a kind of depression crossing back over that same barbed-wire fence on my return trip. I knew that I would soon be enduring more institutional regimentation and assaults on my individuality.

I will never forget my first mini-safari to what would soon become a group of special places that would sustain me through that whole unpleasant period of my life. Though I had some information from my brother George about which direction to take to get off the Lawrenceville grounds and on to the farmland, I was still hazy about what kind of natural world I would find on the other side of the boundary fence. My first exploration took place only a couple of weeks after arriving on campus in the fall of 1956 and began with an effort to get away from Perry Ross unnoticed. This was important, since my trips were unauthorized, and if caught, I might have received some sort of disciplinary action.

Heading southeast and skirting the edge of the golf course, always making sure to use the cover of trees and bushes as much as possible, I passed some large maintenance buildings and finally arrived in a wooded area the school used as a trash dump. Along the southern end of the dump is a creek called "Shipetaukin" (actually the Lower Shipetaukin), a name I only learned recently. It runs east out of the school pond and past the Lavino Field House before leaving the Lawrenceville property and entering the farmland beyond. Finding this small stream delighted me, for I knew that any land that has permanent running water on it is probably rich in wildlife, both above and below the water's surface.

Almost immediately, I saw that there were tiny fish in the main channel of the shallow creek, as well as many different kinds of animal tracks in the exposed mud flats along the bottom edges of the banks. On that first trip, I had no idea what creatures had made those footprints, but in time, I would be able to identify them all, from great blue herons and wood ducks to muskrats and raccoons.

Following Lower Shipetaukin, I came to a primitive bridge across the stream that the farmer evidently used to take his tractor or other machinery across. It consisted of heavy wooden planks resting on top of two metal beams embedded in the ground. From the concentration of tracks going in and out under the structure, many animals apparently found the cover provided by the bridge an attractive hiding place or hunting ground.

Soon after passing under the rustic bridge, the creek emptied into a marsh that I would come to love as one of my most important special places. Even though I was wearing new sneakers and a good pair of pants, hardly the right clothes for wading through a wetland, I felt the explorer's exhilaration at discovering new country, and plunged right into the reeds and mud nearly up to my waist in my determination to follow the watercourse wherever it led. In the future, when I planned to visit the marsh, I wore my chest waders that I had Mother bring from home and kept stored in a waterproof bag that I hid in a brush pile in a patch of woods at the edge of the school property.

As soon as I entered the wetland, I noticed what looked like smaller versions of the beaver lodges I had seen in pictures in books on natural history. Because my brother George had trapped muskrats in this area when he was at Lawrenceville, I knew that these conical mounds, two to three feet above the water and built of marsh vegetation, must be muskrat houses. It was exciting to see these lodges in the marsh and to know that one (or maybe more) of the large rodents with the rich brown fur and long flattened tails was probably inside its home at the same time I was kneeling next to it in order to examine the structure in detail.

After leaving the marsh, I walked up into a forested area adjacent to the wetland. It was a dark, shady woodlot, with a canopy of tree limbs overhead and a lot of bare ground underneath. Some of the trees were huge and looked like they might be two centuries old. On the two sides nearest me, the woodlot had a barbed-wire fence to keep the farmer's black-and-white cows from wandering off. My first sight of the cows among the forest giants, some standing and some lying down, was such a beautiful, bucolic scene that it is still a vivid memory today.

I would later learn that the cows were not always in attendance. On most of my visits they could be seen out in the open pasture, and it was at such times that I enjoyed climbing over the fence, walking out into the middle of the woodland, and sitting for a long time up against the side of a deceased patriarch that had fallen in years past. From this ringside seat, I spent countless hours over the next five years watching the natural world go by.

I didn't like being in the woodlot when the cows were present; they tended to spook wildlife, and to be honest, they made me uneasy. On a couple of occasions when I did share the lot with them, one or two approached me so closely that I had to get up and yell at them while waving my arms furiously, all of which, of course, scared away any animals or birds nearby. Though I wasn't really frightened of them, and sensed that they were simply curious about this strange being in their midst, the fact remains that Holstein dairy cows are really big, *and* intimidating, when you are backed up against a tree trunk and they are pushing their faces right into yours!

When I did have the woodland to myself, I remember how fascinated I was by the different ways in which birds will work over a tree when searching for insects. Two of my favorites are the white-breasted nuthatch, which climbs down a tree headfirst, and the much less common brown creeper, which starts at the base of a tree and then ascends in a spiral pattern around it.

Of the mammals in the woodlot, the most common, of course, were squirrels, which were interesting to watch in any season. In the warm months, I would also often see woodchucks coming back to their burrows along the boundary between the woodlot and the pasture.

In earlier years, in my wanderings around Forest Park, I had learned the identities of many of the common tree species of the Northeast, and during my time at Lawrenceville I developed a deep affection for the large trees of the woodlot, especially the oaks, hickories, and beeches. Of these, the beeches would join the sycamore/London plane tree as one of my two favorite trees.

Both species are, I think, most beautiful on a bright winter's day when the trees are bathed in sunlight reflecting off the snow-covered ground. At such times, the white trunk of a big sycamore seems to shine as the tree reaches up to a blue sky. Under the same winter conditions, the bark of a large beech will have a silvery glow. Many of its elliptical leaves will have remained on the tree, but they are now a golden yellow, and in a breeze they rustle and glimmer in the sunlight.

Sitting for a time alone by an ancient tree, especially but not exclusively sycamores and beeches, has always made me feel better, regardless of what else was happening in my life at that moment. These magnificent living things have been a permanent, peaceful, and reassuring presence in my life when all else seemed chaotic or meaningless.

On that first visit to the woodlot in the fall of 1956, I didn't stay long, because I hoped to have enough time that afternoon to reach my final destination, the "swimming-hole stream," which my brother George had told me was the biggest creek in the area. (In actuality, this is the wider, deeper Upper Shipetaukin.) Although I had little in the way of specifics, I knew that the watercourse must be in the same, more or less easterly direction, I had been following since I left the campus.

Coming down from the higher ground of the woodlot, I skirted the edge of the marsh, crossed a field, pushed my way through a narrow strip of brushy second-growth woods, and came out onto a wide pasture where I could see a meandering line of trees out in the middle that I was sure must be the swimming-hole stream. I could barely contain my excitement as I came up to the edge of its high bank and looked down into water that I knew contained endless possibilities. Unlike the tiny creek coming out of the school pond, the Upper Shipetaukin probably had holes deep enough to sustain some fishes of decent size, perhaps even approaching a pound in weight, and wide enough to attract many ducks during migration. Indeed, soon after I began following the cow path along the top of the bank, I flushed a pair of wood ducks that twisted away though the branches of a large tree.

It was the first time I heard the distinctive, piercing *wee-e-e-e-k*, *wee-e-e-e-k* call of the hen, and I would never forget it. The sun was bright, and the pair was close enough as they flew up off the water for me to see the gorgeous colors of the drake, the most beautiful of all American waterfowl.

Because the afternoon was growing late, I began to walk faster as I followed the winding bank of the creek, hoping to find a particularly wide, deep spot which I could identify as the swimming hole. Just as I was about to turn around to return to Lawrenceville so that I wouldn't be missed at dinner, I found what I was looking for. Here was a wide section of the creek where the dark, slow-moving water looked as if it might be at least up to my chest if I tried to stand on the bottom.

In reality, it didn't take a lot of detective work to know that I had been successful in my quest. On the bank at the edge of the hole was a tree with ropes hanging from a large branch that extended out over the water. A knot had been tied in the ends of some of them so that the Tarzan-imitators would have a secure grip and not drop off before the line reached the end of its swing. While some ropes had only a knot on the end, one had a big tire tied to it that was large enough for a child to sit in. As I stood by the rope-draped tree, I could visualize what had happened on this spot on a hot afternoon only a short time before. There was the small group of kids, maybe both boys and girls, taking turns pushing one of their friends seated in the tire out as far as the line would reach before he or she dropped out into the cool water. How natural it all seemed to me and how I wished I had been with them to join in the fun. It must have been only a summer recreation for a few local children because I never found them using the swimming hole during my many visits between September and May.

It was now time for me to end my first exploration and return to school, but I was a happy boy. I had discovered four new special places—Lower and Upper Shipetaukin creeks, the marsh, and the woodlot—that I believed would bring me great joy for as long as I was forced to go to Lawrenceville.

After returning to campus one year and going out on my first excursion, I discovered with delight that the landowner had built a small, but deep, farm pond on the end of the marsh nearest school and stocked it with largemouth bass, bluegills, and golden shiners. I know what species were there because I caught them all. Out of respect for the farmer who had created this paradise, I released all of my catches except for the first bass, which so surprised me by its size (nearly three pounds) that I kept it and brought it back to one of the African-American kitchen staff with whom I had become friendly.

The pond now joined my other special places. I would fish, bird-watch, or simply roam about in them every chance I got, and I would come to love them as I have loved few places on earth. It wasn't long before I entered these natural worlds with the same feelings I think I was supposed to have—but never did—when I attended the compulsory chapel services at school. They became spiritual oases in a desert of discontent.

*During that first year at Lawrenceville,* my inability to bend to the new demands being placed on me was most obvious when it came to my "performance" in math. Despite the anger I felt at being sent away from home, I couldn't help but be interested in some of my studies, particularly history, literature, and philosophy. But I hated math.

As I fell farther and farther behind in that first-form math class, I began to see, at least for a short time, what I thought might be a silver lining in my failure. Maybe if I flunked the course for the entire year, Mother would be forced to take me out of this high-pressure macho environment and return me to the more genteel, co-ed milieu of Kew-Forest. What I seemed to have forgotten was that my oldest brother Tony had also failed a math course for the entire year, and he had been sent to summer school at a place called Long Lake Lodge in southern Maine to make it up. I also underestimated my mother's determination to get me through Lawrenceville, no matter what it took.

From the beginning of my time there, I had pleaded with her to bring me home, and had even threatened to run away from school. She knew this was a bluff, and warned me that if I became too recalcitrant, she would be forced to find me a place in a military school. As much as I hated the regimentation at Lawrenceville, I felt that being forced to become a cadet at a military institution would probably push me over the edge. And as bad as Lawrenceville was, I had my special places into which I could retreat, and regain my equilibrium. If I were compelled to transfer to another school, I would lose these precious sanctuaries and probably not find any replacements for them.

As a result of my conflicted thinking, I did reasonably well in all my courses that first year except, of course, for math, which I decided early on to treat as if it was a foregone conclusion that I would flunk it. Not only did I fail the class, but I was told that my grade was the lowest anyone had ever heard of a Lawrentian receiving for an entire year's work. I think I took a certain pride in that fact, and thought that in my spectacular failure, I had asserted my individuality; there was at least one hoop my masters could not get me to jump through.

Any hope I might have had about Mother being forced to take me out of Lawrenceville because of poor academic achievement was quickly dashed when she announced that I would be following Tony to the summer tutoring camp in southern Maine. Little did I know then that this would be the first of three summers at Long Lake Lodge. My dislike for that first-form math course would be mild when compared to the loathing I felt for the ever-harder algebra courses of my second- and third-form years.

But rather than being some sort of punishment for not living up to Lawrenceville standards and Mother's expectations, those summers in the semi-wilds of northern New England were among the best times of my boyhood. If I had stayed home, I would have been under the thumb of my older brothers or alone with a mother who often gave me the impression that she was put out by my presence. There were, of course, my local special places that I could visit. Forest Park and the canal between the lakes still held an appeal for me, but I now wanted to explore new country. The ecological diversity of the hundreds of acres of farmland adjacent to Lawrenceville had broadened my horizons, and the very word "Maine" stirred in me visions of wilderness, and endless possibilities.

So it was with mixed emotions that I accompanied Mother on the day that she drove me and my trunk into Manhattan to put me on a train to New England. I felt some anxiety about whether I would be able to make up the failed math course, but I also experienced a sense of excitement and anticipation about the new natural worlds I would discover when I finally reached my destination. I was not to be disappointed.

Located in southern Maine, Long Lake Lodge was a cluster of wooden buildings in woods on the northwestern shore of the lake of the same name, a huge body of water eleven miles long and up to a mile wide. Most of these structures were primitive cabins lacking any of the amenities, including running water; the toilets and showers were up the hill from the cabins, closer to the road. As I recall, my little home for the summer housed two or three other boys besides myself. The only large building on the property was one that enclosed the dining hall and administrative offices.

There were no urban areas of any size nearby. The largest was Bridgton, which had less than three thousand inhabitants according to the 1950 U.S. Census. I remember it as a classic New England town, with attractive white houses and towering, umbrella-shaped elm trees lining the streets.

After arriving in camp—I always thought of the place as more of a summer camp than a school—I discovered that Lawrenceville was only one of a number of private institutions that sent boys there to make up academic work they had failed to complete satisfactorily during the regular school year. After most or all of two months of intensive, personalized study in classes as small as two or three students, we would take a long comprehensive examination, and if we passed, we could return to our respective schools in September without having to repeat the previous year in that subject. While I never failed to pass the big test at the end, there were boys who were not as fortunate. I remember, in particular, another math student I tried unsuccessfully to console after he received the devastating news that he would have to take the same hated algebra course he had flunked the year before all over again.

While most mornings were taken up with math study, the afternoons were almost always available to do just about anything I liked, and it

*A boarded-up, abandoned cabin, possibly one of my own, on the former site of Long Lake Lodge in southern Maine where I spent three summers in the 1950s.*

was the freedom I enjoyed that made Long Lake Lodge so appealing. I even missed dinner many times because of my extensive explorations of the surrounding countryside. One of those early tramps was especially memorable, because it was during that afternoon that I discovered two new special places that would bring me a great deal of happiness. The first of these spiritual retreats was at the northeastern end of Long Lake. Across the stream that empties out of Crystal Lake into Long Lake, beavers had constructed a wide dam and created a shallow pond.

In visiting the pond I would always try to be as quiet as possible when I crept out onto the beaver dam or waded slowly out to their nearby lodge to sit silently on its highest part. I wanted to do everything I could not to spook these animals, who, if they saw or heard me, would sound the alarm by slapping their large, paddlelike tails loudly against the surface of the water. Over time, I learned that I had to be at the pond when it was getting dark if I was to have a chance to see the beavers going about their business. Apparently, they stayed in the lodge during most of the day and only emerged at dusk to look for food plants or to cut down trees and bushes to repair their construction projects and maintain them at the high standard they demanded. How I enjoyed watching them cruise back and forth across the tranquil surface of the little world they had created for themselves. Once, when I was sitting, unmoving and silent, on the edge of the lodge, and there was still enough sunlight to penetrate the clear water of the pond, I thrilled to the sight of a beaver swimming right below me into the underwater entrance to its home.

After discovering the pond, I wanted to know if there were any fish in it that I could catch. Consequently, I always brought along some fishing equipment on subsequent visits except when I was going just before dark to observe the beavers. When the sun was up was a good time to fish, because the beavers were in their lodge and not swimming around, slapping their tails in alarm, or in other ways spooking any fish that might be present.

I soon found that the most deadly, and exciting, lure to use was a black floating plug, about three inches in length, called a "Hula Popper." Made of plastic, it had a rubber skirt hanging off the back (hence the name Hula) and a hollowed-out face that made it dig into the water and gurgle and pop when jerked with the rod tip across the pond's surface. Though it may have been mainly designed to resemble a frog, it could have been any small creature trying to cross safely to the opposite bank. The very first time I tried out this new lure, I knew that its fame as a fish magnet was justly deserved. I don't think I got the plug even a third of the way back before I saw not one but two wakes of fish just below the surface making a beeline for it. I was so excited by the sight of these two miniature torpedoes "running straight and true" toward my lure that I jerked up my rod tip to set the treble hook just as the first fish reached the popper but before it could get it into its mouth. Reeling in quickly, I cast out again, and this time, I allowed the fish to slam into the plug—the splash of water that accompanied its savage attack surprised and delighted me—before I struck back and successfully hooked my quarry.

Because I was using light spinning tackle, the fish was able to put up a scrappy fight, made all the more challenging because I had to lead it away from a profusion of weeds and snags that could have easily entangled my fragile line and broken it. Finally, the fish gave up, and I netted my first chain pickerel, a member of the pike family that includes the famous muskellunge that can reach weights in excess of sixty pounds. My fish was considerably smaller, probably no more than fourteen inches long and between one and two pounds in weight. The reason for the low weight-to-length ratio is that chain pickerel have an elongated shape somewhat like that of a barracuda. The overall body color is a pale green, but the back is darker, with a bronze hue. The fish gets its name from the black chainlike markings on its sides. A long and slender body is not the only thing a pickerel has in common with the barracuda. Like the saltwater species, with which I was already familiar, this inhabitant of my beaver pond had a mouth full of sharp teeth. I wondered what the reason was for these similarities in two unrelated species, one living in a freshwater pond and other in the open ocean.

After catching a few more pickerel and thinking about this question, I developed one of my early hypotheses regarding evolution and ecology. At this young age, I had not heard of either term, but I did possess the common sense to understand that both species had sharp pointed teeth, an elongated body, and a savage, predatory disposition probably because they occupied a similar position in the hierarchy of their watery worlds, and they needed those assets to live successfully.

As would be the case over and over again in my life, I would find that fishing, and later hunting as well, drew me into the natural world and made me an intimate participant in the drama of nature in a way that less direct involvement like hiking and even birding never seemed to do. In each new outdoor adventure, my efforts to capture the quarry, whether it be fish or bird, invariably led not only to a desire to understand its habits and the world in which it lived, but also to a greater appreciation of that species. Every new *active* experience with wildlife pushed me farther along the road to becoming both a naturalist and conservationist.

Besides the pickerel, I don't recall landing other fish of any size at the beaver pond. Because of its legendary fighting ability, which often includes high leaps out of the water, I was especially eager to catch a big smallmouth bass.

That quest brought me to my other special place, one that would remain dear to me during all three summers in Maine. It would also be one of the smallest special places I have ever had. In looking along the shoreline of Long Lake for likely bass habitat, I discovered a tiny public park at its northern end, at the outskirts of the village of Harrison. As I approached the lake on the southern side of this little open area, I could see that there was something dark and round on the water just offshore. It was the cut-off end of a huge log or telephone pole coming up at an angle from the lake bottom with only this last portion visible at the surface. The log was just the kind of cover predators like pickerel and smallmouth bass like to hide under as they wait for shiners, crayfish, or other prey to come close enough to launch an attack. The fact that it was the only obvious cover in that otherwise open water made me believe that it had to be some kind of fish convention center. In my mind's eye, I could see those wonderful game fishes down there under that log, evenly spaced out along its entire length and waiting eagerly for me to cast an artificial lure in their direction.

I soon found out that my imagination had run away with me. Either the objects of my quest were not stacked up like cordwood under the log or they were just too smart to fall for any of the sinking plugs or shiny spinners and spoons I sent their way. One issue I faced was how to get these lures down beside, or even under, the log without snagging them up. But even when I made a perfect cast, and I was sure that the lure was descending right into the predators' lair before I began my retrieve, I was still coming up empty.

One afternoon, as I stood on my favorite flat rock on the shoreline looking out toward the log and contemplating the challenge I had set for myself, I noticed a flash of yellow just below the surface of the water.

*The end of the log (or telephone pole) in Long Lake sticking up out of the water as it looked in July 2005, nearly fifty years after I had discovered it and made it my special fishing place when I was at Long Lake Lodge.*

Casting out a segment of a night crawler on a small hook, I caught a golden shiner, and then another and another. A large school of these scrappy little minnows, not more than six or seven inches in length, had taken up temporary residence just offshore. It suddenly came to me that they could be the solution to my problem.

Remembering how Tommy Gifford had made dead baitfish look alive when trolling off Key Largo, I took the next golden shiner I caught, and instead of releasing it as I had done with the others, I dropped it in the grass next to me. I then changed the spool on my spinning reel to one with heavier line and tied on a large hook. Inserting the hook through the minnow's mouth and out its gills—killing the fish was a necessity in order to control it in the way I desired—I cast the bait out. I think it took two or three attempts before I placed the shiner in the exact spot I was aiming for alongside the end of the log. When I finally succeeded in hitting my mark, I didn't reel back in immediately as I had with the failed attempts, but let the shiner sink enticingly to the bottom before I lifted the rod tip up gently to simulate a crippled baitfish feebly trying to rise to the surface.

How exciting it is in fishing and hunting to devise a scheme that works exactly as planned, to think like the game and fool it into making a mistake. No sooner had I moved the shiner up off the bottom when I saw the line tighten and start to run rapidly up under the log. From my saltwater fishing experience, I knew that I had to give a fish line at such a moment so that it didn't feel resistance, become suspicious, and drop the bait. After going only a short distance, the fish stopped, which is presumably when it

*My rock "fishing platform" at the northern end of Long Lake.*

inhaled the shiner that it was holding in its jaws. After waiting anxiously for about a minute, I jerked the rod tip up with all my strength at the same time I reeled furiously to pull what I could now feel was a heavy fish out away from the log. This was the same technique I had used after hooking big groupers in Florida that made every effort to get back into an opening in the coral, which if successful, always led to a cut line.

For a time, the struggle seesawed back and forth as my adversary kept trying to get back under the log. Given the size and power of the fish, I had no choice but to give it line when it wanted to run to prevent a break-off. More than once, I thought I was about to lose this battle, as it did succeed in reaching its hiding place. Nothing happened, however, for the sides of the log must have been completely smooth, with no branches or snags coming off it to entangle and break my line. Finally, after what seemed like a long fight but was probably only a few minutes, the fish began to tire, and I was able to lead it up toward the flat rock on which I stood. Hoping that my prize would be a large smallmouth bass, I was surprised to see the long form of a chain pickerel coming up to the surface. Any disappointment I might have felt quickly vanished when I realized just how big it was. After an anxious moment or two trying to land the trophy—I could only get it part way into my small net—I was at last able to grab it by the tail, lift it up, and drop it in the grass behind me.

Gathering up all my fishing gear and putting a length of cord through the fish's gills that I formed into a loop for carrying it, I hurried back to camp to show off my magnificent catch. Taking it right to the kitchen, which I knew must have a scale, I was delighted to learn that this giant of its species weighed just over four pounds. That night I shared the fish with those at the camp director's table, and he toasted me as the angler par excellence of Long Lake Lodge. It was a day I'll never forget.

During all three summers at the camp, I stopped frequently at my special place to fish in that tiny part of Long Lake between the log on the south and the shoreline on the north. Because a school of golden shiners was only rarely present, I didn't have many opportunities to use the same angling technique. On the few occasions when I was able to obtain a shiner for bait, I sometimes caught pickerel, but all of them were much smaller than the first one. I was also finally able to catch a number of smallmouth bass near the log, though none as large as I would have liked.

The summer of 1959 would be my last one at Long Lake Lodge, and looking back over those months I spent in southern Maine, I remember nothing but good times. Even the anxiety I must have experienced before taking the big examination at the end that would determine if I could proceed to the next level of math at Lawrenceville has faded away completely.

*In calling to mind my remembrances* of Maine, I found myself recalling other memories relating to my time at Lawrenceville. It was at the start of my third year of what I still look upon as imprisonment that I became a third former (the equivalent of the tenth grade) and left Perry Ross House and Lower School to move into Kennedy House, on "the Circle." Though still unhappy, I felt a vast improvement in my life as compared to the one I experienced in my first two years. For one thing, I no longer had to endure living in a cubicle without a door, with nothing between me and whatever unpleasantness I wanted to escape. For the first time, I had my own room! Though very small, it had a real door, which I could close whenever I wanted to retreat into my sanctum. I could now lay out and organize the gear for my next outdoor adventure without worrying about a master or student barging in to my cubicle to "see what I was doing." The handling of the various items and the selection process of what to bring and what to leave behind have always invoked feelings of anticipation and even excitement as I recalled the joy of past outings. Depending on the season, that equipment might now include binoculars, the Peterson *Field Guide to the Birds*, fishing tackle, and after I began to hunt, shotgun shells as well.

While it was my father who started me on my career as a fisherman, it was my oldest brother Tony who introduced me to hunting with a shotgun, another avocation that would last a lifetime. As already noted, it was seeing that pile of wooden duck decoys on the boat dock near our grandfather's bungalow just before he set off for a day of shooting that piqued Tony's curiosity about how hunters used these lures to bring ducks and geese within range of their guns. Soon afterwards, he made friends with a dedicated "waterfowler" who transferred much of his vast knowledge to Tony, who then shared it with his brothers.

My initiation into the sport came in December 1958, during the Christmas vacation of my third-form year. I was visiting my father, who had moved to Sewall's Point in the Jensen Beach area on the southeastern coast of Florida. Tony was also living in Florida, and by this time, he had become an ardent duck hunter who wanted his father and brothers to experience the excitement of successful waterfowling. So instead of fishing at the Ocean Reef Club or out on my father's boat, we now went duck hunting nearly every day of the vacation.

Our hunting destination was the western shore of the incomparable Lake Okeechobee, wellspring of the Everglades. When filled to capacity, this saucer-shaped body of water that the Seminole Indians called "Okeechobee," or "big water," covers over seven hundred square miles. About thirty-five miles long and up to twenty-five miles wide, it is one of the largest purely freshwater lakes entirely within the borders of the United States. Despite its size, Okeechobee is never more than about fifteen feet deep, even out in the middle, and in the great marshes along its western side it is, or was, shallow enough to wade. When my family began hunting that part of the lake in the late 1950s, Okeechobee seemed pristine, but that was only true once we were out in its marshes. After driving to it from the east, we were in sight of a high levee much of the time as we proceeded around its southern border to Fisheating Creek on the western side, where we launched our boat. The purpose of the levee was to hold back the lake's water and prevent the kind of flooding of towns and drained ("reclaimed") agricultural lands in the Everglades to the south that had killed approximately two thousand people in the hurricane of 1928.

While we were aware of the levee and the several drainage canals we crossed on the way to Fisheating Creek, I don't think we understood their significance. All we knew was that large-scale engineering projects had been built on the lake's shore. It was only after I became a professor at the University of Miami in the 1970s, specializing in environmental history, that I realized just how shortsighted most of these efforts had been to manipulate the southern flow of water out of Okeechobee on its way to the end of the Florida peninsula at Florida Bay.

In the 1950s, despite the large-scale damage that had already been done to the Okeechobee-Everglades ecosystem, the lake remained a wildlife paradise and was probably far richer in animal and plant diversity than it would be in later years. There was still some natural movement of water in and out along Okeechobee's shoreline before the levee was extended completely around the lake. And the Kissimmee River, which gently flowed into Okeechobee's northwestern corner after meandering through extensive marshes that filtered out the nutrients from agricultural lands and cattle ranches upstream, had not yet been "channelized" by the U.S. Army Corps of Engineers. After their work was done, the marshes were all but destroyed, and the once beautiful Kissimmee became little more than a deep, wide ditch that brought such an overload of nutrients directly into the lake that massive eutrophication was the result.[6]

But all this was in the future, and in December 1958 the wildlife, especially birds, was on the lake in incredible numbers. Most of all, there were the coots (*Fulica americana*). Slate black with a chickenlike ivory bill and white patches under the tail, coots were everywhere. Even when some high vegetation hid a flock of these birds from view, we knew they were nearby. As one ornithologist observed, "Coots seem to be almost constantly giving vent to a babble of indescribable sounds, accompanied by much splashing and fussing." These noises "have been variously described," he continued, "as croaks, toots, grunts, cackles, coughs, quacks, coos, whistles, squawks, chuckles, clucks, wails, and froglike plunks and grating sounds"![7] In my memories of Lake Okeechobee, the calls of the coots are as vivid as the image of the birds themselves. Though they are about the same size as some duck species and superficially resemble them at a distance, coots are very different in how they move about on the water and in the air. When swimming, they pump their heads back and forth, and they would much rather skulk off into tall reeds than have to fly. But if they are forced to take wing, they skitter along the water before rising slowly in labored flight, their big feet trailing behind.

While some ducks are able to jump straight off the water when flushed, others, like coots, have to run along the surface for a short distance before becoming airborne. But in all cases, ducks move at a much faster pace than coots. The short time it takes for any species of duck to get out of good shotgun range, which is usually considered to be no more than about forty yards, never fails to surprise the novice waterfowler. A coot, on the other hand, is content to fly only a short distance, as little as ten yards or so, before dropping back down into a thick patch of vegetation.

I'll never forget the huge flocks of coots I saw the first time we went out of Fisheating Creek in Tony's boat on the way to a hunting spot he had located earlier. Though there were many kinds of birds along the waterway, like several species of egrets and herons, gallinules (*Gallinula chloropus*), a relative of the coot, pied-billed grebes, and numerous others, the coots outnumbered them all by a wide margin and were constantly skittering along the surface of the water in front of the boat. For the birder and naturalist in me, as well as the hunter, it was thrilling to see this seemingly primordial abundance.

Our small boat, no more than fourteen feet long, was weighted down with the four of us, our shotguns and shells, and a bag or two of decoys. Still, the ten-horsepower outboard managed to move us along at a respectable clip until we came to a small pond within the marsh almost completely surrounded by high vegetation, not far from the edge of the open lake. Tony shut off the engine, and the boat glided silently into the pocket just as a flock of ducks rose into the air with amazing speed. Hustling us out of the boat and into the nearby head-high reeds that we used to hide both ourselves and our boat, Tony then waded out (we were all wearing chest waders) and placed the cork and balsa-wood decoys in a pattern that resembled two groups of contented waterfowl swimming on the surface of the pond with an open space between them for incoming ducks to land.

It wasn't long before the waterfowl that we had spooked coming into this hideaway returned. Apparently, it was a favorite feeding area. Perhaps eight or ten of them came zipping back in like miniature fighter planes and made a beeline for the decoys and the spot Tony had prepared for them. (Tony explained that we should shoot at them when they were in good range, but before they actually landed on the water.) They would have come all the way in except that one or more of us got so excited when we saw them that we rose up to shoot too quickly and scared them just before they reached the open area between the two groups of decoys. I think everyone but me fired—they were simply too fast for me to follow with my gun—and one of the flock came down dead, hitting the water with a splash.

I waded out to pick up the bird, a drake ring-necked duck (*Aythya collaris*). As I examined it for a moment before bringing it back to our hiding place, I remember thinking how neat it would be if I was able to shoot and physically possess one of these lovely creatures and perhaps preserve it mounted flying on a wall, just as my butterflies and moths and rainbow runner had been preserved. It was so much more satisfying to have the actual bird in my hand and be able to examine it closely, rather than simply looking at it for a few minutes at a great distance through binoculars. Though not as striking as some other male waterfowl, like wood ducks and eiders, the ring-neck is still a handsome bird. It is, however, misnamed, for the chestnut-brown ring on the dark neck of the male in breeding plumage can barely be seen, even when the bird is in the hand. It should be called the ring-billed duck, for the white bar across the gray-blue bill is much more obvious.

As I would soon discover, ring-necks were by far the most common duck in the area of Lake Okeechobee we hunted and the species toward which we directed almost all of our efforts. Even though Tony's decoys were carved and painted to resemble scaup (*Aythya affinis*), they were close enough in shape and color to ring-necks to lure them in without hesitation. This species has several attributes appealing to the hunter. For one thing, they are incredibly fast and difficult to hit with any kind of consistency. They are, in other words, a sporting challenge. And after you do manage to bag a few ring-necks and take them home, you discover that they are very good eating. In fact, these ducks are among the best-tasting waterfowl I've ever had.

Ring-necks also decoy readily, and to me, hunting over decoys is the best type of waterfowling. Instead of blindly walking through a swamp or paddling a canoe down a stream, where you hope to encounter a duck and flush it within shotgun range, the waterfowler using decoys lures the birds into an ambush of the hunter's own design. It is a far more cerebral and creative form of hunting.

In order to be successful, one has to learn the habits of the target species and scout its natural world ahead of time to locate the feeding areas and the traditional flight paths, and then set out the decoys in exactly the right spot, at the right depth, and within the right distance from the blind. Too close, and the birds may see you before they get to the decoys, and flare off, and too far, they may be out of good shotgun range by the time you rise to shoot. What is probably most important is the wind direction. It should always be blowing from behind the blind or from either side. Since waterfowl land into the wind, they will almost never come into decoys when the wind is blowing across the front of the rig and into the face of the hunter in the blind. Flare-offs are the inevitable result.

While ring-necks tend to be unwary, at least at the beginning of the hunting season, other species, like black ducks and pintails, are always wary, and the setup has to be perfect to bring them in. They will often circle the rig two or three times out of range looking for anything, however small, that seems suspicious. The glint of the sun off the brass end of a spent shotgun shell lying on the mud near the decoys or the slightest movement of the hunter's head above the blind will cause them to change their flight path in an instant, and all the frustrated waterfowler can do is to watch them disappear out of range and wonder what he or she did wrong.

Hunting ducks and geese with decoys is, in essence, a kind of exciting game, albeit one in which the loser may suffer the ultimate penalty. If I use all of my knowledge and experience to create what seems to be the perfect arrangement of my decoys, and the waterfowl fly by all morning long without once swinging into the rig, then I have lost the game on that particular day. If on another morning, however, I design a set that looks exactly as it should, hide myself and my boat effectively, place the decoys in relation to the blind at the appropriate distance, and provide a space inside the rig or at its front where incoming birds will want to land—and the waterfowl come to me like moths to a light—then I have won the game that day. Even if I miss most of my shots, I have still solved the problem at hand. By satisfying myself that I know enough about the ways of waterfowl to enter their world and fool them, I have become connected to them in a mystical way that I believe only a hunter can fully appreciate.

But in December 1958, all of this intimate involvement with waterfowling was years away. During that first Christmas vacation hunting ducks on Lake Okeechobee, all I wanted to do was to learn the basics of the sport and see if I could even hit any of the legal waterfowl that flew my way. In this effort, I was handicapped by the gun Dad bought for me. Despite the fact that I was physically large enough to have easily wielded a 12-gauge, which is what I wanted, he bought a shotgun two sizes smaller that would have only been suitable for an expert shooting at very close range. Though some duck and goose hunters may disagree with me, I believe that a general waterfowling gun for an adult should never be less than 12-gauge in size.

When a hunter swings and fires at a game bird on the wing, he or she has an ethical responsibility to use the most powerful gun that the shooter can handle, because the purpose is to make a clean, quick kill, and not have the bird escape crippled. With the greater number of pellets and larger amount of powder in the shell of a 12-gauge shotgun, as compared to a 16-gauge or 20-gauge, the chances of hitting a duck or goose with sufficient BB's moving at enough velocity to make a clean, humane kill go up considerably. I'm sure my father understood this basic ballistic reality, but he simply didn't care. Despite his great wealth and early retirement in his late forties, Dad always endeavored, and usually succeeded, in spending as little money as possible on his youngest son. The only reason he bought the 20-gauge Mossberg for me, and not one of the other guns we looked at in the store, was that the Mossberg was the cheapest of the lot.

As I recall, it had been on sale for a long time, with no takers until my father came along. Its lack of appeal was probably not only because it was underpowered, at least for duck hunting, but because it was an awkward, bolt-action gun, instead of the faster, smoother—and more expensive— pumps and semi-automatics that I liked much better. After haggling with the salesman, Dad managed to get the already low sale price even lower, and I'm quite sure that the gun was no more than fifty dollars. Because of the way in which it was purchased, I never liked that Mossberg, and I had no qualms about bringing it back to Lawrenceville and keeping it hidden in a brush pile in a waterproof bag in some woods at the eastern side of the school property. I knew that because of trapped moisture in the bag, the gun was going to become rusty, but I simply didn't care as long as it still functioned.

The buying of a boy's first shotgun so that he can join in the hunt with his elders is a long tradition in America and should be special. But my father had a way of turning every occasion that should have been full of joy and generosity into something that was sad and stingy. Despite the bad taste I had in my mouth from how the 20-gauge was purchased and the feeling that I was undergunned for the job at hand, I was determined to use the Mossberg as effectively as I could to become a good shot, or at least an adequate one. I quickly discovered, however, that I had no chance of reaching this goal as long as I was in the blind with Dad and George, who were my usual companions since Tony's job only allowed him to accompany us on the weekends.

Instead of taking turns shooting at individual, incoming birds, as is the appropriate etiquette in a blind, they used their longer-range 12-gauges to blast away at every duck that came anywhere near our decoys. Many times, they couldn't tell who had shot what, since they fired at the same bird simultaneously; they then argued over who could claim the prize. This constant competition between Dad and George meant that I rarely had the opportunity even to put the gun up to my shoulder.

Though my father had hunted ducks a few times before, in the 1940s, when he was on fishing trips to Florida and it was too windy to take the boat out in the ocean, it wasn't until Tony introduced us all to waterfowling on Lake Okeechobee that he became seriously involved in the sport. But from the start, he was an excellent shot because of an uncanny ability to calculate lead. (Because pellets leave a shotgun not in a broad front, which most people seem to think, but in a "shot string" like water coming out of a garden hose, and because a duck or goose travels some distance before the pellets arrive, a waterfowler has to shoot ahead of the game in order for the pellets and the bird to intersect, and this is called "lead.")

When my father and George were in the blind with me, I was relegated most of the time to retrieving their (mainly Dad's) ducks. Once, I distinctly remember standing in waist-deep water and leaning over to pick up one of my father's ring-necks just as he shot another one right over my head that came down hard and splashed water in my face. When I expressed the thought that shooting at low-flying ducks when I was in the middle of the decoys might not be a good idea, he simply laughed.

Because of this intolerable situation, I quickly decided that I had to go off on my own if I was to get any shooting at all. As usual, Dad didn't care where I went or how long I was gone, as long as I was back by the time he had set for us to return to the launch ramp. The first time I started out, heading off from behind the blind and into the unknown, I must admit I was a bit anxious. After all, I knew that there were probably many hundreds of acres of waist-deep marsh out in front of me, with no trees or any kind of landmark to guide me out and back; when I had gone too far away to hear the gunshots coming from the blind, all I had to go by was the position of the sun in the sky. But even more stressful, at least on that initial trip, was my fear of encountering some potentially dangerous wildlife, namely alligators and water moccasins. Both were present, especially in the patches of thick, head-high reeds of an unknown species that I frequently encountered and had to fight my way through to get to the more open water on the other side.

On those rare occasions when I quietly waded up to one of these patches and surprised an alligator that splashed loudly as it quickly exited the scene, I'm sure I uttered an expletive and wondered, if only for a moment, what the hell I was doing wandering around in such a place. Because the alligators were always at least partly submerged, I usually saw only a tail and maybe part of the back as they splashed away. But I could tell by the area of water covered by the splashing approximately how large they were, and some were longer than I was! Yet, in all the countless hours I spent wading around in the habitat of these large reptiles, first in Lake Okeechobee and later, when I was a history professor at the University of Miami, in Lake Trafford southwest of Okeechobee, and in the Everglades, I never had a single nasty experience with any of the many sizable alligators I met along the way. I don't think they evolved to eat big, two-legged creatures moving vertically through the water. Mammals swimming on the surface, including dogs and children, are, however, a different matter, and after I came to live in south Florida in 1970, I read about several such attacks.

In my wanderings in the marshes of Lake Okeechobee that first duck season, I encountered many more water moccasins than alligators. Sometimes I'd see them swimming ahead of me, and at other times, I'd find them coiled up on a thick mat of vegetation at the edge of one of those dense patches of head-high reeds I had to traverse; I quickly learned how to tell the difference between the potentially deadly moccasins and the more abundant but harmless banded water snakes (*Natrix sipedon fasciata*). The moccasin has a much fatter body and bigger head than the water snake, and on more than one occasion I met one that opened its mouth in that wide, flat head to show me its white interior and why it is called the "cottonmouth."

After some initial anxiety over being bitten on the upper body by an animal that could kill me, I got over my fear, at least in the daylight hours. The scariest times were when I had to push my way through a patch of high reeds, but even then, I went slowly enough that I thought I would always be able to see a moccasin in time to avoid it. My growing confidence was also the result of the supposed protection my chest waders gave me. Because they were loose fitting, I reasoned, probably incorrectly, that a cottonmouth striking out at me as I waded in waist-deep water would catch its fangs in the rubberized fabric and not penetrate all the way through to the skin.

Aside from any dangers, real or imagined, that I faced slowly moving through the grassy shallows and hidden ponds bordered by tall reeds, I loved my solitary wading. When I was in the boat, I didn't feel as if I was completely a part of the natural world; I was only on its fringes. But when I slipped over the side into the water, I experienced a surge of delight. Now I was immersed, literally and figuratively, in nature. I could feel the bottom below my feet, come surprisingly close to large, unidentified fishes before they finally dashed away, and glide my hand over lily pads as I passed by.

Because there was no loud outboard motor to spook the birds and because I was low in the water, moving slowly and silently through areas that often had enough high vegetation to screen my approach, I found that it was an easy matter to get within good shotgun range of the flocks of coots that seemed to be everywhere. While it was no problem to get within twenty or thirty yards of them, it often proved difficult to get the coots to fly, at least high enough off the water to present a challenging shot. At first, I fired at them when they were running along the water or just after they got airborne, but I quickly became disenchanted with this kind of shooting. It was too easy, and I had a vague feeling that I was taking unfair advantage of them. It wasn't long before I resisted the temptation to shoot at any that weren't high enough up in the air to be going full speed.

These coots were the first birds I had ever killed, and even though I had experienced some misgivings in the past about taking the lives of fishes, butterflies, and moths, I don't think I had any such qualms about shooting coots. At least that was true if the bird I fired at was quickly killed. Then, as now, the loss of a crippled game bird bothers me greatly, ruins an otherwise memorable outing, and sometimes even causes me to end the hunt and go home.

Then why continue hunting, knowing that at least some of the "sensate beings"—to use a phrase favored by animal-rights advocates—I shoot at may escape to "suffer" for a time? There are several reasons. If I use the appropriate gun and ammunition, practice enough to become competent with my firearm, am careful only to take shots when game is in good range, and search diligently for downed wildfowl, preferably with the help of a retriever, I am going to lose very few birds. But if one does manage to get away from this predator, it is often consumed by other predators, like raccoons, mink, great black-backed gulls, and bald eagles. Nature "wastes" very little.

There were also both familial and societal supports for waterfowl hunting. The fact that my grandfather had loved this exciting sport in the past, and my oldest brother loved it in the present, made it a natural activity in which to engage. And in the 1950s, unlike today, duck and goose hunting seemed to be almost universally accepted by society as a traditional, legitimate avocation, particularly for young males. While anti-hunting sentiment had been developing for some time in regard to the pursuit of larger mammals like deer, I can recall no opposition to waterfowl hunting until the late 1960s when I was in graduate school at Northwestern.

But the main reason why philosophical arguments about the morality of hunting would have seemed irrelevant to me that first duck season in 1958 was that I or other humans consumed every single coot or duck I bagged. I knew no vegetarians then, only people who ate meat, including domestic ducks, chickens, and turkeys killed by strangers in a slaughterhouse. If any of these meat-eaters had opposed my hunting, which they didn't, I think I would have wondered how they could condemn me for legally obtaining my own food.

During most of that Christmas vacation, when we drove over to Lake Okeechobee nearly every day, Dad and George, and Tony when he could get off work, satisfied our hunger for ducks, almost entirely ring-necks, while I supplied the coots. Despite what many waterfowlers I've met seem to believe, these "mud hens," as they are contemptuously called, are excellent eating when properly prepared. While the coot shooting could be exciting, I still hadn't proven to myself that I could be a real waterfowler, that I could down the much faster, more challenging, ducks. Without the advantage of decoys, I found it difficult to approach any ring-necks I saw. Unlike coots, the ducks I encountered usually flushed well out of range. The few that didn't flew on unscathed after I fired, probably because I had shot well behind them.

Early one morning, at the beginning of a wading trip, I remember thinking to myself that this would be the day when I would finally solve the problem and become a successful duck hunter. If I saw a duck flying in range, I would control my excitement and force myself to do everything exactly right before firing at it. This meant that I would have to bring the gun up quickly, but smoothly, so as not to snag it on my loose-fitting clothes, push the butt snugly up against my right shoulder while lowering my cheek onto the stock in order to have a straight line of sight down the entire length of the barrel, swing onto the passing duck and catch up to it with the end of the barrel, follow along with it for a moment, and then pass it with the muzzle and fire, while continuing my swing, only when I could no longer see it over the end of the barrel. This is the tried-and-true technique of the proficient "wing shot" ever since hunters began to "shoot flying" in Europe in the seventeenth century. Tony had described the method in detail, and I had, of course, already used a variation of it to bring down coots. But because ducks are far swifter on the wing, I had to execute the technique perfectly, swinging the barrel more quickly and giving the bird a much greater lead.

On that special morning, it hadn't been even an hour after I left the blind when the moment of truth arrived. I was just emerging from a patch of head-high reeds on the edge of a small pocket of open water when, out of the corner of my eye, I spotted a duck coming from behind my left shoulder. When it saw me, it went into high gear, and its speed seemed phenomenal. With complete concentration on following every step in the prescribed shooting method, I swung on the bird and fired.

Just like Aldo Leopold, in his account of bagging his first duck in *A Sand County Almanac*, I experienced the same "unspeakable delight" when the ring-neck folded up and came down with a splash, belly up and stone dead. I hurriedly retrieved the bird, and headed back to the blind to show off my trophy.

It was probably a weekend, because Tony was off from work that day and had joined us on the hunt. He was standing at the near end of a patch of high reeds we were using for the blind. As I came up to him, he looked suspiciously at me, and the first words out of his mouth were: "Did you shoot it in the air or on the water?" I was, of course, indignant at hearing this accusation presented as a simple question. Only after I convinced him that I had, indeed, bagged the young ring-neck drake (one that had not yet attained its full breeding plumage) in a sporting manner, shooting it while it zipped along at about sixty miles per hour[8] rather than sitting still on the water, did Tony accept it as a legitimate kill and my first duck. To

*Holding my first duck, shot flying, on Lake Okeechobee in December 1958.*

commemorate this special moment, he photographed me with my prize, and when I ate it that night, I can still remember how good it tasted.

Less than ten years later, after starting research on my Ph.D. dissertation on pathbreaking environmentalist George Bird Grinnell and the genesis of American conservation, I kept finding historical references to what I would soon call the "code of the sportsman." The development of this self-imposed set of rules in the nineteenth century meant that a sport hunter or fisherman should adopt a kind of contract with his quarry. Eventually, this one-sided "agreement" would mean that game should not be killed in the breeding season or sold for profit; that it should be taken only in reasonable numbers, without waste; and that it should be pursued only by means of sporting methods. The individual fish, bird, or mammal was to have a "fair chance" of escape, even though its capture was made more doubtful as a result; sportsmen came to condemn fishing for trout with worms instead of artificial flies, shooting at waterfowl on the water before they could take flight, or hunting white-tailed deer on snowshoes when the animals were mired down in deep snow.

When Tony asked me that deceptively simple question in December 1958, at the beginning of my career as a hunter, I had no idea that I was joining a kind of fraternity, with a long tradition of sporting ethics that would come to include a sense of responsibility for both the game and its habitat. In time, however, my experience in hunting and fishing and the adoption of the code of the sportsman would be the keys to my understanding of the central role of hunters and anglers in the growth of environmental concern, and the basis for my major work, *American Sportsmen and the Origins of Conservation* (1975, 1986, and 2001).

It was probably fortunate that Tony had been present when I came back to the blind with my first duck. Rather than treating the event as something special, the start of my life as a hunter who had obligations to the game he pursued, my father's reaction was to tell me that he had already shot three ring-necks while I was away. Dad almost never knew when to stop competing with his sons and act like a loving father. Despite the claim in recent years by my brother George that our father adhered closely to ethical sporting standards in our hunting on Lake Okeechobee, I recall just the opposite. In fact, the contrast between the statements and actions of Dad and Tony was an important learning experience for me on the way to becoming a sportsman-conservationist.

When my oldest brother was absent, which was most of the time, our father had no hesitation about violating the code of the sportsman by breaking rules to which Tony always adhered. When, for example, Dad thought no one was around, he would put George or me in the bow and demand that we shoot at birds flushing ahead of the boat moving at full speed. Not only is hunting from a boat under outboard power against the sporting ethic, because it closes the range between the game and the shooter so quickly that it gives the hunter an unfair advantage, it is also against the law.

It would have been bad enough if the only birds he told us to shoot at were legal species like coots and ring-necks. But what caused me tremendous stress was my father's incessant browbeating of me to shoot at *every* large bird that flew up in front of the boat. Green herons, great egrets, and snowy egrets were all legitimate targets as far as he was concerned. I knew very well that this was wrong. Aside from the fact that killing these stunning nongame species was against federal law and an act of vandalism, since the birds would not be picked up for fear of arrest, there was the issue of the egret's persecution only a few decades earlier for the feather trade.

I'm not sure exactly when I joined the National Wildlife Federation, but I know I was a junior member by 1958, and all of my early guidebooks on insects, birds, and mammals have the beautiful Federation wildlife stamps (with copyright dates of 1952 or 1954) pasted into them. It was from the publications of this large environmental organization, founded in 1935 as a consortium of sportsmen-conservationists, that I had learned the full history of how the "plume birds," especially egrets, had been slaughtered for the millinery trade almost to the point of extinction. After several decades of protection, these species were still in the process of recovering their former abundance in 1958, and I didn't care what my bullying father wanted. I wasn't going to shoot at them simply because—in his words—they would make "good practice."

Because my father was not a man to be disobeyed, I did get up in the bow and fire my gun when a heron or egret flushed ahead of the boat, always making sure, however, to shoot to the side or below a rising bird. Every time I missed another easy shot, Dad would mutter "stupid kid," which was his favorite phrase for me during my teenage years when I failed to live up to his ideas of competence.

While my father's cavalier attitude about killing nongame birds bothered me greatly, I would discover that Christmas vacation that his disregard for life extended to mammals as well. One afternoon, as he and I were traveling in the boat out on the edge of the open lake looking for new hunting locations, I spotted something dark and round on the surface well off to the side of the direction in which we were going. I asked Dad, who was in the stern running the outboard, to change direction and go and see what this strange thing was.

About that time, the object disappeared below the surface, and we knew, of course, that it had to be a living animal. As we got closer, it came to the surface again, and I was thrilled to discover that it was a river otter, the first wild one I had ever seen. It had apparently been swimming for a long time, because it seemed exhausted and was only able to stay under water a short time between dives. When it popped back up again, it would look around to see where we were, and though I may be imagining it, that winsome face seemed to radiate fear.

What I wanted to do was simply follow the otter at a respectful distance, to observe it until it got back into the marsh where, I hoped, it would find a resting place, perhaps in a thick patch of reeds. Just as I was about to ask my father to slow down and not press the animal too closely, I heard him shout, "Shoot it—shoot it!"

I was incredulous. Turning around, I yelled something like, "I'm not going to shoot it and neither are you."

He glared at me for a moment and then whispered, "Just watch me." The next couple of minutes were among the worst in my young life. The more I pleaded with him to put his gun away and slow down the boat, the more determined he became to kill the otter and torment me. Finally, he raced ahead of the animal after it made a dive, put the engine in neutral, and waited. With tears in my eyes, I was making one last plea when the otter surfaced right next to the boat, and my father fired. Luckily, I was looking at him at the moment the gun went off and didn't see the otter's face as it received the entire charge from his 12-gauge.

When I refused to take the animal out of the water before it sank, Dad came out with his usual "stupid kid" comment and pulled it in himself. I couldn't bear to look at the otter's mangled head, and of all the many examples of my father's abuse of me when I was a boy, I think this was the worst one. It's safe to say that I hated him at that moment, and the incident haunts me to this day. In fact, as I write these words, I am once again experiencing some of the same anguish I felt over fifty years ago.

Why did I react so strongly to my father's killing of the otter? For one thing, these mammals were, even then, very special to me. I had been fascinated by them from the first time I saw a pair in the Bronx Zoo in New York City. I never got tired of watching them chase each other around their cage and in and out of their artificial pool. We all know some of the descriptive terms for otters, like playful, inquisitive, and cute. However unscholarly it sounds, I like cute best. For me, shooting that otter was like murdering an inoffensive stray dog.

Another reason the act bothered me so much was that, in some spiritual way, the killing of this uncommon animal, which Dad did not intend to use for food or any other purpose, was an affront to the natural world and a breach of ethical behavior. We had received a present from Nature in encountering the otter, and the gift had nothing to do with our duck hunting. But instead of appreciating the meeting as something special, my father's automatic response was to dominate and destroy.

In later years, I've thought about that otter, especially when I've had encounters with others of its kind. On two separate occasions several years apart, while I was duck hunting on Lake Trafford southwest of Okeechobee, one of these animals popped up in the middle of my rig, swam over to the nearest decoy, and poked the counterfeit duck's side with its muzzle. Each of the otters seemed to know that even though these birds looked real, they probably weren't, but they had to make sure just in case! Perhaps these intelligent mammals had already learned about the strange, immobile waterfowl, with no feet showing below the surface, from visiting other hunters' decoy rigs before they called on me.

I've had very similar experiences with another aquatic mammal, the harbor seal (*Phoca vitulina*), while hunting in the Northeast, once when I was rigged out for brant geese near Point Lookout on the South Shore of Long Island and another time when I was trying to lure in eiders in

Lynn harbor on the Massachusetts coast. As in the case of the otters in Florida, I was delighted when the seals visited me, and shooting them was the last thing on my mind. Those four days with the otters and the seals were among the most memorable I've had waterfowling, and I don't even remember if I bagged any birds.

Because my father's killing of the otter made me so angry, the next time we went hunting on Okeechobee, I wanted to get away from him as soon as possible to start my wading trip. I think that my emotional state clouded my judgment, for I paid little attention to him when he gave me the time I was supposed to be back at the blind. Neither did I think about the fact that Dad had decided to go out in the afternoon rather than at dawn, which was his usual custom. Instead of many hours of daylight ahead of me as I set out, I would have only a limited amount of time before it got dark.

We were in a new hunting area in the endless marsh, one that had many little pockets of open water fringed by head-high reeds. About an hour after I left the blind, I waded slowly and noiselessly almost completely through one of these reed patches and peered out of the thick vegetation into a hidden pond. What a sight! Coots were everywhere, and several gallinules walked over lily pads near me, while a small flock of ring-necks, with some pretty drakes among them, swam out in the middle. The scene reminded me of one of the dioramas of mounted aquatic birds I had seen in the American Museum of Natural History in New York.

After watching the ring-necks for a few minutes, trying to figure out if I could sneak around the border of the pond to get within good range, I noticed some movement behind them, right on the edge of another patch of tall reeds. I could barely control my excitement when I saw one and then two mottled ducks (*Anas fulvigula*) swim out in plain view. About the size of a hen mallard, which it strongly resembles except that it is darker in color, the mottled duck is considered by some ornithologists to be merely a subspecies of the mallard. Of the various kinds of waterfowl most likely to be seen, and bagged, on Okeechobee, the mottled duck, which is also called the Florida duck or Florida mallard, was the ultimate prize. Forgetting the ring-necks, I now had only one goal in life: to get close enough to the mottled ducks before they flushed to get a good shot.

My plan was to back out of the reed patch I had just come through and skirt the perimeter of the pond to come up behind the ducks without them seeing or hearing me. Bent over almost to the point where water was starting to come over the top of my chest waders, I crept slowly along behind a screen of high vegetation, knowing that it would be some time before I could turn back toward the pond and hopefully emerge from cover close to the Florida mallards. I had probably gone not more than a third of the way on my circuitous route when something happened for which I was totally unprepared. With my head down and my gun resting on my left shoulder pointing backwards and up to keep the muzzle out of water, I flushed another pair of mottled ducks not more than ten yards in front of me. They jumped straight up into the air with loud splashing and quacking, and so startled me that I blew what should have been an easy shot, or shots.

One of the great appeals of wingshooting is that in order to become a good shot, a certain degree of athletic skill, akin to using a racket to serve in tennis or a driver to tee off in golf, is consistently required. But unlike tennis and golf, or skeet and trap shooting for that matter, the "player" in the sport of wingshooting with wild birds is often caught off guard when the waterfowler has to perform the necessary athletic skill to make a "dead shot."

So it was with those two mottled ducks. Instead of bringing my gun up smoothly and covering the nearest bird with the muzzle, while continuing to move the gun upwards, a technique that would have provided the correct lead for rising waterfowl that close, I hurriedly pointed the gun directly at the duck, fired, and undoubtedly shot under it. Now I was completely flustered, and feverishly working that awkward bolt-action mechanism, I wildly fired a second shot at the rapidly retreating birds, which were, by then, almost out of range. Unscathed, they flew high out over the marsh and finally disappeared from view.

An almost overwhelming feeling of despair came over me. I could not have asked for an easier chance to bag the greatest trophy there is for the South Florida duck hunter. In fact, if I had been any damn good as a waterfowler, I should have downed both mottled ducks with two well-placed shots and achieved what is called a "double." My frustration at feeling like a loser was compounded by the knowledge that all the waterfowl, including the two original Florida mallards I had been stalking, had flown out of the nearby pond when I fired my futile shots.

Because these four mottled ducks were the only ones I had seen in all the wading I had done before that afternoon, I reasoned that there must be something about this part of the marsh that they found appealing. There had to be more in the area, and if I just kept pushing on through other ponds and patches of reeds, I would flush at least one more. Then, I would shoot carefully, redeem myself, and return to the blind with the quintessential trophy.

So I waded on through that seemingly limitless wetland, obsessed with my quest and paying no attention to the time. Though the afternoon wasn't hot, I was still sweating profusely in my chest waders. This part of the marsh also had denser, head-high patches of reeds, and more of them, than I had encountered before, and after struggling through a number of these thickets, I felt very tired. With a keen feeling of failure, I finally decided to turn around and head back. Almost immediately, I sensed that I had probably waited too long, for the sun was already low in the west. Not long after that, anxiety started to creep over me when I discovered that I wasn't sure what direction to take to get back to the blind. Soon that anxiety turned to fear when I realized that I was hopelessly lost.

My situation was indeed precarious and getting worse all the time. As long as I had daylight, I thought I had a chance, somehow, to find my way back to the blind or to be found by my father and George, who, I presumed, were out in the boat looking for me. Daylight at least allowed me to see where I was going and to avoid any alligators or moccasins I might meet along the way. I was, however, losing the light even more quickly than on most days, because as the afternoon had progressed, the sky had clouded up and become ever darker. Once the sun was down completely and the twilight gone, I found myself in the midst of an endless, and trackless, belly-deep marsh, under a moon that was almost completely obscured by cloud cover. Exhausted, all I wanted to do was to sit down and rest, but, of course, I could not. Everywhere the water was at least waist deep, and when I stepped into a depression on the bottom, it was a few inches deeper than that, coming right up to the top of my waders.

I kept hoping that I would find the remnants of a dead tree or a reed patch so thick and intertwined with vines and other vegetation that it would somehow support my weight. Then, I could simply wait out the night, with some confidence that I would be located the next day. I knew that this hope was a long shot, however, since I had never encountered any such resting places on my previous wading trips. As I forced my tired body to move forward in almost total darkness, I remember thinking how lucky other poor fools had been when they had found themselves lost in the wilderness. They could sit down, rest, and wait for help. If I had sat down and stayed there, I would have drowned, since I was sure the water was over my nose. Even if I managed somehow to raise my nose above the surface and keep on breathing, my chest waders would have filled up with heavy, surprisingly cold, water, chilling me and further reducing my ability to move my exhausted legs. The waders were always hard to pull off, and I knew I couldn't remove them without falling back in the water and getting completely soaked. With them off, I would have had no protection for my abdomen, legs, or feet and been completely vulnerable to moccasins on the surface and big snapping turtles on the bottom.

All I could do was to keep moving as long as my legs held out. While I was scared all the time, as I staggered around blindly in the blackness, I was absolutely terrified when I had to force my body through one of the patches of dense, head-high reeds. Once or twice, I heard loud splashing right in front of me as I pushed my way into one of these islands of tall vegetation, and I knew that noise came from a startled alligator. Though the presence of these animals didn't alarm me in the daylight, when we could see each other, nighttime encounters were a different matter. What if the next alligator I met decided not to flee, but to attack?

As I became more and more tired, I started to lose all hope of making it out of the marsh alive. I had now been wading continuously for several hours, and my legs felt like lead. I was at the point where I could barely lift them high enough to put one foot in front of the other. I knew that very soon, I would no longer be able to keep moving, or even standing, and once I sat down on the bottom of the lake, I wouldn't be getting up again.

It was then that I heard an outboard motor and saw a red light off in the darkness coming more or less in my direction. I realized, of course, that it was one of the bow lights of a boat. As excited as I was by the sight, I still didn't feel I'd been saved. I could tell by the light's movement that if the unseen boat continued on its course, it would pass well out in front of my position and miss me entirely.

From the moment I fully comprehended that I was lost, I had occasionally fired off three, evenly spaced shots, which is the signal for someone in trouble, and I had only a few shells left. I knew it was now time to use them!

Because I thought that my hoped-for rescuer would be more likely to hear my shot over a loud outboard engine and because I was sure the boat was well out of range, I pointed my gun high in the air in the direction of the moving light, and fired. Immediately after pulling the trigger, I saw the light change course and head directly toward me. At that moment, I think I was happier than I had ever been before in my young life. I was not going to sink down in the water and drown—I was going to live!

As the boat came closer, a searchlight went on, and I could see a man standing up, sweeping the light from side to side. Finally, the beam came over me, and I think I yelled out something stupid like HELLO! Because I was barely able to move my legs at that point, my rescuer had to bring his large johnboat right up next to me and literally pull me in over the side.

My deliverer was a commercial fisherman, who had grown up on the western shore of Okeechobee and who knew the watery wilderness intimately. He had been out on the lake checking on his fish traps for, I think, catfish, and because he had gotten a late start on his return trip, he had decided to take a shortcut across the marsh. I'm not sure now whether the fisherman said he heard my shot over the noise of his engine, but I do remember him telling me that it was the firelike muzzle flash from my gun that drew his attention. (When a shotgun is fired on a dark night, the mouth of the barrel looks like it has a flame coming out of it.)

The fisherman didn't hold back his understandable contempt for my stupidity. How could I have wandered miles away from my father and brother on a weekday with no other hunters or fishermen around, and without a flashlight or even a compass? And did I know just how lucky I was that he had happened along? Though I think I was in a kind of daze from my ordeal, I began to understand how providential our meeting had been. If the fisherman hadn't gotten a late start on his return trip and decided to take a shortcut through my part of the marsh, if he hadn't been facing in my direction and seen the muzzle flash in the distance, and if I had been lost the night before or the night after, I would have been finished. What really made an impression on me was this last point. The fisherman told me that he only checked his fish traps in this section of the lake's western shore on three evenings a week, and this night happened to be one of those times.

Strangely, I'm not certain now exactly where I rejoined Dad and George, who were out in the boat looking for me. It may have been somewhere along Fisheating Creek on the way back to the launch ramp. While I don't recall where the two boats met, I remember very well Dad's reaction. Instead of expressing any joy at all at learning that his youngest son hadn't drowned somewhere out in the darkness, he was angry that he and George had wasted so much time looking for me. On the way back, I know that I received at least one "stupid kid" comment, and George, who was always eager to ingratiate himself with our father, also added a few nasty remarks about my lack of judgment. Yes, I had been stupid, but their joyless reaction to my salvation hurt me. Still, it was not unexpected. I had become pretty much inured to their verbal abuse by this time, and I was just happy to be alive and to have a future.

*With the end of my Christmas vacation* in South Florida in January 1959, I returned to Lawrenceville for the rest of my third-form year. I was a changed individual in the sense that I now thought of myself as both a fisherman *and* a hunter. The avocations of fishing and hunting, practiced in an ethical manner, would prove to be key in creating my identity, while fostering a love of the natural world and a commitment to its perpetuation.

Coming back to Kennedy House, I brought the 20-gauge shotgun with me, concealed in a nondescript cardboard box. At my first opportunity, I took it apart and sneaked it out of Kennedy in a waterproof sack that looked like an ordinary laundry bag. I then put the sack under the same brush pile on the eastern edge of the school property that hid my chest waders.

When I retrieved the 20-gauge from its hiding place in the following two hunting seasons I was at Lawrenceville, I was often reluctant to fire it because of my fear that the landowner might hear the shot. After all, I was trespassing on his or her farm, a fact that didn't seem to bother me at the time. But there were occasions when I could see that no one was around and when the shot was just too tempting. One of those times was when a crow, or crows, flew over in good range, and I was hidden in brush along one of the Shipetaukin creeks or behind a tree in my favorite woodlot.

Crows were then considered vermin that should be killed whenever possible to reduce crop depredations. These "bad" birds were very common in my special places east of the campus, and even though their flight is slower than a duck's, it is more erratic, making crows surprisingly hard to hit. Still, I did manage to down a number of them.

As noted earlier, I felt a bond with Aldo Leopold when, a couple of years after leaving Lawrenceville, I read the account of his "unspeakable delight" at bagging his first duck, the same emotion that had come over me when I downed my first one, the drake ring-neck. But there was another component of the Leopold story, one that went well beyond the simple fact of a successful shot, and it was this deeper element that had a particular relevance for me in my experience of bagging a wood duck at Lawrenceville. For like the young Leopold, I, too, had "formulated" what he called an "ornithological hypothesis" that led directly to my capture of this lovely prize.

In Leopold's case, he had noticed a small area of open water (on an otherwise snow- and ice-covered lake) created by the warm-water discharge from a windmill. He correctly reasoned that if there were any ducks around that had not yet migrated southward, at least one of them would probably visit this patch of unfrozen lake before the day was out.

In my case, the story began when I was on a return trip back to the campus in the fall, just before sunset, when I spotted a little flock of ducks flying low through some woods and dropping into a large pocket of thick brush along the upland, northeastern border of my marsh. While I thought I knew every part of this special place, I had somehow missed this spot, probably because it was surrounded by a dense tangle of undergrowth.

I had not yet shot any ducks in New Jersey, though I had seen both mallards and wood ducks on a number of my excursions, but always when they were out of range or when I wasn't carrying the Mossberg. This evening was one of those times when I was without the 20-gauge, but I knew it wouldn't have made any difference even if I had had it, because the waterfowl (I wasn't sure what species they were) would have heard me crashing through the thicket long before I got in range. My own "ornithological hypothesis" was that the ducks probably used this nocturnal hideaway on a regular basis because there was standing water in it, and if I was there the following evening with my gun, I could ambush them when they came back.

The next day I headed out well before sunset to make sure I arrived at the roost before the waterfowl returned. Pushing through the dense growth of bushes, vines, and small trees, I was delighted to discover that the first part of my hypothesis was correct. In the center of the thicket was a tiny pond less than a foot deep with some feathers floating on the surface. After finding a good spot to hide in the thickest part of the undergrowth, I cut away branches and vines in front to give me the ability to swing the 20-gauge to either side or up and down, depending on what kind of shot the ducks offered me. Then I waited.

Right on cue, just before sunset, I first heard the *wee-e-e-k, wee-e-e-k* calls of the hens followed by the whoosh of wings as four or five wood ducks swirled down and splashed into the water right in front of me. Even though I was well camouflaged and hadn't moved, the birds seemed to be aware of my presence. Their heads remained up in the alert pose, and I knew that they would probably jump at any second.

While waiting for them, I had rehearsed over and over again in my mind how I would point the gun if the shot was at a duck that saw me after coming into range and then flushed straight up. I would cover the bird with the muzzle of the 20-gauge and not shoot under it as I had done with the Florida mallard in Lake Okeechobee. Focusing on the closest drake, I threw the gun to my shoulder as it leaped up off the water, covered it, and pulled the trigger. Even though it was fifty years ago, I can still recall the exultation that swept over me as the duck stopped in flight and fell back, hitting the water with a splash. Rushing out into the shallow pond, I got my feet wet (I hadn't worn the chest waders because I thought they might be torn by the briars in the thicket), but I didn't care. Picking up the drake, smoothing down the feathers, and examining it in detail, I couldn't believe how colorful it was. I had bagged the ultimate duck trophy and had done so by conceiving a stratagem that had worked perfectly. I was proud of myself as a developing naturalist and hunter.

Later, when I read Leopold's account of his duck hunt, I understood that my plan had not been as creative as his, for, after all, I had actually seen waterfowl using this spot the evening before. But the fact that my scheme was more self-evident than his didn't lessen the bond I felt with him as a fellow waterfowler who had known the joy of the successful hunt.

How I would have liked to have had the wood duck preserved ("stuffed") and mounted in a flying position on a wall. But I had no contact with a taxidermist, and even if I had known of one, I had no way of getting the bird to him or her, or paying for it once it was done. Reluctantly, therefore, I gave it to my friend on the kitchen staff who received it with great joy and who later told me it was delicious. I did, however, photograph the trophy before giving it up.

After downing that wood duck, I would never again have a good shot at one at Lawrenceville when I was carrying my gun. But I did "harvest" (the term preferred by "game management" biologists like Leopold) a number of others in later years, particularly after I came to southern Ohio in the late 1980s.

The wood duck is, in fact, one of the great success stories of wildlife management. After being eliminated from most parts of the country by the early 1900s, the species is now common almost everywhere in wooded wetlands in its original range. In addition to hunting restrictions, the most important reason for its recovery has been the popular campaign to provide nest boxes to replace the increasingly rare natural nest sites in hollow trees.

While the bagging of the wood duck may have been the single greatest moment in all of my many excursions to the special places east of Lawrenceville, I was grateful for every hour I could escape the unpleasantness of my life back at school. But even though I continued to despise certain aspects of my *indoor* life there, like the unrelenting pressure to excel in the classroom and the absence of females, I experienced a reduction in stress every time I stepped outside. The campus is, after all, beautiful. The reason is simple. The school's "enhanced natural setting" was the creation of Frederick Law Olmsted, Sr., the most renowned landscape architect in the country in 1883 when he completed his campus plan for Lawrenceville.[9]

Earlier, I had benefitted from the Olmsted family's skill in harmonizing human and natural environments by being fortunate enough to have spent much of my early childhood in Forest Hills Gardens, that exquisite suburb designed by Olmsted's son. Now, I was the beneficiary of the more famous father, whose aesthetic vision at least allowed me to be unhappy in a lovely setting.

Though I now recall far more about the natural world in and around Lawrenceville than I do about most of the masters who taught me, there are two who stand out in my memory. They were individuals who supported me in my developing love for nature, and in the process, helped me survive my institutionalization.

The individual for whom I had the greatest affection in my five years at the school was Gerrish Thurber. He was both the school librarian and the adviser to one of the honorary organizations, the Library Associates. I was honored to be chosen by him to join this select group and felt even more privileged when he asked me to evaluate the holdings on hunting and fishing and develop a bibliography of new books that Lawrenceville should buy. After I completed this enjoyable undertaking, Mr. Thurber accepted all of my suggestions, and then surprised, and touched, me by saying that I could select one of the older volumes for myself as a reward. (He would then replace it with a later edition.)

The book I chose was William Bruette's *American Duck, Goose, and Brant Shooting*, first published in 1929. After returning to school after the end of my first season of waterfowl hunting on Lake Okeechobee, I remember sitting cross-legged for hours on the floor of a hidden alcove in the library, reading and rereading every part of Bruette's volume. Especially interesting was his account of hunting small black-and-white brant geese, a species that had intrigued me from the first time I saw a group of these birds while fishing in my father's boat on the South Shore of Long Island. Even though I don't think I was more than about eleven years old, I can still remember how impressive they were, with their extra long wings, as they flew with astonishing speed right over my head.

In future years, the brant would become my favorite waterfowl to hunt. For me, there is no more exciting moment in the outdoors than the sight of a large flock of these geese dropping rapidly from a great height and swinging in over the decoys, loudly calling *rronk-rronk* to their counterfeit brethren below. Because my memories of Gerrish Thurber and reading about brant hunting in a hideaway in the Lawrenceville library are among the most cherished I have of my years in prep school, the Bruette book became a precious keepsake, the most important material object I would take away from my time at Lawrenceville.

A few years after I left the school, in June 1964, as I was busy packing for a summer-long camping trip to Europe, my brother Tony, now living in Alaska, made one of his periodic visits back to Forest Hills. Since we both loved waterfowl hunting, I thought that he might appreciate the story of how I happened to acquire the Bruette volume. As in virtually every case when I have tried to share joy with my older brothers, the effort backfired. When I removed the check-out card from its sleeve in the back of the book with Tony's name on it (as well as George's and mine), he grabbed the book out of my hands, declaring that since he had introduced me to waterfowl hunting, it should, and must, be his. Focused on my imminent departure for the airport, I didn't resist, and Tony, without so much as a thank-you, turned on his heels and rushed out of the room with his prize. This seemingly uncontrollable need of both of my brothers to exploit me and transform every opportunity for shared happiness into one that they must dominate or disparage has been a great source of sadness in my life.

While I had the most fondness for Gerrish Thurber among my masters at Lawrenceville, I will also always be grateful to one of my math teachers, Philip Gordon Pratt. After three summers in southern Maine making up the pre-algebra and algebra courses I had flunked, I was ready for a change and the possibility of discovering new special places. Master Pratt would help me achieve this goal by taking me aside at the start of the fourth-form year and explaining how geometry and trigonometry were different from the math I had taken before, and that if I applied myself for once, I could get through the course satisfactorily and not have to go to summer school. His fatherly encouragement was the first I had received from a math teacher at Lawrenceville, and there is no doubt that it inspired me. In addition, geometry and trigonometry really did seem different from algebra; they were more "visual," and I could see some application to the world around me. For these reasons, I passed the last math course I would be required to take at Lawrenceville with a respectable grade—in that period before grade inflation—of, I believe, 74.

*I would now be able to enjoy the summer* of 1960 without any schoolwork, and it would be a memorable time in my life, the "summer of the big fishes." My father and his new wife Helen, who had been his chief nurse, would be traveling abroad, and they had left their house in Florida to Tony and his wife June, who were then living in the state, to watch while they were gone. Dad had also granted permission to his other sons to join Tony and June if we wanted, and both George and I jumped at the chance. We hoped for good fishing. As it turned out, it would be far better than that.

A major reason for our success was the location of my father's home. On the east bank of the St. Lucie River near its mouth, where it joins the Indian River before entering the ocean at St. Lucie Inlet, Dad's house was in the center of one of the best saltwater fishing areas in Florida.

Because Tony had to go to work during the day, he was only with George and me for night fishing. So it was with George that I spent most of my time angling, and the special place I would share with him was the St. Lucie Inlet. It was only a short run there in our father's boat, a small craft of less than twenty feet in length. Our chief targets were sharks, of whatever species were available. As we discovered, the most common types were great hammerheads (*Sphyrna mokarran*), lemons (*Negaprion brevirostris*), and particularly bulls (*Carcharhinus leucas*).

I remember my special place, this fish thoroughfare between the rivers and the ocean, as being pristine and beautiful in 1960. Although there was quite a bit of boat traffic traveling back and forth to nearby Stuart, a major saltwater angling center, we drift-fished for sharks close enough to the northern shore that boats going by rarely bothered us. Only on a few occasions, when we hooked an especially large fish, one that we had to follow because it threatened to strip all the line off the reel, did we have an encounter with a passing boat. Even then, our two craft usually managed to get by each other without cutting off the shark.

*With one of the sharks George and I caught in the St. Lucie Inlet near Stuart, Florida, during the summer of 1960. A bull shark, it is an aggressive species that is unique in being able to live in both saltwater and freshwater environments, and it has been implicated in many attacks on humans.*

That summer was memorable not only for these big fishes, but also because it was the only extended period in my life when George and I got along without bickering. He had recently finished up at Princeton with a degree in English, and I was still at Lawrenceville, about to enter the fifth form, my senior year. I had not yet achieved anything that my middle brother felt a need to compete over, no prestigious college degrees, authored books, or public recognition. I was content to be the passive little brother, and he felt secure in his role as the captain of the boat and the leader of every shark-fishing expedition. The fact is we needed each other on these trips, because capturing, and unfortunately killing, these magnificent animals was definitely a two-person operation.

Our usual method of fishing was to drift with the tide close to the northern side of the inlet with a bait like a big chunk of bonito or a whole mullet suspended from a float about halfway down to the bottom. The float moved along with us, close to the boat and parallel to it, and because the engine was off and we were quiet, the sharks would often take the bait only a few feet from where we were sitting.

The rod and reel we used were the biggest Dad possessed. I don't recall now the weight of the line, but it was probably at least fifty-pound test. And despite our use of steel wire leaders, to keep them from being cut by those wicked teeth, sharks sometimes rolled in the leaders, causing them to kink and break.

While many anglers in 1960 looked down their noses on shark fishing, George and I found it exciting, and sometimes even thrilling. I can still vividly remember seeing the dorsal fin of a shark circling the float just before it plunged below the surface and George's tense face as he watched the line run off the open-faced reel. In order to make sure the fish had the bait well back in its mouth, we usually counted up to twenty before yanking the rod up as hard as we could to set the hook. Then the real excitement began! Whoever's turn it was to fish sat in the bow, holding the rod high and only attempting to recover line, by lowering the rod and reeling furiously, when the shark turned or stopped its run. Though we lost some fish because they were just too big and couldn't be slowed, much less stopped, we were successful in many cases in getting these apex predators up to the boat. It was at that point when the fishing could go from exciting to thrilling.

In later years, we came to understand the key role of sharks in marine ecosystems and lament their catastrophic population declines around the world, but during that summer of fifty years ago, we foolishly saw them as not only dangerous, but worthless. Like Dad, Tommy Gifford, and his friend, Ernest Hemingway, George and I had both lost trophy game fishes to sharks, and I think we had the same view of them as the Cuban fisherman in Hemingway's *The Old Man and the Sea* (1952), who returned to port with nothing more than the skeleton of his giant marlin. Because of our ignorance, we usually tried to kill our sharks when we got them next to the boat by shooting them with our father's shotgun.

Even before we brought them close enough to the surface for a shot, I was always thrilled when I first saw clearly just how big many of them were. When the sharks were well down in the water, the fact that they are dark on top made them hard to see when I looked over the side of the boat. But as they came up closer to the surface, they would roll over, and their white undersides made them visible for the first time. It was as if these ominous behemoths, some of them over eight feet long, had suddenly materialized as if by magic.

Once a shark was exhausted and lying next to the boat, one of us would hold the leader and try to maneuver the fish into position while the other brother would shoot it. After some trial and error, we discovered that a quick kill could only be achieved with a brain shot, which meant aiming for the center of the top of the head. If we hit the mark, the shark would thrash around violently only for a few moments before it stopped moving.

We would then either cut the wire leader and let the fish sink to the bottom or tow it to the little-used public beach on the northern side of the inlet. After one such deposit, a concerned citizen reported us to the local police by giving them the boat's registration numbers on the bow, and we were forced to return and tow the shark well out to sea before cutting it free. I also seem to remember having to pay some sort of fine and receiving a lecture on how bad it was for tourism to have visitors find a large dead shark in the very place they planned to set up their beach umbrella! I recall thinking later that the local authorities would have been even more upset if they had known that the fish was a bull shark, which has probably been connected to more shark attacks on humans than any other species except perhaps the tiger and great white.

The other huge quarry that my brothers and I pursued during the summer of the big fishes was the jewfish or "Goliath grouper" (*Epinephelus itajara*). The origin of the first name is still being debated, but it apparently had nothing to do with anti-Semitism. Largest of the groupers, this species can reach a weight of at least seven hundred pounds and may live as long as fifty years.

The challenge of catching jewfish after they have grown to substantial size has never been in hooking them, for they readily accept all sorts of large baits if the leader is not too heavy and the hook is well hidden in the offering. The problem is what does the rod-and-reel angler do after he or she achieves a "hook-up"? Invariably, the grouper immediately ducks back under a ledge from which it can't be extracted or swims behind a bridge or dock pile covered with barnacles that cut the thin fishing line.

To overcome this challenge, some fishers in the past resorted to rope hand lines, with a chain for a leader and a huge hook that even the biggest groupers couldn't bend or break. An unlucky fish would then be literally pulled out of its hideaway. The downside of using this brute-force method was that the heavy leader and giant hook could make these intelligent fish wary of taking the bait, which could never be alive since the thickness of the hook would soon kill any fish that it impaled. This unfortunate reality posed a real dilemma for Tony, our resident jewfish expert, because he knew that an active, live bait, like a sea catfish weighing a pound or two, was most effective in allaying the suspicions of even the oldest, smartest grouper.

Like all successful fishing and hunting, which are first and foremost intellectual endeavors, Tony thought hard about how he could combine the use of a rope fishing line, chain leader, and huge hook with a live-bait presentation, and came up with an ingenious solution. He would insert a short length of thin steel wire under the dorsal fin of a catfish, which seemed to have little effect on it, and then twist the ends of the wire around the bottom of the hook. Both the catfish and the business end of the hook would be facing in the same direction, and when he lowered this rig down into the water, the lively, but stationary, catfish would be swimming directly below the curved portion of the giant hook. Because there seemed to be no direct connection between the hook and chain above, and the catfish swimming in place below, jewfish apparently had few qualms about taking the bait, and because their mouths are so large, they inhaled not only the catfish but the big hook suspended just above it.

Though I was initially skeptical about the effectiveness of this rig, Tony was determined to show George and me that it would work. He would prove its worth from the A1A bridge over the St. Lucie River, located a short distance upstream from my father's house.

Taking a sea catfish that George or I had caught on one of our light fishing outfits, Tony would connect it to the bottom of the big hook as described and lower the live-bait offering down off the bridge midway between two rows of piles, so that the current took the catfish back under the structure and kept it stationary, about halfway to bottom. He would then tie the top end of the rope to the bridge railing, and all of us would sit with our backs against the railing and get ready for the action we hoped was to come. Unfortunately, on most nights, that action never arrived, and we all endured long, boring hours of fruitless waiting.

There was, however, one trip to the bridge that was anything but boring. As usual, I was half asleep when Tony shook me awake. It seems that a powerful force was pulling the rope back and forth along the outer edge of the railing. George came to our help, but all three of us, tugging together, could barely move whatever it was that had inhaled our catfish offering. Finally, we were able to get our adversary up to the surface long enough for me to shine my flashlight down on it. I will never forget that sight! What was down there in the darkness didn't look like a fish at all, but more like a huge hog with fins and a gaping mouth.

Tony was, of course, elated that his clever system had worked, and that we had hooked one really big jewfish. But as we soon learned, hooking it and landing it were two very different things. Even with all three of us tugging on the rope, we quickly grew tired in our efforts to drag the monster fish on the surface down the northern side of the bridge and up on the beach. Our problems were the piles we encountered on the way. Pulling the hard-fighting grouper across the open water between the rows of these bridge supports was difficult enough, but when the jewfish reached the end pile in each successive row, it would wedge itself behind the concrete structure, making it almost impossible to budge. As the struggle went on, we were becoming ever more tired, and it began to look as if we were going to lose this tug of war.

It was at this point that George came up with an idea that sealed the fate of the hapless jewfish. He would get our shark-fishing boat and pull on the rope down below while Tony and I continued to pull from above. After driving to Dad's house and making the short run back to the bridge in the boat, George tied the rope to a cleat and used the boat's engine to tow the grouper out and away from the pile. Once it was free, we all pulled together and quickly managed to drag the great fish into the shallow water and up on the beach. It was only after we got it on shore that we could see just how big it was, and I think all of us were amazed by its size.

I wish we had simply photographed ourselves with the jewfish in the shallow water and then released it back into the river. That is, in fact, what we would have to do today, since the Goliath grouper is now a legally protected species in Florida. But fifty years ago, it was neither protected nor uncommon, and there was no way Tony was going to release our hard-earned, once-in-a-lifetime catch.

*Tony, John, and George with the 300-pound jewfish (Goliath grouper) caught from the A1A bridge over the St. Lucie River.*

After taking the fish back to the house and having June photograph the three triumphant fishermen with their trophy, we wondered what we should do next. There was, of course, far too much meat for us to consume. It was Tony who decided on the perfect solution. We would give the fish (which was very good eating) to the local, poor African-American community, and they could divide it up as they saw fit.

In that day of overt racial aggression of whites against blacks in the South, it must have been a disturbing sight for the black people in town to see three white men driving down the main street at night with a gigantic fish hanging halfway out of the open trunk of George's Plymouth. But once they realized that we had nothing but good intentions, they became very friendly and directed us to some scales where we weighed the jewfish before it was cut up by the gathering crowd, all of whom wanted at least one grouper steak to take home. Not only did we feel good that none of the fish would be wasted, we were also happy to get an accurate weight for our catch of right at three hundred pounds.

With the sharks and jewfish, the summer of the big fishes would be one of the most memorable and exciting periods of my life. I now thought of myself as an expert angler, and because I had been an active participant in successful operations against worthy opponents, my confidence in my ability to solve all sorts of other problems had risen to a new height.

*Despite my satisfaction with our success*, I didn't despair when it was time to return to Forest Hills to get ready for my fifth-form year in prep school. Given my dislike for the place, I was puzzled at first by my new, somewhat more positive attitude toward Lawrenceville, but I soon came to understand its genesis. Now, at last, I realized that I was probably going to make it to graduation and then on to a new life at a college of my own choosing.

All I had to do was to get through my final year, which I correctly believed was going to be less stressful than any of the last four. For one thing, I would now have the elevated status that came from being a senior and a Lawrentian who had some accomplishments, both athletic and academic, to his credit. Among these were playing on the Championship Kennedy House soccer and fifth-form football teams. As for my academic record, I had enjoyed a number of my courses despite the unpleasant milieu and had done very well in some subjects like history and English and reasonably well in all the others except the earlier math courses, which now had little influence on how I was to be evaluated for college admission. With this kind of record coming out of Lawrenceville in that time of far fewer applicants to college, I was a viable candidate for admission to almost any college in the country except perhaps the big three: Harvard, Princeton, and Yale.

Unlike both my brothers, I had no interest in those three universities or, in fact, any of the Ivy League. After five years in the perverse, all-male, macho environment of prep school, I had no intention of enduring another four years of more of the same. My first requirement for a college was that it had to be *fully* coeducational. While some of the Ivy League institutions did not admit women at all, those that did usually accepted them in far lower numbers than men. Around the beginning of that last year at Lawrenceville, I decided to make a break with the preppy-Ivy League subculture and go in the opposite direction despite my mother, who seemed to believe that if a Lawrentian could gain admission to an Ivy League college, he would be foolish not to accept.

Another proponent of this thinking was the Lawrenceville dean of students, David Douglas Wicks, a history master and graduate of both Lawrenceville and Princeton. In the conference with me on where I intended to apply, he seemed irritated when I told him I had no interest in his guarantee of admission to the University of Pennsylvania, an Ivy League school located in nearby Philadelphia that has always accepted a large number of Lawrenceville graduates. That irritation turned to overt, almost angry, frustration when I informed him that my goal was to go to a Southern institution, maybe the University of Virginia or the University of North Carolina, but most likely Duke, which I had heard was the best college in the region.

It must be remembered that in the northern prep-school world of fifty years ago, none of these places, not even Duke, had the prestige of *any* of the Ivy League universities, and for Dean Wicks, who had, I'm sure, only my best interests in mind, going South was tantamount to throwing away an opportunity for a truly excellent college education. I doubt if he could ever have imagined a time when the widely used college rankings of *U.S. News & World Report* would place Duke at the same level as, or above, some of the Ivy League schools.

My reasons for wishing to attend the university in the piedmont of North Carolina with the cool name were more complex than simply the fact that it was fully coed or because I wanted to turn my back on the prep school-Ivy League subculture and its assumptions of innate superiority. One of those other reasons was my desire to go to college in a small city, unlike Philadelphia, close to a vast rural region. There had to be, I thought, abundant opportunities for hunting and fishing in the Durham-Chapel Hill area and for locating new special places. I had already found some of those opportunities in another Southern state, Florida, and assumed that I would discover even more in North Carolina.

One final reason for my choice of colleges was a fascination with my Southern roots, particularly my great-grandfather and Civil War hero, Private Wesley Mayes Dance of the 59th Virginia Infantry, who was killed during the Battle of the Crater near Petersburg on July 30, 1864. The igniting of explosives at the end of a tunnel dug by Union soldiers under the Confederate lines not only made a huge crater in the earth, it might also have led to a major Southern defeat and an early end to the war if only it had been carried out correctly. Before he was killed, Wesley's regiment played a key role in holding up the Union advance until Confederate reinforcements arrived.

When I was still a small boy, our cousin Pauline Dance, a proud Virginian and the historian of the Dance family, gave my mother and me a tour of the Petersburg battlefield, and it was a day I will never forget. As we walked slowly up to the Crater, which intrigued me immediately because its contours were still clearly visible, Pauline began to speak in a solemn voice. I don't remember her exact words, of course, but I vividly recall the three points she stressed, with tears in her eyes, about Wesley Mayes Dance: first, that he died tragically, but gloriously, for "The Cause"; second, that his sacrifice was part of my own personal heritage; and third, that his death and that terrible war were still with us, part of the present and not so long ago.

That emotionally charged experience with Pauline at the edge of the Crater was one of those life-changing events that a person only comes to understand many years later. It had much to do, I'm sure, with developing my early fascination with history and my acceptance of those well-known lines from William Faulkner—even before I read his *Requiem for a Nun*—that "The past is never dead. It's not even past."

Probably the best example of the truth of Pauline's third point, that Wesley's death was not so long ago, was the fact that his son, George Washington Dance, was born in 1858, shortly before the start of the war, and George was the father of my mother, who was born in 1905. In other words, Wesley was only my great-grandfather, and many people today know their still living great-grandfathers, and some even know their great-great-grandfathers. Perhaps, by going to college in the South, I could come to understand the region in which Wesley grew up and his sacrifice in the not so distant past. With this reason added to the others, I went ahead and applied to U.V.A., U.N.C., and Duke with the hope of beginning a new stage in my life in the American South.

When the written responses from the colleges arrived in my Lawrenceville mailbox within a day or two of each other, I knew right away by the thickness of the envelopes that all three institutions had accepted me. Hoping for congratulations from my parents, I immediately contacted them and received the usual lack of support. Even though he wasn't paying for tuition, Dad wondered why I didn't want to go to a much cheaper, public college, and my mother, who was still disappointed that I hadn't taken up Dean Wicks' offer to go to Penn, said she would talk to a Kew-Forest teacher she knew well before deciding whether or not Duke was a worthy institution. After consultation with this sage adviser, Mother informed me that she now believed that Duke was one of only two "respectable" colleges south of the Pennsylvania-Maryland border, the other being Georgetown, where my friend and former Kew-Forest student, Chuck Pucie, was going.

After sending my acceptance letter to Duke, I spent the rest of my senior year in a kind of holding pattern, just waiting for graduation. Finally, on June 10, 1961, which also happened to be my eighteenth birthday, the big day arrived. My mother came over from Forest Hills, and my father arrived as well, driving up to Upper House on a rented motor scooter with Helen hanging precariously off the back. The two of them had been traveling around the country in his big recreational vehicle and decided to fit me into their itinerary. The only thing I now recall about any of their reactions to my graduation was my father's response when I asked him if I was going to get a nice gift like the new Corvette and Jaguar automobiles parked in front of Upper House, presents, I had been told, for two of my classmates. He answered this attempt at humor with one of his own and said that his mere presence should be enough of a gift. I told him I would have preferred the Jaguar.

At last, the five-year ordeal during that formative period of my life was finally over. As I strode up the aisle of the chapel to receive my diploma from the headmaster, I felt triumphant and still defiant. Despite my antipathy for the place, which had lessened somewhat over time but never disappeared entirely, I had not only gotten through, but had been able to choose the university I wanted to attend. And, of course, the whole point of going to prep school was to be admitted eventually to the "right" college and be prepared, after a rigorous course of study, to do well at that institution.

As the graduating seniors filed into the chapel, I recall being surprised by how few of them had been with me in Lower School five years earlier. I recently checked with the Lawrenceville archivist to find out how many students were in the four houses of Lower School in September 1956, and then I went through the 1961 school yearbook to see who had made it through to the end. I was amazed by what I discovered. Of the one hundred fourteen boys who began with me, only twenty-five, including myself, were there for graduation!

Obviously, there were a variety of explanations for why they had left Lawrenceville, but I am willing to bet that a significant percentage of those reasons had to do with their inability to cope emotionally, as well as their good fortune in having caring parents who listened to their cry for help and removed them from the stressful environment. The only difference between their response to prep school and my own was that they could leave and I could not.

Though I had survived outwardly, I sensed that I would never be as whole again psychologically as I was when I began my institutionalization at age thirteen. At the time, all I knew was that I seemed to be different emotionally from other teenagers who had stayed at home and gone to local schools. It was only after reading an article by psychologist Joy Schaverien in the *Journal of Analytical Psychology* on "Boarding School: The Trauma of the 'Privileged' Child" that I came to some understanding of the lifelong impact of the Lawrenceville years. Though the study deals specifically with British schools, she makes it clear that her conclusions apply to all such institutions since "the British exported this system all over the world."[10]

While there is no corresponding organization in the United States, as far as I know, to the British "Association for Boarding School Survivors," perhaps there should be. Like Dr. Schaverien's patients, I survived physically but was damaged psychologically.

I don't think I have ever gotten over my sadness as a boy abandoned by his parents to the social control of strangers in a rigid world without females, love, or familial intimacy. Particularly difficult has been my feeling that I am always on the fringe of every social situation, a permanent outsider "looking in," but never a full participant. Dr. Schaverien found this condition common among her patients. As she observed:

> The psychological impact of boarding school on the developing child affects the core of the personality. As a result of the sudden loss of early attachment figures, the vulnerable self needs protection. Therefore, a form of acquired and defensive encapsulation may occur. One adult patient described it as feeling as if he were "trapped in a bubble," which isolated him from other people. This type of personality structure, which serves a necessary protective function at the time, is difficult to reverse and leads to problems with intimate relationships in later life.[11]

In the future, this sense of alienation, which became a permanent part of my mental outlook, may have led me to insights I wouldn't have had if I had been happily adjusted. It may even have made me a better teacher-scholar. I don't seem to possess the same need as many professors to adopt, without question, the "groupthink" on a host of issues from the urging of animal rights for *all* species to the elimination of required courses in Western civilization and American history because of their supposed ethnocentrism. Nor have I been willing to accept the interpretations of other scholars, before doing my own research, simply because they were considered the "definitive" versions of historical truth.

There were other, more obviously positive, aspects of the Lawrenceville legacy, like the development of my love for history and the books that record it. When I took an honors course in ancient history, I was amazed that we can read today about events that took place two thousand years ago, even to the point of knowing something about the sex lives of Roman emperors! From that time onward, I've seen books in an almost reverential light, as objects that give their authors and their ideas a kind of immortality. In another history course, this one on the American past,

I found role models that I desperately needed to replace the older males in my own family, who, sad to say, I had little desire to emulate. (The only exception to that statement was my initial introduction to hunting ethics by my oldest brother Tony.) Particularly inspiring were men in combat, fighting for what they believed was a worthy cause, like the defenders of the Alamo in 1836 and the torpedo-bombers in the Battle of Midway in 1942 attacking the Japanese carriers, who knew they were probably going to die and faced their fate with a courage I can hardly imagine.

One final source of my love for history was my belief that all of American nature was more abundant in earlier times. When I was a foolish teenager (and didn't know how precious my later years would be!), I used to say that I would gladly have given up a year of my life to have had the opportunity to see a bison herd miles wide stretching to the horizon when that magnificent animal still numbered in the millions, or a flock of passenger pigeons flying over at noon and turning the day into night as their innumerable hordes blocked out the sun.

It was in these years that I developed a fascination with the wildlife and people of East Africa. This seemed to be the one place on earth where I could still witness the kind of abundance that used to exist in America. I longed to see the Great Migration of hundreds of thousands of wildebeest and zebra through the lands of the famous Masai, who seemed to be impervious to the influence of the modern age.

The future of my own country seemed to me to represent nothing but ever-greater destruction of the natural world, a viewpoint I expressed, apparently, quite often to my fellow Lawrentians. One of my nicknames at Lawrenceville in my senior year, as recorded in the yearbook, was "Black John." This title had nothing to do with supposed African ancestry, but rather with my constant complaining about what would later be called "environmental issues," everything from the poisoning effects of radioactive fallout from nuclear tests to the seemingly imminent extinction of the whooping crane.

I have sometimes wondered whether my love of books and history, and my early interest in "saving" nature, would have developed as strongly in those five formative years if I had stayed home and gone to school at Kew-Forest. I could have then avoided the misery brought on by my institutionalization at Lawrenceville. While I can never know the answer to that question, one thing is certain. If I had not had my special places to escape into and be emotionally calmed and spiritually refreshed, I would have had a much more difficult time making it all the way through to June 10, 1961, when I reached out my hand to receive that hard-won diploma.

One question I don't have to wonder about is whether the Lawrenceville of today is a better place than it was when I went there. With coeducation, a female head master—something I don't think anyone could have conceived of fifty years ago—an emphasis on recruiting a diverse student body, and strong efforts against hazing and other forms of bullying, the school has come a long way, and all of it in the right direction.

# CHAPTER FIVE

# Becoming a Sportsman-Conservationist:

## *College Years in Colorado, North Carolina, the American West, and Europe, 1961-1965*

The summer of 1961 was a busy one as I prepared for my new college life in a fascinating, but unknown, part of the country. I was, however, able to take off a couple of weeks to visit my Lawrenceville friend Britton ("Brit") White, who I had gotten to know only in the last months of my senior year. Brit lived in Denver, and he also loved hunting and the outdoors. Even though Mother would have preferred that I stay at home and work at a summer job, she finally gave in and reluctantly allowed me to accept Brit's invitation.

The hot 1,800-mile bus trip—Mother said that since I wasn't working that summer, she would send me by the cheapest means possible—from New York City to Denver was a grueling experience, made all the more difficult by a four-hour breakdown in Kansas. Though it was an unpleasant journey, especially at night when I couldn't sleep, I did enjoy some of the daylight hours because of the chance to see new, open country and the mammals and birds that lived in it. Particularly interesting were the jackrabbits and badgers, many of which, unfortunately, were dead alongside the road. I also recall the first black-billed magpies I spotted and being surprised by the Westerner sitting next to me, who said they were considered vermin, no better than crows "back East." To me, these striking black-and-white birds with long, greenish tails streaming behind had to be better than ordinary crows!

After I met Brit at the bus station and got settled in, we planned the next day's adventure. Like so many other young males of that time, I couldn't get enough of the television "westerns" like *Bonanza*, *Gunsmoke*, and *Wagon Train*, and now I had my chance to be in that romantic land, walking on ground that had been fought over for centuries by both indigenous peoples and Euro-Americans. Since Brit had accompanied me on some of my tramps along the Shipetaukins, he was aware of my attraction to running water and the wildlife that invariably congregates near it. He also knew that I hoped to see an unspoiled section of the South Platte River (not the part that ran through Denver), because of its historic associations with western expansionism.

Strangely, I don't remember our trip to the South Platte, but I do recall very well a walk along the banks of Cherry Creek. Near the confluence of these two streams, gold was discovered in 1858 that led to the founding of Denver. It was on Cherry Creek that I felt as if I was in "real" western country. There were the cottonwoods and willows on the banks, just as I had seen in movies about the West, and numerous black-billed magpies flying in and out of the stream corridor. These large, dramatic birds, with their loud, harsh calls, also seemed emblematic of the West.

Having experienced, at least in a small way, Colorado's High Plains and riverine ecosystems, I was anxious to visit the most dramatic of the state's natural environments, the Rocky Mountains. The trip to the national park of the same name, less than eighty miles northwest of Denver, was the highlight of my visit with Brit. As everyone knows who has taken that drive, the snow-capped peaks rising up like a jagged wall in the distance are an awe-inspiring sight. Once we were in the park, the stops along Trail Ridge Road were exciting not only because of the scenery, but for all the wildlife I was seeing for the first time. There were mammals, like the western version of the woodchuck, the marmot, stately elk, and mule deer, which ran off with their bizarre jumping gait that made them look like they're riding pogo sticks. And, of course, there were many new, often beautiful, birds, like the Steller's jay and mountain bluebird. Circling high in the sky were two species I had long wanted to observe in the wild, the legendary raven and that icon of the western mountains, the golden eagle.

The trip to Rocky Mountain National Park was a day I'll never forget. Thanks to Brit, I had seen and experienced more of the natural world on my visit to Colorado than I had ever expected when I boarded the bus in New York. I knew, however, that I had barely scratched the surface of what nature in the American West had to offer, and I vowed to return for a much longer stay.

What was left of the summer was spent getting ready for the move to North Carolina and my new life at Duke University. I arrived in Durham shortly before the start of the fall term, full of anticipation and a little scared about whether I would be able to cut it. Even though the school wasn't in the Ivy League, I kept hearing it referred to as the "Harvard of the South" and that made me think that I might have to work harder at my studies than I had originally intended.

After getting my room set up, finding out where everything was on campus, and scheduling my classes, the most important order of business was to meet women to date. After all, at Lawrenceville I had not been able to experience the normal high-school life of a teenager in the 1950s to date, "go steady," and enjoy the company of the opposite sex on a daily basis. Even though I knew I could never make up for those lost years, I planned to do my best to try. I recall very well my first class at Duke when I walked into the room, and there they were, real live women sitting in the seats! That was the first time I had been in a coed classroom since the seventh grade—when I was twelve.

Very quickly, I discovered that the mere presence of females didn't mean that I could connect with them. Like in other colleges I'm sure, there was a definite hierarchy at Duke in the competition for dating coeds, and as a freshman with very little money to spend, no involvement with sports, and no interest in joining a fraternity—to be forever a "G.D.I." ("God Damn Independent")—I was at the bottom of the pecking order. Still, I did manage to wrangle some dates with Duke coeds, but found the procedure for picking them up to be so formal and restrictive that I quickly rebelled against it. I had to wait in the "parlor" until the young lady descended the stairs from the upper floor like some Miss America contestant making a grand entrance. She then had to write her name in the sign-out book, tell where she was going, and promise to return by a set hour.

This archaic system of regulating the behavior of adults over eighteen became a bit freer over time. Later, a female could visit a male in his dorm room during certain limited hours on the weekend, but the door had to be open, and if the couple was on the bed, each of them had to have at least one foot on the floor at all times to make sure that full hanky-panky would be difficult, if not impossible.

Because of what seemed like almost puritanical restrictions imposed by Duke on dating its coeds, I decided early on that I would go off campus for my social life. I met another like-minded freshman from New Jersey who kept his Ford Thunderbird in the big parking lot behind our dorm (freshmen were not supposed to have cars), and we tooled around Durham, hitting the drive-in "restaurants"—I especially remember Shoney's Big Boy—in an effort to meet local ladies. Neither my friend (who had to leave Duke later under mysterious circumstances) nor I were shy in these endeavors, and we found that some of the female "townies" were as eager to date Dukies as we were to date them.

All of this active social life interfered, of course, with my studies, but I didn't care. I had my priorities, and doing well academically, at least in the first couple of years, wasn't one of them. Along with trying to make up for the social life I had lost at Lawrenceville, my other top priority was finding new special places for wingshooting. They had to be near campus, because I knew no one with a car who liked to hunt. I especially wanted to bag the two traditional game birds of the South, the bobwhite quail and mourning dove.

To show how attitudes have changed over time, I thought nothing about keeping my still relatively new shotgun, a Remington, 12-gauge, "Wingmaster" pump, in my dorm room or walking with it on campus as I explored nearby woods and fields for hunting spots. And though I kept the gun in a cloth case, avoided the most heavily traveled parts of campus, waited until cars had gone by before crossing a road, and generally maintained a low profile, it still seems amazing to me today that none of the students or faculty I passed questioned me about what was in the obvious gun case held in my hand or resting on my shoulder.

The area I hunted in that first fall at Duke was probably not much more than a half-hour walk from my dorm, beneath some high voltage power lines, and with a great variety of wildlife habitat nearby. I especially recall the thick pine woods where doves liked to roost in the late afternoon and the brushy fringes of small agricultural plots managed by African-American farmers, who, I suspect, didn't actually own the land they farmed. It was in this hunting paradise that I bagged my first doves and quail, which I gave to one of the farmers with whom I became friendly. In later years, on two different occasions, I visited Duke and tried to find this piece of the natural world where I had been able to escape the stresses of an academic workload harder than I would have liked. I failed in my quest, and the only explanation I have is that the expanding campus or nearby residential neighborhoods had obliterated any remnant of my special places.

With all the time spent pursuing my social life and hunting new species of game birds, I had little left for my courses, even when all I wanted to get at the end of the term was a midrange, "gentleman's C," something, in other words, over a 2.0 grade-point average. I didn't quite make it that first semester, ending up with a 1.81, the result mainly of an "F" in logic, a course a bad adviser told me to take to fulfill part of the math/science requirement. He said logic wasn't real math since it was colisted in both the philosophy and math departments. Though there was another option to fulfill the complete requirement, which was to take three courses in geology (called "rocks for jocks" because it was considered the easiest of the natural sciences) instead of the usual two, the adviser pushed logic despite my telling him I didn't like anything even slightly resembling math.

After sitting in three classes, waiting for the philosophy component to kick in, I realized that I had been conned, and that this boring course really was math! Unlike at Lawrenceville, where I was forced to take the hated subject, I discovered that I could simply drop it, though I received an "F" because I had kept the class beyond the official drop period. It would be the first and last time I received a failing grade or went below my target of a 2.0 grade-point average. In looking over my official transcript from Duke, and then checking my class rank upon graduation, it is easy to see the growth of grade inflation in the intervening years. The twenty-one Bs I received were the most frequent grade, followed by sixteen Cs, four Ds, and only *two* As. A record like that in college today, whether at a public university or a so-called elite institution like Duke, would probably be considered mediocre. Studies show that at many schools, the B has now become the average grade, and As are common to the point of absurdity.

So, with all those Cs and only two As, what was my class rank at graduation? Was it near the bottom, as it would be today? No, it was right in the middle, a rank of 221 out of 441. Apparently, in the early 1960s a C really did mean "satisfactory" and a B really did mean "good."

Not only did I avoid math by taking three courses in rocks for jocks, I enjoyed the geology classes, particularly the last one, geomorphology, on the origin and evolution of earth's landforms. The class gave me an understanding of the history of topographical features and a greater appreciation of every natural environment I entered. It was also in one of those geology courses that I heard an analogy between a long-playing record and our planet's history. This was the idea that if the record's running time corresponds to the billions of years of earth history, the record would play on for hour after endless hour, and modern humankind would only appear in the last minute. This analogy had a profound impact on me. I no longer thought twice about whether our species, *Homo sapiens*, had evolved from other life-forms, or whether the Genesis version (actually there are two versions in Genesis) of human creation was correct. This new knowledge seemed to bring me closer to the natural world and make me love it even more. I and my kind had come out of nature—at least in a physical sense—without the necessary intervention of God, and we had endured while so many other species had become extinct.

At the same time I was studying the various eras of earth history, I learned of the 1925 "monkey trial" in Dayton, Tennessee, when a biology teacher, John Scopes, was put on trial for teaching evolution. Still vivid in my memory is a student discussion in geology class in my sophomore year a few minutes before the professor arrived, in which we all agreed that the trial was an exercise in ignorance and that we were lucky to be living in an enlightened period of American history where scientific truth would soon prevail.

How naïve we were! The Pew Research Center in Washington D.C. conducted a poll in 2009 and found that only 32 percent of the American public believed "that humans and other living things have evolved over time and that evolution is the result of natural processes such as natural selection." In addition, the news media has reported on school boards in different parts of the country fighting over whether "creation science" or "intelligent design" should be incorporated into the teaching of high-school biology, and in recent years candidates for the Republican nomination for president have proudly, and publicly, stated their belief in the biblical version of how *Homo sapiens* came into existence.

Besides my geology classes, there was another course I took in my sophomore year that would have a lifelong influence on me. It was "Introduction to Art History," taught by Professor Sidney Markman. Like all great teachers, he had a certain flair for the dramatic, and I can still see him in class on the first day telling us that even if we later forgot everything else we'd been taught in his course, he would have done his job if we remembered one, overarching principle for understanding human creativity: "AN ART OBJECT IS A SOCIAL DOCUMENT."

He then went on to develop this concept in a way that it seemed to explain much of human history. If we want to understand the results of the creative process, from something as grand as the building of the Parthenon to something as mundane as the writing of a news release, we have to go back into the past to study the social and cultural "milieu" in which it originated.

To make his point, he suddenly stopped his lecture and asked the class if anyone present could tell him why the sculptures high up on the Parthenon were as beautifully carved on the back, where they couldn't be seen, as they were on the front. After several of us tried, and failed, to explain this strange impracticality, Professor Markman spoke in a reverential voice: "It was because the gods could see them."

Even now, I can remember clearly how deeply moved I was by his answer. What a wonderful principle to live by. In later years, when I researched subjects in history and archaeology to preserve my findings in everlasting print, I tried to emulate the sculptors of Ancient Greece in making my finished work "perfect" in both conception and execution. I realized, of course, that I could never attain their level of creative perfection, but I knew I had to try. For me, it wasn't the gods who were watching, but Posterity, and I was sure she would find out if I cut corners and failed to complete the statues.

In teaching as well as research, I found Professor Markman's emphasis on the need to understand the social and cultural atmosphere of the times when interpreting the past so persuasive that I adopted the concept when I began my own teaching career as an assistant to historian Robert Wiebe at Northwestern in 1967. Ever since, the first class in all my courses has contained a discussion of the importance of the milieu in analyzing history.

*My sophomore year was memorable* not only because of my courses in geology and art history, but because it was the first time I had an automobile of my own, a black 1958 Bel Air Chevrolet. An inexpensive, *very* used car that frequently needed repairs, it was, nevertheless, my ticket to adventure. Now that I had the delicious freedom that came with "wheels," I could explore the North Carolina countryside as far as my gas money (and gas was then very cheap) would take me. From the moment I left the lot in that Chevy right up to the present, I have loved driving, even for many hours at a stretch, in regions free of industrialization where I only pass through an occasional small town.

Now that I had a car, my social life picked up as well, and I discovered that one of the advantages of dating townies was that their male relatives or friends sometimes had information about hunting spots that they were willing to share. This was how I found out about a backwater area of the sprawling, 50,000-acre John H. Kerr Lake created by a dam completed on the Roanoke River in 1952. Straddling the North Carolina-Virginia border northeast of Durham, it provided excellent waterfowl hunting for ring-necks, mallards, and hooded mergansers. It would be one of my most important special places for the rest of the time I was at Duke.

Often, I hunted it alone, wading through flooded timber to an open-water area in which I carefully set out the rig of inexpensive plastic decoys I had purchased. Hanging up the burlap bag I carried them in on low limbs as a screen, I sat on a stump in waist-deep water and waited for the ducks that were usually not long in coming. I can still see myself rising up from that stump and in the same morning making perfect overhead shots on a drake mallard and drake hooded merganser, both of which were species I had never bagged before and both of which hit the water with a splash. This was the first waterfowling with decoys that I had done on my own, and I felt exhilarated by my success. It was—to quote from William Faulkner's "The Bear"—"the best of all breathing."[12]

It was a little later at Duke when I began to comprehend why duck hunting would always be at the center of my active participation in nature. Every outing was an adventure and a chance to get away from the anxieties of studying and test taking, as well as the humdrum routine of daily life. But it was more than that, and my new thinking about hunting was the direct result of my discovery of Aldo Leopold.

I first learned of this seminal figure one day in 1963 while visiting a favorite section of the main library, the new acquisitions exhibit. After spotting a book called *The Quiet Crisis* by Secretary of the Interior, Stewart L. Udall, I sat down with it at a nearby table, and I don't think I got up again until I had read the entire volume.

That experience in the college library transformed my thinking about nature. Udall seemed to be speaking to me directly in his historical narrative of the use, and abuse, of the natural world, and his call for the development of a conservation conscience. Particularly moving was his final chapter, "Notes on a Land Ethic for Tomorrow," which began with a quotation from Aldo Leopold's *A Sand County Almanac*: "We abuse land because we regard it as a commodity belonging to us. When we see land as a community to which we belong, we may begin to use it with love and respect."

While most environmentally committed people today have probably heard of Leopold, and many of them can even paraphrase that well-known passage from his book, he was not a famous figure in 1963. Though *A Sand County Almanac* first appeared in 1949, a year after his death, it sold only moderately well until 1966, when Oxford University Press published a paperback edition that rode the tidal wave of rising environmental concern sweeping America. I don't believe it would be an exaggeration to say that the volume became the "bible" of the environmental movement, a position it still holds today.[13]

After reading Udall's book that day in the library, soon followed by Leopold's classic work, I had found my cause, one that would be at the center of my life from that time to the present. My worldview now included not only a sense of responsibility to the game wildlife I pursued as a sportsman, but to the entire natural world.

In *The Quiet Crisis* Udall had included sections on a number of the great nature writers of the past, including, of course, Henry David Thoreau and John Muir, but neither of these individuals appealed to me like Aldo Leopold. After reading his *Game Management* (1933)—dedicated to his father, Carl Leopold, "Pioneer in Sportsmanship" (meaning what I would later call the code of the sportsman)—and *Round River* (1953), I realized that Leopold was the perfect model for me of what an "environmentalist" should be. In addition to his philosophical orientation toward nature, represented by the land ethic, he combined both aesthetic and utilitarian components in his conception of conservation, the hands-on, everyday work of managing natural resources like wildlife and forests to allow human use while preserving their ecological integrity.

As a twenty-year-old, agnostic undergraduate in 1963, searching for inspiration, and maybe even religion, the discovery of Udall and Leopold was just what I needed. I knew that I loved the natural world and wanted to preserve it, but I had no models in my personal life to guide me in this effort.

In 1963, my retired father now seemed indifferent to any issue that wasn't related to setting aside money for his worldwide travel adventures. Tony had some interest in wildlife conservation, but it never went beyond saving ducks and geese in his part of the country (he had moved to Alaska) for his own future hunting opportunities. And in the early 1960s, George had even less environmental concern than Tony. Like our father, my middle brother was busy with travel, as well as graduate school in English and coming to terms with the military draft; he would soon join the navy and go to Vietnam as an intelligence officer.

After I read Leopold's *Round River* in 1963, I think I understood better why I loved duck hunting so much. I knew already that almost every trip contained exciting moments, experienced within a natural world that I liked better than most human-made ones. In addition, there was the escape from stress and boredom, and the athletic challenge of consistently shooting well, even to the point of possibly becoming a crack shot. But Leopold's second posthumous book, much less well known than *A Sand County Almanac*, suggested other reasons for my fascination with waterfowling.

In *Round River*'s first essay, "A Man's Leisure Time," he asserted that leisure time was critical to having a happy life, for regardless of the level of formal education, "the man who cannot enjoy his leisure is ignorant." And the best way to experience that enjoyment, he believed, was to be dedicated to a hobby. But Leopold wasn't talking about just any hobby. It had to be a "defiance of the contemporary," an activity that "is an assertion of those permanent values which the momentary eddies of social evolution have contravened or overlooked." The true hobbyist, he argued, "is inherently a radical, and ... his tribe is inherently a minority."

His declarations leave little doubt as to how he would have felt about attacks on hunting as a hateful anachronism. He would have disliked what we today might call the "political correctness" of these attacks, their entanglement in "the momentary eddies of social evolution." After Leopold's death, his fishing and hunting partner, Robert A. McCabe, remembered that "in the years that I knew A.L. (and before), he tried with a skill possessed by no other to articulate the compatibility of a hunter's love for the object of the hunt."[14] In Leopold's thinking, it is precisely *because* hunting is an atavistic activity, a throwback to an earlier, primitive time, that makes it so appealing. As he knew, all hunters are, in a sense, rebels, swimming against the tide of modernity and fashionable thinking. After reading his essay in 1963, I felt confirmed in the intrinsic rightness of my favorite outdoor activity, and I was proud to be a member of his ancient tribe. Those sentiments have remained unchanged to the present day.

*While the Kerr Lake backwater* was my favorite inland spot for water-fowling, I discovered another special place for duck hunting along the coast, a section of the famed Outer Banks of North Carolina. It did have one drawback, however; it was straight east over two hundred miles away, requiring about four hours of driving. Even after reaching the Banks, I then had to travel about thirty miles more down Route 12. My hunting area was south of the village of Salvo in a portion of the marsh that extended farther west into Pamlico Sound than the sections north and south of it. I would park my car on the side of Route 12 and head out with my gun and bag of decoys, wading straight west through mud and thick vegetation until I finally broke through into the open marsh bordering the Sound.

Sometimes, I placed the decoys at the edge of the marsh where it met the open water, and lay down in the grass, hoping to lure in a "puddle duck" like a pintail or black duck. On other trips, I waded farther out into the Sound and took advantage of one of the wooden box blinds raised up on piles whose owner wasn't home. The target species then were "divers" like scaup and redheads.

While I occasionally went with Ralph Monaghan, another Duke student who liked hunting, most of these mini-expeditions were made alone, enabling me to experience, without distractions, the joy of hunting in a vast and beautiful natural world. Compared to the benefits I received, the long drives seemed like a small price to pay. On the return trips to Durham, I often thought about how lucky I was that this healthy ecosystem (I was already aware of that term) had been preserved in the Cape Hatteras National Seashore and was reminded once again how much better it is when land is saved from private despoliation through public ownership.

The Chevy that enabled me to make these excursions back and forth to the North Carolina coast also gave me the opportunity to follow up on the goal that I had set for myself after my visit with Brit White in Colorado. I could now explore a much larger portion of the American West than my short vacation with Brit had allowed—if I could only raise enough money to make the trip.

The solution to the problem came with the news that the Green Giant food company needed summertime workers in their huge cannery in Dayton, in the southeastern corner of Washington State. I'm not sure now how I learned about this opportunity, but several Duke students I knew, including my friend Richard Linnemann, thought it would be cool to go out to Washington, work for a time in the cannery, and then travel around the West.

In return for their paying for my gas, I would drive three of these Dukies, including Richard, in a very crowded car out to Dayton. Because all the other students lived in North Carolina and I was coming down from New York, we agreed to meet in a location more-or-less equidistant between the two, Washington, D. C. We would rendezvous at the Washington Monument at high noon. When I rolled up in the Chevy exactly at 12:00 p.m. on a sunny June day, I was delighted to find my passengers standing almost at attention, packed and ready to go. Quickly loading up the car, I set out on one of the great adventures of my life.

In America of the early '60s, it was still the heyday of the automobile. Cars were big, gas was cheap (no more than thirty cents a gallon for regular), and roads uncongested, at least outside of the big cities. As I passed through all the different states and changing topography, I felt exhilarated, and free, somehow proud to be living in a country where I could drive all the way to the Pacific Ocean without interference. With the windows down and a breeze blowing through (most cars didn't have air conditioning in 1963), my left arm resting on the top of the door, and the radio blaring away with the latest rock and roll, I thought I was king of the road!

The trip was endlessly interesting, even when we were going over terrain in western Maryland and Pennsylvania that didn't look that different from what I was used to in New Jersey and New York. I was especially eager to see the new streams and rivers we passed over. When driving, I have never stopped being amazed by how few passengers in my car "bother" to look down into the water when we are driving on a bridge, even if it is over a great, and historic, river like the Susquehanna or the Ohio. My passengers' lack of interest in moving water usually reveals an apathy toward the natural world in general.

As we traveled into country that looked more and more like what I had seen in television programs and movies about the West, I became increasingly excited by the topography. In my romantic imagination I could see potentially hostile "Indians" (they had not yet been renamed Native Americans) riding their pintos along a ridgeline in the distance. What was most striking was how abruptly the terrain changed after crossing the one-hundredth meridian and the Missouri River. I began to see such characteristic topography as buttes standing alone in a plain stretching to the horizon, and I knew that I was now really in the West.

I don't recall much about the wildlife we saw on the trip with one great exception. In Montana we spooked a small herd of pronghorn antelope right next to the left side of the road, and they ran parallel to us for a time, reaching a speed of nearly sixty miles per hour!

Finally arriving in Dayton, we found that the promised work in the Green Giant cannery was waiting for us, and we immediately began one of the most mind-numbing jobs I've ever had. I don't remember anything about it except for the tedium of standing for hours over endless rows of cans of asparagus, corn, and peas as they moved along for packing in big cardboard boxes.

After several weeks of this, Richard and I decided we could take no more, and we left to find new employment to accumulate enough money for traveling. Our new work had one advantage over the cannery job—it was outdoors and not in a hot, smelly building. That was, however, its only positive feature. In every other respect, it was more difficult, and just as tedious. Richard and I now joined the ranks of migrant farm workers, mainly Mexicans, laboring in the pea fields. The only part of our labors that I can even vaguely recall was feeding the pea vines into some sort of a machine, the ultimate purpose of which I suppose was to remove the peas from the pod.

What I do remember with greater clarity was being loaded into the back of a truck like cattle and taken out to the pea fields for the night shift, where we worked in such thick clouds of whirling dirt kicked up by the machinery that our faces were black when we came back to the trucks. We then returned to the "labor camp," a wooden, barrack-like building that I assume now was also owned by Green Giant, showered, ate, and slept until it was time to climb back in the truck for another work period. Richard and I kept this up for another couple of weeks until one day he returned from the shower room to tell me that one of the migrant workers had some kind of terrible skin condition over most of his body, and that Richard didn't want to stay in the place a minute longer! And so we collected our earnings and left.

An occasional skin condition notwithstanding, I learned to have nothing but the greatest respect for these Mexicans, who had crossed the Rio Grande, legally or illegally, to labor long and hard to harvest American crops. My experience with them in the pea fields in Washington State and later in the apricot orchards in California influenced all my future thinking about the "illegal alien problem" in the United States, especially when I heard Americans complaining about them who can't imagine doing the kind of work they perform on a daily basis.

Richard and I now started out on our outdoor adventure, the fun part of the summer of 1963. Because I had read that Glacier National Park had the most dramatic mountain scenery south of the Canadian border, and because it was also a good place to see a grizzly bear, we decided to go there first. It wasn't long after arriving at the west entrance to the park and starting up Going-to-the-Sun Road, which many consider one of the planet's most spectacular mountain highways, that I knew we had made a wise decision. This was one time when that overused term "breathtaking" really was applicable. I appreciated the mountains and lakes in the park not only for their indescribable beauty, but also because they were dramatic examples of what I had learned about in my geology courses at Duke. Here I could see up close how all-powerful glaciers had transformed the land.

We stopped many times on the road, but some stops were more memorable than others. One of these was on snow-mantled Logan Pass, atop the Continental Divide. Here Richard and I had a brief snowball fight. I was fascinated by the phenomenon of the Continental Divide—that a raindrop falling west of the divide would eventually join waters flowing into the Pacific Ocean, while a raindrop falling east of it would eventually join waters emptying into the Arctic or Atlantic Oceans. On Logan Pass I felt that I was standing astride North America.

Somewhere beyond the pass, I decided to leave the road and take a hike to the north while Richard napped in the car under a thick layer of blankets. I still hoped to see that symbol of the western wilderness, the grizzly bear. If there were any bears around, I thought I'd be able to spot one at a great distance with my binoculars, because the country I was hiking up into was open terrain, with only a few patches of small conifers here and there. Since the conventional wisdom of the day was that only sow grizzlies with cubs were dangerous, I wasn't particularly apprehensive when I came across one set of very large bear tracks in the snow.

After following the trail for a while, I noted that it seemed to be heading in the direction of one of those little islands of vegetation some distance away. I remember thinking to myself that I hoped the animal hadn't gone into the patch, because then I wouldn't be able to see it. As I got closer, I was frustrated to find that, indeed, the tracks disappeared into one end of what was a short, narrow strip of brush and stunted trees. Thinking the grizzly might have simply passed through the patch and continued on its way, I walked entirely around it and was excited to discover that there were no tracks coming out. *Ursus arctos horribilis* was still inside, only a stone's throw away! That expression describing a short distance has always been one of my favorites, and it may have given me the idea for getting the bear to do what I wanted it to do, and that was to show itself. I had no intention of returning to the car defeated in my quest for a grizzly sighting.

What I did next would be considered insane today, but it seemed to make sense at the time. I don't believe that there were any recorded instances of fatal bear attacks in Glacier in 1963. Since 1967, when two young women were killed in unprovoked attacks by two different bears miles apart on the same night, there have been a number of such encounters. Still in all, what I did was pretty stupid.

Picking up a large rock, I chucked it into the brush where the tracks had gone in, thinking that the curious, but probably placid, bear would stick its head out of the vegetation to discover what had caused this minor commotion. Nothing happened, so I continued to work my way along the patch, throwing in a rock about every few feet. Because the short strip of brush and small trees was so narrow, most of my projectiles seemed to go right into the middle of it. After throwing in about a dozen stones, I was running out of brush when I heaved in a particularly large rock that didn't clatter down through the dead branches but hit something soft. At the same moment, I saw some brush move and heard a sound I will never forget. It was a long growling roar like some mythical giant clearing his throat.

Suddenly, terror swept over me as I could visualize the grizzly bursting forth from the brush with the speed of a racehorse, and I wheeled around and ran down the mountain at a pace I know I have not attained before or since. The whole way back to the road I never looked around, thinking that the bear might be right behind me. Probably running away was the most ill-advised action I could have taken, since it might have triggered the predatory instinct to give chase, and that's one race, of course, I could never have won. But I was lucky. My grizzly was a good-natured bear that stayed put. He or she simply didn't like getting hit with a rock! I would have to wait until some years later, on a trip through Alaska's Denali National Park, before I saw my first *horribilis* in the wild.

Before leaving Glacier, I had one more memorable experience, not as dramatic as the bear encounter, but still one that has stayed with me all these years. Not long after starting to drive along the shore of St. Mary Lake, we pulled off the road, and I got out to view the beautiful scenery. Out in front of me was a tiny bit of tree-covered land completely surrounded by water, which I later learned is called Wild Goose Island. Standing on the lakeshore, looking at the island, I had the longest, most powerful *déjà vu* of my life. It may not be rational, but I *knew* I had stood on that spot before, looking at the island in exactly the same way. I even had the intense feeling that I had camped for many days, right there, at the edge of the lake.

Did that *déjà vu* experience have anything to do with my choice of a dissertation subject four years later, when I selected George Bird Grinnell, who first came to the area in the 1880s on hunting trips and who later led the campaign to preserve it as a national park? That question will always remain unanswered in my mind.

While the trip through Glacier was definitely one of the high points of that summer, there were other exciting western locations I felt lucky to be able to see firsthand. After leaving Montana, Richard and I traveled across Idaho and reentered Washington State, visiting two national parks, snow-capped Mount Rainier and its endless meadows of alpine wildflowers, and Olympic, with its mountains, dense rain forests, and rugged Pacific shore. We then decided it might be cool to see something of nearby British Columbia, and so we crossed the Strait of Juan de Fuca to Vancouver Island and traveled up the east coast, stopping in a tiny fishing community called Deep Bay, just north of the much larger Qualicum Beach. When I told one of the local fishing guides how much I wanted to catch a chinook salmon, he surprised me by offering to take us out if we paid for his gas and allowed him to keep any fish we caught. What a memorable trip it was, trolling slowly in his boat along that beautiful coast, and we even caught three salmon, one a respectable twelve-pounder.

Another memory I have of Vancouver Island that was not nearly so pleasant was my shock at seeing extensive clear-cutting being done in the

*In the summer of 1963, with Richard Linnemann and our chinook salmon on the east coast of Vancouver Island. The contrast between the clear-cutting in Strathcona Provincial Park and the protection given American national parks made a deep impression on me.*

middle of the island, in Strathcona Provincial Park, which I assumed was a nature sanctuary. When I asked a local resident about this "outrage," he simply shrugged his shoulders and said something like "That's the way it is up here; we don't have the same restrictions in our provincial parks that you Americans have in your national parks." Apparently, this destruction was being carried out by private timber companies. I couldn't help thinking the obvious: what's the point of having a nature preserve if you're not going to preserve it?

After leaving Vancouver Island and returning to Washington State, we drove down the spectacular Oregon coast, most of which I was delighted to find had been kept open for public use and out of the hands of private developers. At Florence, we headed inland to see Crater Lake National Park. I will never forget what can only be described as my amazement when I walked up to the edge of the volcano's mouth on a bright sunny day and looked in at that shining body of water. Of course, I had been told it would be blue—but not that blue! The inky color is so dark and deep that it is, literally, indescribable, and the lake has to be one of the most beautiful sights in all of American nature.

Crater Lake was the last national park I visited that summer. My money was running low, and I was eager to get down to the apricot orchards near

San Jose, California, where there were supposed to be lots of jobs picking fruit. Richard was done with this kind of work, and we split up shortly before I began my last stint as a migrant farm laborer. I remember standing near the top of a ladder leaning precariously out to pull the apricots off the branches and dropping them into a big basket. As fast as I worked, I could never compete with the Mexicans picking fruit from adjacent trees. Despite their small size and shorter arms, they seemed to have a rapidity and elasticity in their picking that I could never duplicate. When I asked one of them how he could be so quick, he answered by saying that if I had six children back in Mexico, I'd be quick too.

After only about a week or two, the opportunities for work began to decrease rapidly, and finally dried up entirely. I then had to bite the bullet and do what I never wanted to do, which was to call Mother to wire me enough money to get home. Despite the fact that I had successfully combined work and western travel over most of the summer, she was still unpleasant on the phone and reminded me that I wouldn't be in this "fix" if I had stayed in Forest Hills and taken a local summer job. With the one hundred dollars she sent, I made it back across the continent, barely. Because I knew that most of the money might have to go into my repair-prone Chevy if I had a breakdown, I slept in the car, rather than motels, and ate thirty-cent hamburgers and five-cent candy bars. I got all the way to eastern Pennsylvania before the only major mechanical problem occurred when the muffler fell off. Still, the Chevy kept running, though the car was now so loud that Mother said that—despite being deaf in one ear—she could hear it coming down the street even before I arrived in front of the house.

The importance of the 1963 summer trip in crystallizing my attitudes about a number of issues is, I think, hard to exaggerate. I was inspired by the as yet unknown men and women who had saved these beautiful natural places I had enjoyed so much. What a tragedy it would have been if the same kind of clear-cutting I saw in Strathcona Provincial Park was being permitted in Olympic National Park, and would Crater Lake have been as stunning if it had been encircled right up to the rim by private businesses like hot-dog stands and souvenir shops? Preserving these natural oases, which were like my own special places except that they were not just for me but for all people, for all time, seemed like an effort to which I should be committed.

That summer, I also found out what it was like to do hard physical and monotonous labor, devoid of any creativity or intellectual input on my part. I knew now that whatever my future career would be, it had to include those latter two elements to keep me even reasonably happy. Finally, the summer was important for putting me together for the first time in my life with poor people. Because we worked daily side by side and in one part of the summer even lived together in a labor camp, I got to know many of these migrants and came to appreciate their seemingly endless capacity for hard work. The contrast between them and the students I had known at Lawrenceville and often still encountered at Duke, who were irritatingly smug about their wealth and high social status, couldn't have been greater. I developed a deep empathy for the migrants, who were forced to lead such difficult lives in poverty. They made me feel very lucky that I could go to a place like Duke without having to work outside the college to pay for tuition. At least partly because of my experiences over the summer, I returned to school in the fall of 1963 with a greater awareness of, and sensitivity to, the problems of those less fortunate than myself.

While these experiences brought my feelings of empathy and concern up to the surface, they had been developing for some time. Because of what I had gone through during my institutionalization at Lawrenceville and the syndrome I believe I developed there of always feeling like an outsider, on the fringe of society and every social situation, I was naturally attracted to psychology as a possible major. But I wasn't just interested in my own development, but in how society as a whole evolved over time. To best understand why and how this growth took place, I decided to combine history, the study of the past and long my favorite subject, with sociology, the study of present-day society and the processes that govern social interactions. When forced to pick one of these disciplines as my major, I chose sociology rather than history simply because it seemed to be the more practical of the two. Not thinking that I would ever teach, I saw no way to turn a history major into a foundation for a career, what my father called a "tool of life." Sociology, on the other hand, might lead to a number of possibilities, from social work to the creation of strategies for the marketing of consumer goods.

It was during my junior year at Duke that I developed an insatiable desire to experience European cultures and compare them to my own, to visit the historic sites I had read about in my history courses, and to view, firsthand, some of the magnificent works of art I had studied in Professor Markman's art history classes. By the spring semester of that year, I decided that unless I got to Europe that summer, which was presumably the last time I would have for an extended visit before having to go to work fulltime, my college education would be incomplete, regardless of what I decided to do after graduation.

To make sure this didn't happen, I decided to sell almost everything I had of value, like an outboard motor and some wooden factory decoys (unlike the nearly valueless plastic ones I used for hunting), and to borrow money from my father and mother in order to accumulate the necessary funds to make the trip. My plan was to hook up with a Duke friend who was also willing to travel on a shoestring, rent a car in Paris, and camp out across Europe, sleeping nearly every night in a tent. My traveling companion for the trip would be Al Meyer, a pre-med student who agreed to split the cost of the rental car, including the gas, down the middle.

Before starting the main portion of the adventure, when we picked up the car in Paris, we decided to fly to London first and stay in England for a week. I was excited when the plane touched down on June 17, my first time on another continent. I hadn't purchased our tent yet, and our stay in London was one of the few times we slept indoors during the summer. Our lodging was a "really primitive" room on the fifth floor of a youth hostel. I know these details, because of all the trips I have taken in my life, this was the only one on which I kept a diary.

After seeing many of the great artistic achievements of Western civilization in London, like the Elgin Marbles in the British Museum, sculptures from the Parthenon that were, indeed, carved in the back as well as the front, and Sir Christopher Wren's masterpiece, Saint Paul's Cathedral, I wanted to get out of the city and visit the town of Windsor. Windsor Castle has been an important royal residence since the days of William I, and across the Thames from Windsor is the famous English "public school," Eton, a model for American boarding schools like Lawrenceville. I hitchhiked the twenty-five miles west to Windsor and was surprised by how quickly London gave way to an almost rural environment. While my time at Windsor Castle was brief, I spent most of the afternoon wandering the countryside around Eton. With lots of trees and cows grazing along a stream running through their pasture. it was the perfect pastoral scene and reminded me of my special places east of the Lawrenceville campus. I wondered how many of the boys then enrolled at Eton took advantage of this beautiful natural world on their doorstep.

After a week in and around London, and eager to reach Paris to begin the main part of our adventure, we waited impatiently on the evening of June 24 for the train to leave at eight that night. Our first destination was Newhaven on the English Channel. From there, we crossed on the ferry *Falaise*, named after a key site in the Normandy campaign of World War II, and after reaching Dieppe, we boarded another train for Paris.

Arriving in the French capital early on the morning of the 25th, our first order of business was to pick up the automobile that would be our chief means of transportation for the next two and a half months. We had arranged for the least expensive vehicle we could find, a Citroën *Deux*

*Chevaux*. As it turned out, the car fit our needs very well with one glaring exception. With an engine of only seventeen or eighteen horsepower and a top speed on *level* ground of probably no more than fifty-five miles per hour, it was woefully underpowered at times.

This problem became obvious driving in the Alps of West Germany and Austria and particularly in the Pyrenees of Spain and Andorra. In this last country, where the elevations around us were at seven to eight thousand feet, the road was so steep that "it became a bit tense for a while, due to the fact that it looked for a short time as if our car wouldn't be able to make it." Only by keeping the Citroën in first gear "the whole way up" did the car "finally pull us through." The issue of being underpowered in the mountains was more than made up for by its great fuel economy, high ground clearance for off-road driving, and sturdy construction. With that wonderful little car, we drove 10,300 kilometers (6,400 miles) on a journey that took us across parts of France, Luxembourg, West Germany, East Germany (on the Soviet-controlled highway to Berlin), Austria, Italy, Monaco, Spain, and Andorra.

Most towns and cities we visited that were tourist destinations seemed to have a campground on their outskirts for the hordes of young people also traveling around Europe on a meager budget. As I recall, these places charged something between fifty cents and a dollar for a space to pitch a tent and the use of their bathrooms and showers. Many nights we paid nothing at all for lodging. Because I didn't want to drive in the dark and miss seeing the countryside, we would stop even if a campground wasn't nearby, and simply drive out into a field or into some woods to pitch

*Al Meyer leaning against our sturdy, but underpowered,* Deux Chevaux *somewhere in the wilderness of the Pyrenees of Spain. During the summer of 1964, we drove 6,400 miles across Europe, and there were few nights when our sleeping accommodations were other than the small tent to Al's left.*

our tent. I don't remember being hassled, even once, by a landowner for following this unorthodox practice.

In going over my one-hundred-page diary for this once-in-a-lifetime trip that lasted until early September, I think I can see now what impressed me the most in our travels. One discovery that kept on surprising me was the abundance and beauty of unspoiled nature, even in thickly settled regions. I believe that 1964 summer odyssey solidified my commitment to preserving natural spaces for public enjoyment, for all time, even in the midst of large human populations. Most of the time, this loveliness was of a subdued, pastoral kind, like what we saw on the road from Paris to Reims: "The countryside is more beautiful than practically any I have ever seen—in the East at least [eastern part of the United States]. There are few if any billboards; the road edges are free from rubbish, and the view from the road is unobstructed and beautiful." And later in the trip I wrote: "Most of the roads that we traveled on in France have tall sycamores [probably London plane trees] planted on either side that completely shade the road and add a great deal of charm to the countryside." The people of France seemed to know how to live harmoniously with nature far better than Americans.

At other times in our travels, the topography was anything but "subdued." Some of the mountainous country we drove through was as dramatic and awe-inspiring as anything I had ever seen. In the Bavarian Alps we took a cable car to the top of the nearly 10,000-foot Zugspitze, the highest mountain in Germany. As I wrote on July 13, "the view was, of course, magnificent," and "I'm told that the snow-covered peaks we were seeing all around us were some of the mountains of Switzerland, Austria, and Italy, as well as those of Germany." While the Alps were well settled, at least at their lower elevations, the Pyrenees of Spain and Andorra were part of a vast wilderness region that even contained bears and wolves. On August 22, I wrote: "The Pyrenees ... and the flat, plateau-like country on the other side [in Spain] are both just about the wildest and most fabulously beautiful country I've seen this summer."

In addition to the sublime nature I discovered on the trip—I thought it would be grand to have another summer-long visit to Europe just for the nature alone—there were several places we visited that stand out in my diary and memory above all the rest. In the chronological order of our visits, they were Verdun, France; Berlin, in West and East Germany; Pompeii, Italy; and the Cro-Magnon cave of Font de Gaume, near Les Eyziers, France.

The first of these places, the World War I slaughterhouse of Verdun, where hundreds of thousands of Frenchmen and Germans were killed or wounded in 1916, had a profound impact on me. Seeing the countless white crosses stretching down the slope and looking through the windows into the cellar of the huge mausoleum on the hill that contained tens of thousands of skulls and scattered bones of unknown soldiers, I wondered at the futility of it all. How incredible, I thought, that one man or a handful of men could have been the cause of the demise of so many other men who probably had little idea of why they were fighting or for what they were about to die. I vowed then and there that if I ever supported a war, or actually participated in one, I would have to have well-thought-out, concrete reasons for fighting and possibly killing other human beings.

The second place to remain vivid in my memory was the divided city of Berlin. On July 6, I wrote: "Well, here we are in Berlin, and I must admit that I was quite excited about actually being able to see the 'Wall' and other manifestations of this political struggle I've lived with my whole life." Though there were many sights to see in Berlin, I kept coming back to the Wall, the very symbol of the beleaguered city. First erected in 1961 and made steadily higher and more fortified in the years leading up to our visit, the structure "was as ominous looking as I thought it would be—complete with East German guards armed with automatic weapons, tank traps, great coils of barbed wire, and broken pieces of glass fastened to the top of the Wall in places where it comes near to buildings on the East Berlin side." After some hesitation because of the supposed danger involved, we decided on July 8 to cross over through Checkpoint Charlie into East Berlin and "actually walk around in this capital of probably the most closely guarded of all the Eastern European countries under Soviet control."

The contrast between the two Berlins couldn't have been more marked. "The Western sector is full of life—with many new buildings and an atmosphere of gaiety," while "the Eastern sector looks very much like New York City's garment district about 5 in the morning; there are few people on the street, and the streets themselves, as well as the general surroundings, are bland and spiritually degenerative." Another striking contrast between them was that in the West, I don't recall seeing any rubble remaining from the bombings that ended in 1945, but in the East, there were whole blocks that hadn't yet been cleared. It was strange to look at the front of a large building that looked intact, except for the doors and windows, and then to go around the side and discover that it was simply one wall, with nothing behind it.

"The most interesting and educational part of our walk occurred when we went into the German Democratic Republic's museum of

German history." Everywhere we looked in that depressing building were reminders of "the omnipresent and omnipotent communist spirit." There were busts of Marx and Lenin, huge maps showing the "imperialistic" and "socialistic" nations, and a special section called the "room of capitalist development" that emphasized the terrible working conditions in factories. The one incident I clearly remember, and recorded in my diary, "occurred while we were talking to the old woman who was supervisor of the 'room of capitalist development.' Since this was the 'capitalist room,' we asked her where the 'socialist' or 'communist' room was?" In an almost threatening voice, she loudly answered that there was no single room, because it was "ALL AROUND YOU!" As the woman talked to us, "she kept looking anxiously over her shoulder toward the supervisor of the next room, then abruptly cut off the conversation and walked away."

On the way back to Checkpoint Charlie, I tried to speak with some of the few people we encountered in the streets. Without exception, they fearfully waved us off even before we got close to them.

Those hours spent walking around East Berlin, especially the time spent in the so-called museum of German history, made a deep impression on me. For one thing, the experience intensified my desire to study history in order to understand how and why this once beautiful city had been divided, with a large part of it reduced to such a sad state. Before that day, I had wondered many times whether or not what I had constantly heard about how little freedom there was for Eastern Europeans under Soviet communism was the actual situation or simply propaganda. "Now I found that it was really true! This made me feel good in the knowledge that I and the West, as a whole, are not being duped by their political leaders (at least in this respect)."

When the Wall finally fell in November 1989, I wept with joy. How I would have loved to have been there to share in the celebration.

The third place that summer of 1964 that affected me, both intellectually and emotionally, more than almost any other, was the archaeological site of Pompeii, the Roman town in southern Italy buried by the eruption of Mt. Vesuvius in A.D. 79. On August 10, I wrote in my diary: "Spent most of the day at Pompeii—I could have spent a week." It was as if I had been transported back in time to another world:

> In the streets, there are openings on either side of the stone, pedestrian, crossing blocks through which the wheels of carts passed almost 2,000 years ago; the original water pipes paralleling the streets; nearly perfectly preserved frescoes and mosaics; implements of daily life such

as frying pans, fishing rigs, anchors, nutcrackers, and bronze heating units—all looking very modern; a perfectly preserved amphitheatre where the gladiatorial games were held; and even notices on the sides of the walls paralleling the main streets advertising the soon-to-be-presented gladiatorial contests.

As good as the whole day was, the very best moments came when I wandered away from the crowd and ducked behind a fence and into a part of the town I wasn't supposed to be in. Passing through a dark opening, I suddenly found myself walking out into the arena of the amphitheatre. No one else was around; there were no planes flying overhead, and I could hear no sounds from outside. What an experience! As I stood alone in the middle of the arena where so many gladiators had fought and died, I thought I could almost hear the yelling of the spectators and the clash of weapons, metal against metal.

From the time I read H. G. Wells's *The Time Machine* (1895) at Lawrenceville, I had been fascinated with the concept of time travel, but unlike Wells's hero I would go back in time, not forward. That day in Pompeii, I thought I had come as close to time travel as I would ever get—but I was wrong.

There was one last place on my summer trip that would outdo even my experience in the arena at Pompeii. It was the "Grotte [Cave] Font de Gaume," near Les Eyziers in southwestern France, which I visited on August 25. I had wanted to see the more famous Lascaux, which I had studied in Professor Markman's art history class, but found that it had been closed to the public the year before. Outside air, light, and the breath of its many visitors were damaging the delicate paintings. The people at Lascaux told us that there was another, similar *grotte* called Font de Gaume, only about twenty-four kilometers away, and that's where we headed.

That night, I exuberantly recorded my feelings about what I had seen:

> The tour through this cave has been the most enthralling experience of the whole summer. Inside, the passageway was very narrow and the ceiling extremely high. The entrance to the cave is on a hillside and looks exactly like every painting or drawing I have ever seen that has endeavored to reproduce what life must have been like in that prehistoric period.

I was amazed to think that the artwork I was looking at was *at least* seventeen thousand years old and that along with the bison and horses depicted on the cave walls, there were also giant Irish deer and woolly mammoths, species that had been extinct for thousands of years. I was also fascinated by how "the artists [had] ... incorporated the contours of the walls of the cave into the painting itself in order to give the subject more of a feeling of movement and life—this attempt at realistic depiction is clearly preconceived and not the least bit accidental."

It is difficult now to describe how much I admired these early Europeans, with whom I felt a strong affinity, both as a fellow hunter and as a theoretical descendant. Their "unquenchable desire to recreate— or perhaps to control—their environment" through artistic expression touched me deeply. I could "imagine two or three of these human beings crouching next to that same cave wall 17,000 years ago, with one or more holding a torch, while the respected artist traced his wet, stained finger over the surface and created something looking very much like the bison the group had killed the day before." Then, "when the artist was finished, the entire group came nearer, holding their torches ever closer to the masterpiece, and all murmured satisfaction and, undoubtedly, joy."

After the visit to Font de Gaume, we still had nearly two more weeks in France before we had to return our Citroën in Paris and depart from Orly Airport on September 7. Though I saw a great deal in that time, like the famous Loire Valley châteaux, Chambord and Chenonceau, the magnificent Chartres Cathedral, which "appears from a distance to rise literally out of the wheat fields of the surrounding area," the palace of Versailles, and the many treasures of the Louvre, like the *Venus de Milo* and the *Mona Lisa*, nothing touched me as deeply as the cave paintings of Font de Gaume.

Returning to Duke for the start of my senior year later that month, I began to think seriously about what I would do after graduation, and in my mind, I kept coming back to that cave in southwestern France, as well as the other most impressive sites on the summer trip, Verdun, Berlin, and Pompeii. Even though I had majored in sociology and was grateful for the insights it had given me into how people interact with each other, from small groups to entire societies, I now knew that I couldn't continue my work in that field in graduate school or apply what I had learned to some business pursuit like marketing. The European trip had forced me to recognize, and accept, my passion for history. I wanted to immerse myself in the past and know how it had become the present, and how the present might predict the future.

All of these feelings about wanting to keep history at the center of my life came together one day in the spring semester at Duke in a course on the development of American democracy. I can still see that master teacher and charming Southern gentleman, Professor Robert Durden, wearing his signature bow tie and resting one arm on his lectern, telling us about the country's reaction to the bombing of Pearl Harbor. Suddenly, it dawned on me that this is what I should be doing with my life—like Professor Durden, I would be a college history teacher. Then, I could live in the past, study it, and get paid, all at the same time.

Because of this epiphany in Durden's class, I set about applying to graduate school at the two major public universities in Florida, Florida State and the University of Florida. I picked those two institutions because I thought they were probably as good as any of the other schools in the state and because their tuition would, of course, be far cheaper than at the only other possible candidate, the University of Miami. With my experience in Florida, and affinity for the state, I thought I would probably end up living there after graduation. In addition, I knew that its population was growing at a phenomenal rate and that I would be likely to find many opportunities to teach at one of its numerous junior colleges.

Even though Durden had been my inspiration, I hadn't consulted with him before considering graduate school, and I made the serious mistake, which I only understood later, of applying to the two universities in education, rather than history. I'm not sure why I proceeded as I did; perhaps, it was simply a matter of thinking that because I wanted to become an educator, I should apply to the department of education. In any case, I was quickly admitted to both universities for the fall term of 1965, and I believed that all I had to do now was to choose between the two schools, graduate from Duke, and move to the Sunshine State to begin this new phase of my life.

As my graduation date of June 7, 1965 approached, I naturally thought about what I had learned and how I had changed over the past four years. Certainly, I had much greater confidence in myself than I had when I began college, and that confidence extended into every sphere of my life, from knowing that I could do well when challenged intellectually to interacting successfully with people from other cultures, whether they were young Southern ladies from Durham or the many individuals of both sexes I met along the way during my summer in Europe.

Something else I had now in greater abundance than in 1961 was a commitment to conservation, in both its utilitarian and aesthetic forms. I was a duck hunter, who saw himself as an ethical sportsman who wanted to preserve well-managed, healthy populations of waterfowl that I could hunt in good conscience, as well as a "tree-hugger," who loved national parks and other protected natural areas where hunting was forbidden.

In my worldview, I had also become a committed Progressive. From that time forward, I have seen myself as one dedicated to public service and to the idea that government should be for the people as a whole and not simply the wealthy and politically connected. Indeed, I understood by the time of my graduation that in many areas, like managing migratory wildlife and creating, and protecting, national parks, the only power capable of controlling the avarice of real estate developers, giant corporations, and others—through scientifically based regulations—was the federal government. Given how the two major political parties approached the issues of the day, from civil rights to conservation, I had no choice but to be a Democrat, starting with my first election in 1964, when Lyndon Johnson beat Barry Goldwater in a landslide.

After my graduation from Duke, three days before my twenty-second birthday, I spent most of the summer working at various odd jobs and getting ready to move to Gainesville; I had chosen the supposedly better University of Florida over Florida State. Finally, it was time to go, and I packed up my white Volkswagen Beetle and headed south to start my new life as a graduate student.

# CHAPTER SIX

# Becoming a Historian:

## *Graduate School Years in North Florida, Illinois, New York City, and Long Island, 1965-1970*

O n my way down to Florida, I stopped at Duke to thank Professor Durden for inspiring me to go into teaching. At our meeting, he seemed pleased at first, but then turned somber when I told him I was entering the school of education rather than the history department in the college of arts and sciences. He urged me to do everything I could to transfer into history. I would then have a much better chance of getting a good position teaching history full time (as distinct from general social sciences or humanities) at a junior college, where certification of teaching ability was not required, as well as possibly going on for a history Ph.D. at a later time. With this new information, I drove south the whole time worried that the history department wouldn't take me, and then I'd be in a kind of limbo, not knowing what my next step should be. As it turned out, I had cause for worry.

When the chair of the history department, John K. Mahon, accepted my request for a meeting, I found him to be a distinguished, no-nonsense individual who intimidated me without even trying. From the start, he was less than enthusiastic about my chances of entering the program. After all, I was applying at the eleventh hour and had bypassed the admissions committee. In addition, he was not the least bit impressed by the fact that I had been admitted to the school of education, stating that in his opinion its standards were far below those of the history department. He also took hold of the Duke transcript I had given him, and with a great flourish, circled the many grades below a B and told me that these were not the kind of grades he would have expected from an individual hoping to enter graduate school!

Professor Mahon then leaned back in his chair behind a very big desk and waited for my response. By this time in the meeting, I was more determined than ever to get into the history department, especially after his disdainful remark about the standards of the school of education. It would, I thought, be like accepting an inferior product when the superior one was right at hand.

So I decided to go for broke. Leaning forward in my little chair in front of his desk, I told Mahon that if I could get Cs at a school like Duke in courses I wasn't particularly interested in, I could certainly get Bs and As at the University of Florida in courses on a subject that I loved and wanted to teach for the rest of my life. I ended my passionate plea with a pledge. If he would take a chance on me, I would sign a kind of contract before I left his office stating that if I didn't have good grades at the end of the first term, I would immediately leave the University of Florida and never look back.

For a moment, Mahon said nothing. Then, a small smile appeared on his face, and he gave me the answer I wanted to hear. He told me he admired my determination, and okay, he would give me a chance. No, I didn't have to sign anything, but he would be watching me like a hawk, and if I didn't do well the first trimester, there wouldn't be a second one, and I'd be out.

As at a number of other critical times in my life, the right person was there at the right moment to move me along the path of success. If Professor Mahon had been a different kind of individual, inflexible and obsessed with following the "correct" procedures for admission to the graduate program, my future career as a teacher-scholar might never have gotten off the ground. I felt lucky and grateful, and immediately set out to prove to him that I would do what I said I would.

Despite a heavy course load and the writing of a thesis that would soon be published in its entirety in three articles in the *Florida Historical Quarterly*, I managed to complete the requirements for the Master of Arts degree in three trimesters, from August 1965 to August 1966. But once again, there were individuals who were as important in achieving this good result as any efforts on my part.

One of these people was Professor Rembert W. Patrick, whose seminar on the Civil War and Reconstruction I took in the winter trimester of 1966. He was completing his monograph, *The Reconstruction of the Nation*, published in 1967, and one of the assignments in the class was that each of his students had to take chapters of his manuscript and critique them in detail. He would later thank us in the preface of the book for "having the professional courage to point out factual errors, question interpretations, and suggest improvements in composition."

Some might think that Patrick was being unethical in using us as free editorial assistants, but I disagree. In addition to the excitement I think most of us felt at seeing our names in print in a book published by Oxford University Press, the assignment itself was a great learning experience. My work on the manuscript taught me just how important it was to be absolutely faithful to the historical record, to judge the veracity of sources with the greatest of care, and to be able to document thoroughly every conclusion. In adopting this scholarly approach, which would carry over into all of my thinking, I was consciously rejecting the values of the other three males in the Reiger family.

My father, and particularly my two brothers, were great raconteurs, whose storytelling about themselves was always entertaining but often frustrating, because I was never able to separate fact from fiction. While my father mellowed over time and could be trusted in his last years to provide an accurate account of incidents in his life, Tony and George have never lost their penchant for telling—often with great earnestness—these tall tales about themselves. They became a model for me for how *not* to approach the study of history, whether it had to do with my own life or the lives of others.

The scholarly method of fact-finding and analysis that I learned in Patrick's course would now be utilized in researching and writing my own monograph, a thesis entitled "Anti-War and Pro-Union Sentiment in Confederate Florida." This topic appealed to me for several reasons. First, I think I was trying to understand the experience of the common soldier in the Confederate army, men like my great-grandfather, Private Wesley Mayes Dance, before he was killed in 1864. In some mystical way, perhaps, I thought my research would bring me closer to him by knowing what Southern soldiers endured during that terrible time.

Second, I was frankly surprised when I discovered how active Florida had been in the Civil War, not only for the soldiers it gave to the Confederate cause, but for its shipments of salt and cattle. Up to that point, I had only been familiar with modern South Florida, and the antebellum history of its northern region fascinated me.

Finally, I also picked this topic because after only a small amount of research, it seemed clear to me that the two chief historians of Confederate

Florida, William Watson Davis and John E. Johns, had been mistaken when they concluded that Florida's internal opposition to the Confederacy had been very small, even during the last year of the conflict. Utilizing the extensive collection of primary sources in the university's P. K. Yonge Library of Florida History, I decided to see for myself whether or not the accepted interpretation of Florida's loyalty to the Confederacy needed to be revised.

What I found was that opposition to Confederate authorities, especially among poorer Floridians, was significant from the beginning and became rampant as the war went on. It was a moving experience to read these original letters between soldiers and their loved ones, expressing their rapid disillusionment with the war effort. I remember one letter in particular. Penned on high-quality paper that didn't show its age, a soldier was writing home about his growing despair when he abruptly stopped because it was raining, and the ink was starting to run. There, on the paper, was a small bump and ink stain where a raindrop had fallen a century before. What a strange feeling came over me! It was as if all the years between our two lives had melted away, and I was sitting beside the soldier, sharing his anguish. For those of us fortunate enough to be able to empathize with people from the past, the study of history never loses its appeal.

Not only was I lucky in finding an excellent thesis topic, I also quickly discovered that the Lincoln scholar, William E. Baringer, who would direct my work, was an extraordinary man who did everything in his power to aid me and make sure I completed the thesis by the deadline I had set for myself of August 1966. He was always available for consultations at his home, even in the evenings, and his enthusiasm for the project made working with him a joy. Like John Mahon and Rembert Patrick, William Baringer was the right person at the right time in providing the essential help I needed to move down the path of success.

Because of the many hours I spent most days studying and working on the thesis, I needed to relieve the stress on occasion by escaping into nature. Not long after coming to the University of Florida, I found the perfect special place, a part of the state already made famous by Marjorie Kinnan Rawlings' novel *Cross Creek* (1942). Only a short distance southeast of Gainesville, the waterway in the book's title connects two lakes, Lochloosa and Orange. What a beautiful area it is, so different from what I was used to in South Florida. I especially remember the cypress trees in the creek and the groves of live oaks in the uplands nearby, their limbs draped with Spanish moss.

While I tried bass fishing in Orange Lake and hooked some very large fish, all of them managed to break my line before I could get them to the boat. I had better luck duck hunting with decoys in the southeastern corner of the lake and in a marsh just on the other side of Route 301, between the road and the Seaboard Coast Railroad tracks. In those two special places I had a number of glorious mornings, bagging, among other ducks, my first drake gadwall and canvasback.

The times I was able to go hunting or fishing were fewer in number than I would have liked because of the need to complete my academic work by August 1966. The reason for the urgency was that I had decided to go on for a Ph.D. in history, but not at the University of Florida, and I planned to start at the new institution in September. Though I was touched by the efforts of the graduate faculty to have me stay in Gainesville for the doctorate, I hoped to enter a program where I could concentrate on the African past, while still studying American and European history. In particular, the people and wildlife of East Africa, Kenya and Tanganyika (which became Tanzania in 1964 when it merged with the island of Zanzibar), had captivated me since I was a teenager. I wanted to learn about the cattle-herding Masai and their reactions to European conservation efforts on behalf of wildlife, like wildebeest and zebra, that shared the Masai Mara and Serengeti plains with their livestock. I also planned on doing more general research on the clash between Europeans and East Africans during the late nineteenth century. Eventually, I even thought that I might want to live and teach in the region for a time.

With these aims in mind, I researched the subject of graduate schools and found that the three universities that seemed to have the best programs were the University of Wisconsin, U.C.L.A., and Northwestern. After receiving acceptance from all three, I chose Northwestern. My decision wasn't based on a thorough knowledge of the African scholars who were there, but rather on the fact that the school was much closer to the East Coast and its history department was quite a bit smaller than the others, which, I thought, might mean that I would receive more personalized treatment than at the larger institutions.

*After what had been a wonderful year* in Gainesville, I hoped for more of the same in Evanston, Illinois. It was a great feeling now to know exactly what I wanted to do for the rest of my life; I was reconfirmed in my identity as a teacher-scholar. Even though I had had no teaching experience yet, I was sure that with my love for history and my desire to share that passion with others, I would be more than adequate in the classroom. I was confident, then, as I drove west, but definitely not cocky. While the University of Florida had been a challenge, I knew that Northwestern would be a bigger one—perhaps a much bigger one.

After finally reaching Evanston, which is the first suburb north of Chicago, I found it something like Forest Hills Gardens, with plenty of large trees and beautiful homes. The campus itself was more appealing than I had imagined, largely because it borders the lake, where there is always a great variety of wildlife present, from alewives and salmon in the water to gulls and ducks in the air.

After finding an inexpensive, furnished room in a home owned by an elderly widow, I went to see the young Africanist who had been preselected as my adviser. From the moment we met, we didn't get along. When I enthusiastically told him about my research interests, he produced a disdainful look and said that I was thinking too much like a white person of European extraction (he was also white). What I had to do was to approach African history strictly from the point of view of the indigenous people; my idea of analyzing the interaction between East Africans and Europeans, with about equal attention to both, was simply wrongheaded.

I was frustrated, and more than a little angry, by his denial of what I felt was my legitimate research approach, but I had no choice other than to go along with him, at least for the time being. That meant taking his "Survey of African History" in that first quarter, the fall of 1966. The whole time I was in the course, he seemed to project an obvious hostility toward me, and I was happy that the class was one of the few at Northwestern that could be completed for credit without having to receive a grade.

But when the winter quarter approached, I knew I might be in trouble. I had to take this second course in the African survey sequence for a grade, and he ominously implied that it would be a critical test of whether or not I was to have a future at Northwestern. The grade for the class was to be based mainly on a paper he required on a large ethnic group in East Africa, which happened to be one of his main research subjects. When I returned to school after the spring break, I was stunned to find that I had received a C on the paper and for the course as a whole.

When I called him up to ask for an explanation of why I had gotten a grade that is unacceptable in graduate school, he told me that I had relied too much on his own work, and that even though I had cited him (repeatedly) in the footnotes, I had come dangerously close to plagiarism. I was, in fact, lucky that he hadn't given me an F! In a later, face-to-face meeting, he disheartened me completely by suggesting that I quit the program and find something else to do with my life.

This self-righteous individual, with his ideologically driven mind-set, seemed poised on the verge of ending my dream of becoming a college professor. I assumed that he would talk to the other members of the department and poison them against me. A classmate of mine at Northwestern, John Watterson, still remembers me sitting in a car with him, tears in my eyes, pouring forth my despair over what looked like the imminent termination of my hopes for the future. But the apparent desire of my antagonist to send me packing would be frustrated by the man who literally saved my career as an academic historian. He was the Americanist, Richard W. Leopold.

In the same winter quarter that I was taking, and virtually flunking, the class in African history, I was doing very well in Professor Leopold's course on the literature of American history. Unlike the young Africanist, Leopold seemed to take a real interest in what I thought and had to say, without pushing any particular ideological agenda. He became, and remains, a model for me of what a college history teacher and scholar should be—an individual who possesses a passion for history that he or she can share with students, turning them on to the subject and their potential for expanding their own knowledge of the field.

While I knew that I had greatly enjoyed both the class discussions and written work in Leopold's course, it wasn't until I received my A and a class rank of number two that I discovered just how much we had clicked in the teacher-student relationship. The timing couldn't have been more fortuitous, for Leopold was not only an eminent historian, he was also the chair of the department. After his class, I had far fewer worries about what the Africanist, a junior faculty member, thought about my potential, or lack of it.

Even though I now moved seamlessly into American history as my area of concentration, I retained an interest in African history and needed it, along with European history, as a secondary field. I had to pass a five-hour written examination in both subjects, and I studied extra hard for the African test to make sure that my antagonist would have no ammunition if he decided to resume his attack. When I learned that I had easily passed, I was ecstatic to be done with this ideologue once and for all.

Though Northwestern had a relatively small history department, it had more than its share of brilliant scholars, and I was privileged to work closely with two of them, the Americanists, Robert H. Wiebe and George M. Fredrickson. I would become Wiebe's teaching assistant, and Fredrickson would direct my dissertation; I was, in fact, his first doctoral student.

Wiebe published his landmark synthesis on the Gilded Age and Progressive Era, *The Search for Order, 1877-1920*, in 1967, when I was his assistant, and the book would make him famous among scholars of

American history. He taught me a great deal about how to research and write history, as well as how to get the best out of my students. I now taught for the first time, lecturing and fielding student questions, in Wiebe's course on "The United States Since the 1890s" and thoroughly enjoyed the experience—just as I knew I would. His approach of giving analytical essay examinations instead of fill-in-the-blank or multiple-choice tests is one that I have followed in all the years since.

Just as I was lucky to have been the teaching assistant, and later friend, of Bob Wiebe, I was also fortunate to have had George Fredrickson for a dissertation director. Although he was one of the younger professors in the department, he was already well known for his first book, *The Inner Civil War: Northern Intellectuals and the Crisis of the Union*, published in 1965. In later years, he would become a renowned historian on the subject of race in America.

Both of the early books of Wiebe and Fredrickson helped me to decide on my dissertation topic. Even before coming to Northwestern, my main chronological interest, whether in Africa, Europe, or America, had always been the latter part of the nineteenth century and early part of the twentieth, the same period covered by Wiebe's synthesis. And Fredrickson's often poignant volume on how the horrors of the Civil War transformed his subjects' thinking about social organization and reform in the decades following the conflict gave me insights into how reformers of all types reacted to a rapidly changing society.

In a class with Fredrickson on the history of racial attitudes in American society, and the reformers who tried to better the conditions of the oppressed groups, I discovered George Bird Grinnell, an important ethnographer of the Plains Indian (the term "Native American" was not yet in common usage). Though his work with Indians interested me to some degree, I became really excited when I learned that he also had a career as a wildlife conservationist. I wondered: would it be possible to write a dissertation that combined my love for history with my commitment to conservation?

Setting out to answer that question, I came across a reference to a book by James B. Trefethen entitled *Crusade for Wildlife: Highlights in Conservation Progress*, published in 1961. It seemed to be a history of a big-game hunter's organization called the Boone and Crockett Club that had been active in conservation since its founding in 1887. Perhaps the volume would show me if Grinnell was worthy of a dissertation. Because Northwestern didn't have a copy, I had to get it from the Chicago Public Library, and the trip back to Evanston on the "El" (for "elevated") train, in the fall of 1967, was one I'll never forget. Finding an empty seat, I sat down and took the book out of my briefcase. After turning only a few pages, I came across a photograph of George Bird Grinnell smoking his pipe, with the caption, "One of America's greatest and least appreciated pioneer conservationists." Somehow, I knew in that instant that I had found my dissertation topic, and a lot more besides. As mystical as it may sound, I seemed at that moment to be taken over by a feeling that it was my responsibility to bring Grinnell out of the shadows—at least as far as academic historians were concerned—and into the light, where I could test Trefethen's essentially undocumented claim for Grinnell's importance.

But before I could research and write a dissertation on Grinnell and his role in conservation, I had to find his personal papers. After some investigation, as well as help from Trefethen, I discovered that the main body of papers had gone to John P. Holman, a Fairfield, Connecticut, Boone and Crockett Club member, and, though much younger, a close personal friend of Grinnell in his last years. But because Grinnell was born in 1849 and died in 1938, I knew that by the late 1960s, if Holman were still alive, he would have to be very old. It was, therefore, with some anxiety that I called Fairfield information to see if they had a current telephone number for him. Imagine my excitement when the operator gave me the number, and after calling and explaining my mission, I heard the elderly voice on the other end say, "Yes, I am John Holman. When are you going to come and see me to talk about Dr. Grinnell?" (Grinnell had received both an A.B. and Ph.D. from Yale, and Holman never failed to use the respectful title when referring to his older friend.)

On arriving at Holman's house, I found that it sat back in a small grove of trees very close to Interstate 95, where the whoosh of traffic could be continuously heard. Despite this intrusion of the modern world, the colonial-style house was filled with old books and furnishings from the turn of the century or before, and it seemed to be a kind of time capsule from an earlier age. I was soon to find that its occupant, the man I had come to see, who was then about eighty, was also from another time. After greeting me, Holman began immediately to talk about how he came to know Grinnell and how they had shared a love for hunting and the outdoors. He was particularly proud that Grinnell had praised his 1933 Boone and Crockett Club-approved book, *Sheep and Bear Trails*, about hunting Dall's sheep in Alaska and grizzlies in British Columbia.

Holman then directed me to sit in a huge leather chair next to his, because that had been Dr. Grinnell's favorite. It was in that "place of honor," as Holman called it, that Grinnell would regale his young friend with stories about what it was like to grow up in a still somewhat rural

157

upper Manhattan, near the home of the late John James Audubon, where Grinnell hunted and fished with the painter's grandchildren and studied natural history with his widow Lucy, who became like a second mother to him; what it was like to cross the continent in 1870 on the just-completed transcontinental railroad and have the train stopped for three hours in eastern Nebraska by bison crossing the tracks; what it was like to join the Pawnee and the famous scout Luther North in 1872 for the tribe's great bison hunt; what it was like to ride with George Armstrong Custer in the Black Hills in 1874 when his expedition discovered gold that would help to lead to his annihilation on the Little Bighorn two years later; what it was like to hear the news that his friends in the Custer command had been wiped out on an expedition that he had nearly joined; and, finally, what it was like to become friends with a young Theodore Roosevelt in 1885, and two years later, to join him in founding the Boone and Crockett Club.

The hours of that first interview with John Holman passed by in a flash, but I still had to know if Grinnell's papers were extensive enough to support dissertation-level research. Holman told me that he had given the papers to the Connecticut Audubon Society, whose museum was just down the hill from his home. After entering the small room where the papers were stored, I found to my amazement that the collection began in 1886 and included thirty-eight letterbooks, most of which contained about one thousand pages of Grinnell's outgoing, copied letters. I assume that Grinnell or his secretary used a "copying press" to make these duplicates, a process described by David Owen in the August 2004 issue of *Smithsonian* magazine: "A user took a document freshly written in special ink, placed a moistened sheet of translucent paper against the inked surface and squeezed the two sheets together in the press, causing some of the ink from the original to penetrate the second sheet, which could then be read by turning it over and looking through its back."

One of the first letters I found in a letterbook picked at random was to "My dear Roosevelt," and I realized that I had discovered one of the great primary source collections of conservation history. It is those letters, and the issues of the weekly newspaper *Forest and Stream* (that has no connection to today's *Field & Stream*), which Grinnell owned and edited from 1880 to 1911, that I would use to document his preeminent role in early conservation. And a huge part of that importance came from his friendship with Theodore Roosevelt, who would go on to lead the movement to preserve and manage—i.e., "conserve"—"natural resources," to use that term in its broadest sense.

*A historical figure who has inspired me and many others was the pathbreaking conservationist, George Bird Grinnell. Here he is, as an elderly waterfowler, in his duck blind on the property of the Narrows Island Club in Currituck Sound, near Poplar Branch, North Carolina. His folding wooden chair is facing left, toward the water and the decoys. Despite what some historians want to believe, this founder of the original Audubon Society continued to hunt birds until the end of his active outdoor life.*

After completing the course work and passing my examinations, both written and oral, I left Evanston in the fall of 1968 and moved into my mother's house in Forest Hills. While she didn't understand what I was doing in graduate school and like the rest of my family gave me zero psychological support, she allowed me to move into an empty bedroom above hers for the time it took "to finally finish my schooling." Even though the arrangement was almost of a business nature, since I paid her rent from my fellowship money by a set day each month, I will always be grateful for her help, however unenthusiastic it may have been.

Now, almost every day, I made the drive in my Volkswagen beetle from Forest Hills to Fairfield and back, and even though the trip, with traffic, could take as long as an hour and a half each way, I looked upon the commute as an exciting time in my life. Each day, as I arrived at the little Birdcraft Museum library room of the Connecticut Audubon Society, where the letterbooks and an almost complete run of *Forest and Stream* were kept, I wondered what new discovery I would make in this treasure-trove of primary source material on early conservation history.

It wasn't long into my research on the dissertation, now entitled "George Bird Grinnell and the Development of American Conservation, 1870-1901," when I received a letter that threatened to derail everything I had been working for. Arriving home one night, I found an official-looking letter from Selective Service and knew immediately what it was. My student-deferment classification of 2-S (for college students making satisfactory progress toward a degree) had been changed to 1-A, meaning that I had to report immediately to my draft board for induction into the army! I was outraged, because I was still a full-time student at Northwestern, being generously supported with fellowship money from the university to complete my dissertation, and Selective Service had promised college students already in school that they could finish their degrees before there would be any change in their draft status.

I had a vision of myself being forced into the military and sent to Vietnam, where I would be compelled to kill other human beings against my will because an American president, Lyndon Johnson, demanded that it be done. My opposition to the war in Indochina was not some new sentiment, acquired simply because it might interfere with my career plans. I had been against it as early as the spring of 1965, when I graduated from Duke.

My brother George had attended the graduation ceremony, not to congratulate me, but to remind me that Princeton, where he had gone, was more prestigious than Duke, and to impress me with the fact that he would soon be going to Vietnam as a naval officer to protect America by fighting communism. I reassured him on the first point, that no one, including myself, would ever think that Duke could compete in prestige with Princeton. But as for his second objective, I just couldn't bring myself to give him the praise he craved. In fact, we got into a heated argument when I told him I thought the United States had no business in Vietnam.

I felt this way because I had studied the history of Vietnam in two courses at Duke, the one with Robert Durden that had inspired me to be a college teacher and an earlier one with Joel Colton on "Europe in the Twentieth Century." In those classes I learned about the long struggle of the Vietnamese people against French colonialism and how the United States in 1956 had gone against one of its most cherished principles—the right of all peoples to self-determination—in helping to block free elections in the country because it was obvious that the "wrong" candidate, communist Ho Chi Minh, would easily win and finally achieve his goal of an independent nation. Then, too, I remembered my feelings when I visited the battlefield of Verdun and the promise to myself that if I were to enter a war, or even support one from the standpoint of a noncombatant, I would need to have good, well-thought-out reasons for doing so. If those reasons were there, as they were in our revolt against British colonialism or the retaliatory response to the Japanese for their attack on Pearl Harbor, then I believe I would have been ashamed of myself if I hadn't joined the military and fought for the righteous cause. But those reasons weren't apparent, if they existed at all, in America's war in Vietnam.

On the morning after I received the draft notice, with an intense feeling of uncertainty about what the future held for me, I reported to the address given on the form. It was in one of the poorest neighborhoods of the borough of Queens, and after I entered the huge building, I was surprised by the mass of young men I saw when I came through the door. There were many hundreds of them, packed together shoulder to shoulder, and as far as I could tell, every one was a person of color, either African American or Hispanic. In fact, the only two pale white people in the place seemed to be myself and a large woman sitting at a desk near the door, who apparently was in charge.

After waiting in line for what seemed like an eternity, I finally got up to her desk and started right in to a rehearsed speech about how I was still a full-time student even though I was no longer living in Evanston and how Selective Service had obviously made a mistake. I didn't get all the way through my prepared statements when the woman stopped me and told me to calm down. All I had to do, she said, was to get Northwestern to send the draft board a letter certifying my full-time student status, and my 2-S classification would be restored. In addition, she pointed out the fact that I would soon be twenty-six years old and no longer eligible for the draft after that time. Then, gesturing with her hand for me to lean in over the desk closer to her, she whispered—and I remember the exact words—"Besides, all these guys in here will go before you will."

As I backed away from her desk to allow the next man in line to move up, I felt a great sense of relief. I would not have to do unimaginable things to people against whom I bore no ill will, and my dream of becoming a college professor remained intact. But relief was not the only emotion I felt. As I was leaving, I stopped just inside the door, turned around, and looked at all those young men and wondered how many of them would suffer and maybe even die in that damn war.

As I write these words, I am once again experiencing the shame that came over me while I stood there for those few moments. It wasn't that I was guilty over not doing my "patriotic duty" in a conflict that seemed like pure folly. Rather, it was because I was part of a corrupt system that allowed privileged individuals like myself to avoid war, while forcing poor people, who couldn't get 2-S deferments, to go through an experience from which, if it entails intense combat, probably few escape mentally unscathed, even if they do return physically in one piece.

In late 1969, about a year after my trip to the draft board, the first lottery was held, which was supposed to do away with the inequities of deferments. It still seemed like an incredibly arbitrary and unjust system to me, and I felt the federal government did the right thing in 1973 when it ended the peacetime draft and went to an all-volunteer army. When I came home that afternoon, I vowed to work even harder to complete my dissertation and obtain the Ph.D. Even though I knew I would not be drafted, I owed it to the men I encountered that morning to be worthy of the privileged status I had been given.

*During those months I lived* in Mother's house, I not only had to research and write the dissertation, I also had to find a college teaching position for the time after I received my degree. Fredrickson was of little help in the search, forcing me to devise my own plan. Purchasing one of the college guides, I selected three hundred possible choices and typed up the same letter of inquiry to the "Chairman, History Department" of all of them, giving my credentials and expressing my interest in their institution.

Since I had already published one article from my M.A. thesis in the *Florida Historical Quarterly* and had another about to appear in the same journal, the only two positive responses I received were from schools in Florida: the University of Miami in Coral Gables, one of the largest private institutions in the Southeast, and Florida Technological University (later the University of Central Florida), a new public school in Orlando. My appeal was less that I had gone to Northwestern and studied under some eminent historians and more that I was a supposed authority on Florida history and could presumably teach a course in that subject. While that attraction was not quite as important in Orlando, it was crucial in Coral Gables, where the opening was for an individual who could replace the retiring Charlton W. Tebeau, perhaps the leading historian of Florida in the country.

Because the bottom of the market for history Ph.D.s had dropped out at the end of the 1960s, I was delighted to receive a phone call from Tebeau offering me an interview. The truth is I would have jumped at almost any opportunity to start my career as a full-time college teacher.

By March of 1970, when the campus visit and interview took place, I had completed my dissertation and successfully defended it, a fact that seemed to please Tebeau and the chair of the department, Raymond G. O'Connor. I guess they were happy they wouldn't have to take a chance on an "a.b.d." (all but dissertation) hire who might fail to finish the degree and have to be fired later as a result. When I received the offer from the University of Miami for what seemed like the grand salary of $10,500 for a nine-month contract (I had been living for years on far less), I triumphantly showed the letter to my mother. After reading it over twice, it suddenly seemed to dawn on her that maybe I had not been wasting my time after all. Perhaps, I really could live in the past and make a living doing so.

That March was also memorable because it was the month I met my future wife. One night, my friend Dick Vahey and I were in a singles bar on the east side of Manhattan when a young man came in and announced that there was a party going on in a nearby apartment and that everyone in the bar was invited. As soon as Dick and I walked into the large living room where everyone was gathered, I spotted a young woman sitting in the corner with someone, apparently a girlfriend. I immediately went over to her and struck up a conversation, while Dick talked to her friend. She told me her name was Andrea (Andi) Becker and her friend was Charlotte Perry, and that they were both nurses at Columbia-Presbyterian Medical Center.

After only a few minutes of talking with Andi, I was thoroughly smitten. I discovered that there really is something called "love at first sight." The two women had to leave only a short time later, but I obtained Andi's phone number, and as Dick and I left the apartment building, I turned to him and said, "You know, I'm going to marry that girl." We were engaged that summer before I left for Coral Gables and married the day after Christmas, 1970. On December 26, 2011 we celebrated our forty-first wedding anniversary.

*While I was still in Forest Hills*, in the time between finishing all of my work for the Ph.D. in March and heading south in the summer to find an apartment near the University of Miami, I worked as a crew chief for the U.S. Census Bureau. It was an interesting experience, enumerating households in Queens for the 1970 census and riding herd on my crew, some of whom wanted to get paid for visiting homes and apartments that didn't exist. The most exciting time on the job was compiling the census data on the inmates of the Queens House of Detention for Men in Kew Gardens. Housing several hundred individuals awaiting trial on a variety of charges, some of them serious felonies, the place was depressing in the extreme. I sat at a table and had each inmate brought up to stand in front of me while I asked the various questions. I had never been in a prison before, and I was probably more concerned about my safety than I needed to be, especially since a guard stood on either side of the table, billy club in hand.

Because I made a surprising amount of money working for the Census Bureau, I could afford to go back to Evanston for my graduation ceremony, which took place on June 13, three days after my twenty-seventh birthday. How I wanted to go! Some of my classmates, who are still close friends, would also be receiving their doctorates, and I was bursting with pride about what I thought was a grand accomplishment. Unfortunately, neither of my parents had the slightest interest in seeing me receive the doctorate, and I didn't want to go alone. Andi and I were not engaged yet, and I felt it improper to ask her to accompany me. And so, I missed out on what should have been one of the most joyful days of my life. Instead of the diploma being handed to me by the president of Northwestern, it arrived in a brown envelope, pushed unceremoniously by the postman through the mail slot in my mother's front door.

*Though I was excited about the new life* I would soon be leading in Florida and the fulfillment of my dream of becoming a professor, I regretted what I assumed would be the permanent loss of some of my most special places, where I had shaken off the worries and stresses of college and graduate school and been refreshed, physically and mentally, by escaping into nature. All of these sacred spots were along the South Shore of Long Island, and they remain intact today, though the wildlife that frequented them has been sorely reduced in numbers.

One of my favorite retreats was along the border of a salt marsh in Bellport Bay on the eastern end of Great South Bay. From the mouth of the Carmans River at Long Point west along the shore to Post Point was a duck-hunting paradise where I had many wonderful dawns decoying a variety of waterfowl, the most common of which were black ducks, widgeon, and greater scaup. This last species, called broadbill by waterfowlers on Long Island, was especially abundant. Though I usually hunted at the mouth of the Carmans at first light, I was there on one occasion after the sun went down and had what can only be described as an ethereal experience. In the minutes before it got too dark to see any distance, a continuous line of broadbill flew north up the river right past and over me. On and on they came, flock after flock, until I could see them no longer, though I could still hear the whoosh of their wings as they passed overhead. I can't begin to estimate how many thousands of birds I saw and heard that evening. It was almost as if I had been transported back to pre-Columbian America, when Great South Bay was a pristine ecosystem and its wildlife existed in numbers beyond our modern imagination. I was spiritually renewed by what I had seen and heard and very grateful that my life and the lives of all those waterfowl had come together at that exact moment in time.

Another of the great appeals of this special place at the eastern end of Great South Bay was that it is just to the west of, and connected by water to, Mastic Beach, the town in which my grandfather had lived and died. Because he loved waterfowling so much, I have no doubt that he must have hunted at, or at least in sight of, my special place at the mouth of the Carmans.

Happily, the lower reaches of the river have been preserved in the Wertheim National Wildlife Refuge. Great South Bay itself, however, is a much-changed ecosystem from the 1960s. It has been terribly impacted by "development" along its northern side and the resulting pollution runoff, like salt from highways and fertilizer from lawns. The huge flocks of broadbill that thrilled me are now rarely, if ever, seen in the bay.

The other two special places that had been so important to me in the 1960s that I thought I would never again hunt or fish in after I left for Florida were Fire Island Inlet and Jones Inlet, and their surrounding waters. I had known about the first of these spots as early as the summer of 1960, when I discovered it on a drive with Mother. Because I didn't have a car and wanted to hunt the inlet in December when I came back from Lawrenceville on Christmas vacation, I had a friend take me out in her vehicle. Before we got stuck in the sand and needed a tow truck to pull us out, I managed to bag several oldsquaw ducks (now increasingly called the long-tailed duck) from the many hundreds that were flying back and forth along the beach on the western end of the inlet. The male oldsquaw is especially attractive and one of only two species of waterfowl—the other being the pintail—to have extra long central tail feathers. It moves swiftly through the air, often twisting and turning, presenting a striking contrast between its dark wings and white body.

But what is most amazing about this duck is that it is the champion diver of all waterfowl. In many documented cases, it has been caught, and drowned, in gill nets of commercial fishermen on the Great Lakes set at depths between one and two-hundred feet! I saw some of the oldsquaw's diving ability during that first hunt at Fire Island Inlet. A small flock of five or six flew by, and when I fired at them, the entire group dropped into the water. For a moment, I thought I had bagged the whole lot! Then I noticed that no oldsquaws were floating on the surface, and after a minute or two, each of the birds popped to the surface farther out in the inlet and flew off unscathed. My shot had obviously scared them and produced the same kind of instinctive response they would have had to being attacked from above by a predator like the peregrine falcon ("duck hawk").

On that first day at the inlet, before I sneaked down to the water's edge and set up a portable blind in which I sat to wait for the old squaws to fly by in range, I had hidden for a time behind a small sand dune, watching and listening to them. The birds make a melodious, yodel-like call that can be heard at a great distance over water and which one ornithologist has likened to "the distant baying of a musical pack of hounds or *ow-ow-owdle-ow*."[15] I was so taken by these wild calls, which seemed to come straight from the Arctic wilderness where the birds breed, that I imitated them in an English class soon after returning to prep school. I got so carried away with my demonstration that I continued it even after the master walked into the room, whereupon he stopped, turned, and sarcastically asked, "What are you, Reiger, some kind of talking dog?!" The nickname of "Talking Dog" stuck and ended up in the yearbook along with "Black John" (for my constant complaining about the state of the world, especially the natural world). Given my attitudes about Lawrenceville, I wore both of those nicknames as badges of honor.

After that first trip to Fire Island Inlet, I returned many times in the following years, right up through the hunting season of 1969-1970. In the summer I fished for fluke and in the winter I hunted with decoys off the Oak Beach jetties and at the mouth of the inlet on its northern side. The waterfowling was sometimes spectacular, especially when Great South Bay was ice covered and thousands of broadbill were concentrated in the inlet as the only remaining open water in the area.

I usually hunted by myself, but sometimes with my friend Dick Vahey, who I had introduced to waterfowling, or my brother George. While the broadbill were the main species taken, it was also at Fire Island where I bagged my first daily limit (two birds) of the wary black duck and my first brant, the little sea goose that I had so much wanted to hunt ever since I had read, over and over again, the account of pursuing brant in the Bruette book that my favorite master at Lawrenceville had given me. Those two hunting trips, when I bagged the black ducks and the brant, were two of my most memorable outdoor experiences. But even when the hunting was not very good, it was still exciting, and even inspiring, to be out at dawn on a cold, windy day in those magnificent surroundings, with the white beaches and sand dunes, rocky jetties, fast-flowing tides and the Atlantic Ocean itself, just outside the inlet, on the other side of Fire Island to the south.

The other special place that I thought I would not be able to fish and hunt in again after I moved to Florida was Jones Inlet, or more specifically its western side along Point Lookout Beach and the mouth of Reynolds Channel. This inlet was farther west, closer to New York City than Fire Island, and when I returned to the area in the 1980s, I was amazed to discover that on a clear day, I could see Manhattan's World Trade Center off in the distance. Because I only found this special place in the late '60s, I didn't fish and hunt in it as much as in Fire Island Inlet, but the times I did go there were always memorable. The fishing for flounders (the flatfish with the small mouth unlike the fluke or summer flounder) was sometimes incredibly good. The bottom seemed paved with these delicious fish, and all one had to do was drop a "spreader-rig" with two baited hooks at either end down to the bottom, wait a few seconds, lift the rod tip sharply, and fight two more scrappy flounders up to the surface. I say "fight" advisedly, because I always used ultra-light spinning tackle, and landing two nearly foot-long flounders pulling in opposite directions against a tiny rod with fragile line was always a sporting challenge.

While the fishing in Jones Inlet and Reynolds Channel could be fun, there were two days of waterfowl hunting off a jetty on the western side of the inlet that went well beyond fun. They remain clearly in my memory as two of my greatest outdoor adventures. The two trips to the inlet occurred back to back in January, during a special "bonus" broadbill-brant season after the regular duck season had ended. Because the temperature had plummeted and remained well below freezing for several days, the creeks and bays in the area had become ice covered, forcing waterfowl to concentrate in the ice-free tidal flow of the inlet. When I walked out onto Point Lookout Beach with my brother George at the dawn of the first day, I was amazed to see one giant dark mass of waterfowl extending all the way from the mouth of Reynolds Channel in the north to where the inlet met the ocean in the south. It seemed as if every broadbill and brant in the world was there that morning.

Setting out my decoys off the end of one of the jetties, we hunkered down in the rocks and waited. I remember trembling in anticipation, like a deer hunter with "buck fever," because of the action I knew wouldn't be long in coming. Flock after flock rose up from the multitude of waterfowl out in the inlet and flew along our lee shore looking for a place to settle in out of the wind. Some groups of birds passed us by, but others acted as if they were being pulled into our decoys by a giant magnet.

The broadbill rocketed by like miniature fighter planes, so fast it was hard to swing the gun on them before they got out of range. The brant came in a bit more leisurely and with a gracefulness all their own. As they

*With my daily limit of brant at Jones Inlet, December 1986.*

swept in over the decoys, calling a greeting of *rronk-rronk* to their false friends down below, I experienced a stirring to my blood that hunters have felt, I am sure, since our species began. It was as if we had been magically transported back at least a century, when waterfowl abundance was beyond modern comprehension. Like everything else that day, our wing shooting was nearly perfect, and my brother and I soon had our daily limits, which, as I recall, were very generous, something like five broadbill and six brant apiece. The day was also memorable because of how well George and I got along, with none of his usual anxiety to compete with me to prove that he was the better shot. This happy situation was probably due to the fact that there were so many opportunities for both of us that he felt no need to compete.

Even though I was a dog-tired hunter that night from cleaning my birds, I knew I had to take advantage of the unusually cold weather and the concentration of waterfowl in the inlet. As soon as it warmed up even a little, the ice sheets on the surface of the creeks and bays would melt, and the broadbill and brant would disperse, making them much harder to pursue. To have one more glorious morning at the inlet, I called up my friend Dick Vahey and invited him to join me on the jetty at dawn. Everything was the same as the day before, just as perfect, the direction and speed of the wind that kept the decoys "swimming" realistically, the concentration of birds in the inlet, their eagerness to decoy, our skill in wing shooting, and the bagging of our legal limits. After we had taken our birds, Dick and I sat back in the rocks, perfectly still, for a long time, enjoying the sight of so many waterfowl going in and out of the decoys. I knew that these would be two hunts that I would never forget and that they would number among the very best days of my life.

# CHAPTER SEVEN

# Life as a Teacher-Scholar and Full-Time Conservationist:

## Mainly South Florida and Connecticut, 1970-1988

H aving received so much joy from my special places, the mouth of the Carmans River and the two inlets on the South Shore of Long Island, I wondered, as I drove south in the summer of 1970 to begin my new life in Coral Gables, whether I would find comparable natural areas in South Florida. From earlier experiences in the region, I knew that there would be excellent fishing, but what about the hunting? Lake Okeechobee, where I began my waterfowling, was a long distance away to the north, and now that I was used to hunting in invigorating cold weather, would I find it enjoyable again to pursue ducks and other game birds in heat and humidity, often with mosquitoes and no-see-ums thrown in as well? There were, of course, other issues on my mind. I wished that Andi could be with me, but we would be separated until my winter vacation, when I returned north and we married in her hometown of Spring Lake, New Jersey.

Though I never had any doubts about whether I would like full-time teaching, or whether I would be pretty good at it, I was curious about what kind of colleagues I would have and whether I would fit in. I also wondered about how I could publish the findings of my dissertation and expand my research on George Bird Grinnell and his allies in the sportsmen's conservation movement. I knew that I was sitting on a treasure-trove of primary sources, some of which, like the Grinnell letterbooks, were unknown to academic historians. It seemed clear to me that this new evidence I had discovered would transform the way in which scholars thought about how and when organized environmental concern began in America—if only my work were published.

One last issue I thought about on that long drive south was how I could integrate my love for history and my commitment to conservation. I wanted to protect the natural world and give something back to Nature for having been at the joyful center of my life since childhood.

Now, at twenty-seven, my self-image and worldview were, I believe, fully formed. I was a teacher, historian, hunter, fisherman, and conservationist, in both the aesthetic as well as the utilitarian senses of that term. I had internalized what I called the code of the sportsman, a responsible way of behaving toward the wildfowl I hunted that had developed in nineteenth-century America and which I had consciously begun to adopt as early as when I bagged my first duck, and my brother Tony demanded to know if I had shot it in the air or on the water. The sportsmen-conservationists I had studied while doing the research for my dissertation, particularly George Bird Grinnell and Theodore Roosevelt, now joined Aldo Leopold, whom I had discovered earlier, in inspiring me to take responsibility not just for the game I pursued, but for all wildlife and the habitat that sustains it. I think I knew from the very beginning of my career as a college professor that I would not always be content simply to teach and write about the great conservation achievements of the past. Sometime in my future, I would, if I ever got the chance, need to have some of my own achievements.

All of these thoughts were in the back of my mind when I walked into the University of Miami's history department for the first time, shortly after arriving in Coral Gables and even before I started my search for an apartment. Not all of the older faculty were back yet from their summer travels, but I did get a list from the departmental secretary of the members, with their basic biographical data, that included not only those individuals I had not met in March on my campus visit but also the new hires like myself. What struck me right away as I looked over the list was the impressive credentials of the faculty. Most had Ph.D.s from well-respected graduate schools in history, and I had fewer concerns, therefore, about being a professor at a renowned "party school," disdainfully referred to by some as "Suntan U."

The other concern I had, of course, was how well would the under-graduates stack up against those I was used to teaching in Bob Wiebe's course at Northwestern? As I soon discovered, many of them *were* at Miami mainly for the sun and fun, but there were very few classes over the next dozen years that didn't contain some excellent students, who responded to my passion for history and opened themselves up to its potential for enriching their lives. Unlike so many of my colleagues, who wanted to have only upper-division and graduate courses, I enjoyed teaching the two surveys of American history, before and after 1877. My aim was to show students how a knowledge of their country's past was essential for understanding the present and even possibly predicting the future.

One obvious reason why we should all study history is to be able to tell when politicians are misinformed or lying about a policy they want us, the voters, to support. By the early '70s, the debacle of the Vietnam War was already an excellent example of that very point. I also argued that it was particularly important for students to know about those brave men and women in many different historical situations who faced daunting challenges and overcame their fear for some greater good. Indeed, one of the central purposes of studying history is to keep those individuals who have inspired us close at hand to help us through our darkest moments in life.

While I taught a variety of courses in United States history, like "Civil War and Reconstruction (1850-1877)" and "The South in American History," my two favorites were "History of Florida" and "Ecology and the American Experience." Most undergraduates seemed to think of the Sunshine State as a creation of the twentieth century, and they were always surprised to learn that it has the longest history of any American state, stretching back to 1513, and that St. Augustine, not Jamestown, Virginia or Plymouth, Massachusetts, is the oldest permanent settlement in the United States.

My "Ecology and the American Experience" class, which I started to teach as soon as I arrived on campus and which, I believe, was one of the first such college courses to be offered in the United States, was always popular in that time of growing environmental concern. I described it in the undergraduate catalog as "An analysis of the evolution, from 1607 [the founding of Jamestown] to the present, of Americans' interaction with their natural environment, including such topics as romanticism, the 'code of the sportsman,' conservation, and the 'land ethic'."

Because I enjoyed teaching so much, my new life as a professor was all that I thought it would be. I also liked all the free time I had, but I understood from the start that the time was not really "free." My department expected me to be engaged in what my Ph.D. training had taught me to do, and that was to conduct research in order to publish findings that would add to the body of knowledge in my field. I needed no encouragement from them to do just that. Eager to have my discoveries about the genesis of American conservation published as quickly as possible, I submitted my dissertation to several publishers, all of whom had essentially the same reaction. Their editors told me that my thesis was so different from the accepted interpretation that it couldn't be right. Everyone knew, they said, that conservation as a movement began in the 1890s, not the 1870s, as I argued; that it was started by a small group of government experts and technocrats, the most famous of whom was Gifford Pinchot, and not by sport anglers and hunters of the upper-middle and upper classes; and that its chief focus was the forest, not wildlife, as I claimed.

Though discouraged, I continued to look for a publisher and became excited when I learned about a New York company called Winchester Press. Its editor-in-chief was William Steinkraus, a well-known Olympic equestrian who had won gold, silver, and bronze medals in the Summer Olympics. The Press produced works on a variety of subjects, everything from horsemanship, hunting, and fishing to wildlife studies, game management, and the history of firearms in the American West. The only connecting thread seemed to be that all of their books had to do with the outdoors.

While Steinkraus was interested in my dissertation, he liked the first part best. That section focused on Grinnell's "Memoirs" or "Memories," as some copies are called, that I discovered among the Grinnell papers stored in the Birdcraft Museum of the Connecticut Audubon Society. The manuscript deals only with the first part of his life, from his birth in 1849 to his early thirties, in 1883, when it ends abruptly in the middle of a word on page ninety-seven. I accepted Steinkraus' offer to create a book around Grinnell's partial autobiography as long as I could do it according to my own design. Instead of simply providing some editorial commentary at the beginning, with explanatory notes at the back, I would splice together my own commentary with portions of the memoirs, set off by quotation marks, along with additional quoted selections from his unpublished letters and *Forest and Stream* articles. My purpose was to produce a flowing narrative, mainly in Grinnell's own words, of what it was like for him to witness, firsthand, *The Passing of the Great West* (as I titled the book)—the destruction in the period 1870-1883 of both the remaining bison herds and the free-ranging Indian cultures that depended on them.

When the book appeared in hardback in 1972, it received mainly good reviews in history journals, and most scholars seemed to understand, and accept, my unusual narrative form. Because the majority of the words were Grinnell's, I opted to call myself the editor, rather than the author, even though I had done far more than most editors. Some historians told me I had been foolish not to describe myself as the author, and George Fredrickson, my dissertation director at Northwestern, was particularly concerned about this point, believing that the lesser status of an editor might diminish my chances for tenure at the University of Miami. As it turned out, he needn't have worried, for I would follow that first book with another, "authored," work three years later. Not only did the department seem to like *The Passing*, but other publishers as well. In later years, it was reprinted in paperback by both Charles Scribner's Sons and the University of Oklahoma Press.

Encouraged by the apparent success of *The Passing*, I set to work on revising my dissertation to go well beyond Grinnell in analyzing how sport hunters and anglers came together to form the first organized conservation movement. I was especially interested in reading the other nineteenth-century hunting and fishing periodicals, not just the New York-based *Forest and Stream*, to see if sportsmen in other parts of the country had coalesced behind the same conservation creed I found in Grinnell's weekly. In a research trip to Harvard, with Andi as my research assistant, I thoroughly studied these sportsmen's newspapers and discovered that the tenets of what I called the code of the sportsman, with its demand for taking responsibility for wildlife and habitat, were widely shared in New England and the Midwest, as well as in New York and the other Middle Atlantic States. With my background in sociology, I understood that this belief system was at the center of a sportsmen's *subculture* virtually ignored by academic historians. If I had not had extensive experience in hunting and fishing myself, I never would have gained the insights, or the inspiration, to set the record straight as to who really began the conservation movement in America.

Armed with this greater documentation for my thesis on how organized conservation started in the United States, I went back to Winchester Press to see if their new editor-in-chief, Robert Elman, was interested in publishing the rest of my dissertation, along with the new findings. He was himself a well-respected writer who authored works on hunting, wildlife, and western history. Elman was enthusiastic about the project from the start, and *American Sportsmen and the Origins of Conservation* appeared in hardback in 1975. Despite the fact that Winchester Press was not an academic publisher, Elman allowed me to publish the book with endnotes and bibliography, both over forty pages long, as well as "A Picture Album of Sport and Conservation" containing ninety-two illustrations, many of them rare and previously unknown, that documented points I had made in the text.

I was fortunate to have *American Sportsmen* widely reviewed in scholarly history journals. Those historians who had at least some acquaintance with nineteenth-century sportsmen's literature tended to give the book very good reviews. Examples were Arthur Ekirch, Jr.'s evaluation in the *Journal of American History* and Richard Bartlett's appraisal in *History: Reviews of New Books*. It was even nominated for the first Forest History Society book award. Not everyone who read the book, however, was complimentary. While some historians had both positive and negative things to say, only one, as I recall, wrote the kind of evaluation of which author's nightmares are made. It appeared as the first review in an issue of the *Journal of Forest History*, the publication of the same organization that had nominated *American Sportsmen* for its book award. Written by Alfred Runte, who had recently completed his Ph.D. dissertation under Roderick Nash at the University of California, Santa Barbara, and who would later become well known for his controversial "worthless lands" thesis regarding the origins of national parks, the review contained almost nothing but harsh criticism. His last words summed up his thinking: "the jury on American sportsmen as originators of conservation must still be out."

Despite this one really bad review, there were enough favorable ones for the University of Miami history department to overcome any suspicions the senior faculty might have had about me publishing my work with a press no one in the academic world had heard of before. My two books, in addition to other publications, and good appraisals of my teaching, would be enough to allow me to rise through the ranks and become a full professor by my mid thirties.

Even Runte in later years seemed to have had fewer problems with my thesis. At a U.S. Forest Service-sponsored conference held in Missoula, Montana, in June 1991 to celebrate the centennial of the National Forest System, I presented a paper on "Wildlife, Conservation, and the First Forest Reserve." During a break, I ran into Runte, and he told me that when the University of Oklahoma Press had contacted him to ask if he would recommend that they publish a new edition of *American Sportsmen*, he had given them a favorable reply. When I asked him why he performed this good deed, given his earlier review, he said that even though there were still aspects of the book he didn't like, my "sources had held up remarkably well." I wanted to chastise him, of course, for not evaluating those sources in greater depth back in 1976, before he wrote his critical appraisal, but I said nothing. I was, in fact, grateful to him, for when the prestigious University of Oklahoma Press published a second edition of

*American Sportsmen* in 1986, it seemed to remove any of the taint that might still have been attached to a book originally issued by a publisher with a famous gun-maker in its name.

In addition to the recognition I had received for *American Sportsmen* from the historical profession, I was gratified to be acknowledged by the professional wildlife-conservation community. These are the men and women who do the actual day-to-day work of preserving and restoring North American wildlife. On March 22, 1976, I was given an award certificate from The Wildlife Society at their banquet in Washington, D.C., during the annual meeting of the North American Wildlife and Natural Resources Conference.

*The strain of researching and writing* two books in my first five years at the University of Miami meant that I had to find new special places where I could escape into nature. In my early searching, I found a location with potential on Key Biscayne, the large barrier island east of Miami that was well known in those years because President Richard Nixon had a home there. The spot was a large vacant lot on the Biscayne Bay side where local anglers sneaked in at night to fish for snappers, snook, and other species.

Because my friend John Berk and I had only limited success fishing off the sea wall, we decided one night to drop my twelve-foot, aluminum boat off the wall and row out farther into the bay to get closer, we hoped, to more productive fishing grounds. As events would prove, I had shown poor judgment in leaving my outboard motor behind and relying solely on oars for propulsion.

Using a chunk of dead mullet for bait and fishing only about fifty yards off the shore, I hooked a large fish that leaped clear of the water right next to the boat. It was at least a yard long, silvery in color, and with a long streamer coming off the back of the dorsal fin; we knew immediately that I had a tarpon, king of the inshore game fishes, on my line. The tarpon quickly threatened to strip all the monofilament off my spinning reel as it raced for the deeper water out in the bay. John did his best to row after it so that I could regain line, but my rod was simply too light and flexible to put any pressure on a fish of that size.

Just as it was becoming obvious that I was going to lose this battle and have to break the fish off, a violent storm, complete with tremendous wind, high waves, and driving rain, came out of nowhere and struck our small craft broadside, driving us out toward the middle of the bay. Cutting off the tarpon and taking over the oars, I rowed with all my strength in an effort to get us back to the sea wall, but it was no use. The wind kept pushing us out, while waves crashed over the side that began filling the boat with water faster than we could bail it out. It soon became clear that our survival was very much in doubt. When enough water entered our little craft, it would no longer stay afloat, and we would have to make an impossible swim through high waves back to the sea wall, which was now over a mile away in the darkness.

Just as we were about to give up and resign ourselves to our fate, I heard a boat's engine, and looking in the direction of the sound, I could see the dim outline of a good-sized craft, probably about twenty-five feet long, running without lights farther out in the channel (we were already on the edge of the Intracoastal Waterway). As we were being pushed southwest, out into the middle of the bay, the mysterious vessel was ploughing the waves in a northerly direction, parallel to us, heading toward Miami. John and I knew immediately why there were no lights on the boat. In the early '70s, South Florida was awash in drug smuggling, particularly for marijuana, humorously referred to as "square grouper" because many of the smugglers were former commercial fishermen who found that "catching" bales of pot was a far more lucrative enterprise than landing groupers and snappers.

From the moment I made out the indistinct outline of a vessel through the darkness, I shined my flashlight at it, frantically waving it back and forth, and repeatedly turning it on and off. Suddenly, the craft turned toward us, and John and I let out a simultaneous shout of joy. We were, however, premature in believing we had been saved.

After coming fairly close, the boat stopped, and with the engine idling, it drifted parallel to us, rocking from side to side with the waves, while two men in the open stern engaged in what seemed to be a nearly violent argument. There was a lot of shouting in Spanish, which we could barely hear over the wind, and the waving of arms, and we realized to our horror that the men were debating whether or not they should interrupt their clandestine voyage to save us or simply continue on their way and let us drown!

I will never know why the smuggler with a conscience won out over his more expedient confederate, but I will always be grateful to him. John and I realized that we were now really going to be saved when we saw that the men had stopped arguing and that the boat was backing down toward us, with one of the smugglers standing in the stern, holding a rope in his hands. When he threw us the line, I grabbed hold of it, and John and I moved to the back seat of my little boat, which was now half filled with water, so that the bow would be kept as high as possible while being towed. Otherwise, it could go under the waves, and we would be swamped.

Our saviors towed us very slowly, and skillfully, back to the western shore of Key Biscayne, which was out of the wind. After I threw the line back to the men, who were now standing together in the stern of their boat, John and I waved at them and shouted thank you, but not too loudly, because we didn't want anyone on shore to hear us. We then watched them head out, their running lights still off, until they disappeared into the darkness.

After bailing out the water, we worked our way back along the sea wall to our starting point in the vacant lot. In the years since, I have often thought about those smugglers. That was one shipment of square grouper I hope got through.

Needless to say, the vacant lot and nearby bay waters did not achieve the status of a special place, and after our adventure with the tarpon, storm, and smugglers, we never went back. The loss of the tarpon frustrated me greatly. I had never had to cut a fish off before, and I now became determined to capture a large specimen of this legendary battler. My chance came when I met and became friends with Earl Gentry, a well-known fishing guide in Islamorada, in the upper Florida Keys.

It all began with the anchoring of Earl's open boat, a craft about twenty feet long, on the edge of Channel Two, on the Florida Bay side, that runs under the Overseas Highway (U.S. 1) southwest of Islamorada. The date was May 30, 1972, the height of the tarpon fishing season in the Keys, and we had only a short wait before we began to see big fish moving at or near the surface as they swam through the deep channel on their way toward the highway bridge and the Atlantic Ocean on the other side. As one broke the surface close to the boat in a behavior called "rolling," I gently lobbed a live mullet about ten inches long that I had hooked through the lips out in front of it. The mullet hit the water and swam down, and for a moment, I thought the tarpon hadn't seen it. But then the great fish rolled again at the surface, and there was my hooked mullet hanging out of the side of its mouth.

Even though the "silver king" took its prey in an almost casual manner, its reaction to the feel of the hook and the restraint of my line was anything but leisurely. Because the inside of a tarpon's mouth has been likened to concrete, fishing guides often encourage anglers to strike a fish repeatedly, and with as much force as he or she can muster, in order to set the hook solidly. This is done, of course, by making sure the line is tight and then yanking the rod tip upwards.

With the first strike, the fish tore line through the water and off the reel with such ferocity that it almost jerked the rod out of my hands and over the side. Because I was trembling with excitement, Earl told me to calm down as it would be a long fight, and when I anxiously asked if I should strike the tarpon again to make sure it was well hooked, he softly responded: "Give him death." It was then that I noticed a kind of sardonic smile on his face, and I began to think that he was secretly rooting for the tarpon.

At the end of its first run, the fish leaped straight up out of the water, so high that there was at least a foot of space between its tail and the surface of Florida Bay. Unlike the tarpon I hooked on that dark night off Key Biscayne, I could see this fish clearly. So surprised was I by its huge size, silvery brilliance, and oversized eyes that seemed to be looking for the source of its torment that I forgot to drop my rod tip down so that it wouldn't fall on a tight line and break it. Earl reproached me by observing that I was lucky that time because the tarpon was still on, but that I must not forget to "bow to the fish" every time it came out of the water; I didn't forget again.

I think the tarpon only jumped twice more. The "giants," defined as individuals over fifty pounds, are less acrobatic than the smaller ones, and Earl told me that this meant that the bigger fish were able to conserve their energy by not jumping and, therefore, took longer to tire out. When he gave me this discouraging information, I once again began to think that he was on the side of the tarpon.

Unlike what most nonanglers seem to think, one does not, of course, simply reel in a large game fish. It has to be "played," meaning that when it wants to run, one has to let it, or break the line, and only after it stops does the angler try to regain line by slowly lifting the rod tip up, called "pumping," and then reeling in slack line quickly as the rod tip comes down, all the while keeping a tight line (except on the jumps) to prevent the hook from pulling out. Except for the technique of bowing to the fish when it jumped, I had known the basics of how to play a big fish as far back as the early '50s when I accompanied my brothers on their trips after king mackerel.

Not being able to sit in the "fighting chair" because of the need to move, standing up, completely around the small boat as I fought my opponent, my back soon began to hurt terribly. After I finally got the fish in close to the boat, the pain in my back now extended to my arms as I worked feverishly to keep it, and my line, from becoming tangled in the anchor rope in the bow or the outboard-motor propeller shaft in the stern (Earl joked with me during the struggle that I would appreciate "victory" more if he didn't raise the anchor or motor).

At several points during the fight, I seriously considered giving up and cutting the line, but my memory of how frustrated I was over the loss of the tarpon off Key Biscayne and the disdain I knew my respected guide would feel for me kept me going for a while longer. At last, the behemoth with the huge, intelligent-looking eyes lay on the surface, exhausted, next to the boat. What should I do now, I wondered? Should I simply release the fish with no record of its capture--I had forgotten to bring a camera—or have it mounted as a trophy to commemorate the most exciting fishing experience of my life?

In 1972 I didn't know that a tarpon that big might be twenty years old, with some years yet to live. Neither did I know that painted fiberglass models, based on measurements of the length and girth of the tarpon while still in the water, were already replacing mounts requiring the skin of the dead fish. The development of this new technique in taxidermy would allow trophy-sized game fishes of every species to be released after being photographed and measured, and help ensure, thereby, the perpetuation of the sport fishery. Whatever I might have decided had I known these things, the situation on that May evening in 1972 gave me only two choices: either release my prize without even a photograph to memorialize a fight that I had nearly lost, or bring this exquisite creature aboard, and have it mounted across a wall in my home. Then, I could admire it for the rest of my life and have a constant, almost living, reminder of one of my greatest outdoor adventures.

It took me probably less than a minute to give Earl my decision. Slipping a huge, barbless hook mounted on a short handle known as a gaff inside the tarpon's mouth and out through the lower jaw, he and I pulled the exhausted fish up and over the side of Earl's boat. Once it was aboard, I was amazed by its size: six feet, four inches long and weighing 117 pounds. The battle had taken nearly half an hour, and though physically drained, I was ecstatic beyond words.

*With the mount of the tarpon of Channel Two.*

181

In the years ahead, I would return many times to Channel Two and fish for tarpon with various friends from my own twelve-foot boat, now powered not by oars but by a 7½-horse Mercury outboard engine. I developed a stratagem of my own design for catching these powerful game fish that illustrates, once more, that successful fishing and hunting are cerebral processes that mere watching of nature from the sidelines is not. We would anchor on the Florida Bay side on an outgoing tide about fifty yards from the bridge over the channel and use live mullet we purchased from a Keys character called "Frank the Net" for his expertise at throwing a cast net. When one of us hooked a tarpon, the other person would quickly pull up the anchor, start the engine, and try to run up behind and as close to the fish—which invariably made a dash for the bridge—as possible. We would then all go through the span together and out into the open water of the Atlantic. Once we were beyond the bridge, and there was no chance of the tarpon cutting the line on some part of the barnacle-encrusted structure, we usually caught the fish.

The whole process had to be executed perfectly, however, and sometimes we lost the game when there was too much line between the fish and the fisherman as the tarpon started through the bridge, and it was able to abrade the monofilament on the side of the span and break us off. Once, on the way to the bridge, I remember being down in the bottom of the boat, trying to move a tackle box and other items out of the way for my friend John Berk, who was fighting the tarpon, when I looked up just in time to see the fish, probably about four feet in length, emerge from the water almost in slow motion right next to the boat and above my head, with its great shining eye looking down on me.

What a magnificent animal is the tarpon! Sportsman Aldo Leopold, who was an avid angler as well as a hunter, sometimes spoke of the "reverent rapport" he had with the game species he pursued.[16] I have no doubt that if he had ever fished for tarpon, he would have experienced that same reverential feeling for the silver king.

Channel Two became my most special of special fishing places in the years I taught at the University of Miami. Though none of the tarpon, which I always released, ever came close in size to the first one I caught with Earl Gentry, I was grateful to them all for the battles they had given my friends and me.

*While fishing in the Florida Keys* was available for some species all year long, the tarpon angling was a seasonal sport, taking place mainly in May and June. And even though one could pursue some species of game birds

*Standing in Lake Trafford deciding on where to rig out the decoys, January 1976.*

like doves and quail earlier, my favorite type of hunting, waterfowling, was also chiefly a two-month activity, occurring during December and January. Just as Channel Two would become my most important special place for fishing, Lake Trafford would be the equivalent for hunting. Located just west of the town of Immokalee and southwest of Lake Okeechobee, Trafford is an oblong, shallow body of water about one-and-a-half miles wide by two miles long. Though it is the largest body of fresh water in Florida south of Okeechobee, it was small enough that I could easily reach, and hunt, any part of it, even with a nonmotorized craft like a canoe or kayak.

When I first visited the lake in the early '70s, I was amazed by the numbers of waterfowl I found there. There seemed to be hundreds of ducks everywhere, with the most common species being ringnecks, lesser scaup, and bluewing teal. What attracted them was the profusion of edible plants, particularly *Hydrilla verticillata*, an invasive originally from Asia. It had probably first arrived in the United States as an exotic plant for aquariums. Broken-off fragments of its stalks on boat trailers, outboard motor propellers, and in fish livewells spread it from one body of water to the next, and it is now found over huge areas of the country. Growing up from the bottom of Lake Trafford, its stalks sprawled over the surface forming dense mats that wound around my outboard's propeller, requiring me repeatedly to put the engine in neutral and lift up the prop to clean it off. Having to perform this continual task was irritating, but the exciting shooting I had over decoys once I finally arrived at my favorite spot in the northwestern corner of the lake was well worth the effort.

All I knew when I first visited Trafford was that the hydrilla seemed to be giving the ducks a reliable, abundant food supply that they obviously relished. It was only after I left Florida that I learned about the disastrous impact of the plant on aquatic ecosystems, in outcompeting and ultimately eliminating native plant communities, and after it dies, causing algae blooms and massive fish kills like the ones that hit the lake in the 1990s. In an effort to restore Trafford, the state of Florida used herbicides to clear the lake of hydrilla. Now the invasive is gone, but so are the ducks that used to feed on it.

But in the 1970s, because of this plant, I thought I had discovered a waterfowling nirvana. In my "honey hole" in the northwestern corner of Trafford, there was a large growth of native pickerel weed (*Pontederia cordata*), tall plants (many of them probably at least three feet tall) with large leaves that made an excellent natural blind for my boat and me. When I pulled up to the edge of the weed patch and jumped out, sometimes from my twelve-foot aluminum craft and sometimes from my fiberglass canoe, I often spooked an alligator at least seven feet long that had taken up residence there. Like all my encounters in Florida with these large reptiles, I found that they seemed to be much more afraid of me than I was of them. I was always amused by the comments of other duck hunters I met on the lake, who stayed in their boats when hunting and who thought that I was either phenomenally macho or just plain crazy to be wading around in "alligator-infested" waters. All of my efforts to assure them that I was neither, and that there was little or no danger, always seemed to fall on deaf ears.

What these other hunters also failed to understand was how joyful it was, almost in some strange spiritual way, to be immersed up to my waist, while remaining completely dry in my chest waders, in the watery habitat of the species I was pursuing. Wading around in what seemed like an aquatic Eden made me feel even more that I was a player in the natural world and not simply a spectator looking in from the outside.

Sometimes, when I arrived at the mini-forest of pickerel weed, I found that a small flock of ringnecks was already there, feeding on their seeds. Rather than shooting at the ducks, I simply flushed them out, quickly pushed my way into the thickest part of the patch, jumped out into the waist-deep water, threw my camouflage netting over the boat, tossed out three or four decoys, hunkered down, and waited. Dressed completely in camouflage clothing, from my chest waders to my wide-brimmed hat, and with a green see-through netting covering my white face, I was invisible to the ringnecks, which invariably started to return in ones or twos only after a few minutes to resume their feeding.

This was real hunting, where I had solved the problem at hand. Instead of shooting at the ducks when I first saw them and scaring them away for the rest of the day, I let them fly off only mildly alarmed by the approach of my boat. Because I had figured out why they were in the pickerel weed, I could anticipate their early return and knew that when they saw what looked like others of their kind already there, any hesitation about dropping back in for more feeding would be eliminated. I had a feeling of satisfaction that I had successfully ambushed the ducks by understanding, and outwitting, them.

When the ringnecks were not feeding in the pickerel weed, I took more time in arranging a large spread of decoys on the edge of the patch, where the open water of the lake began. Because Trafford received a fair amount of hunting pressure on the weekends, the waterfowl could be very wary, and I was not always successful in luring them into my decoys. But just seeing so many ducks, as well as all the nongame birds like swallows, egrets, and herons, made nearly every trip a delight. I say nearly every trip, because there was one that was almost a tragedy for me and a friend I had introduced to hunting.

The friend was Douglas "Cap" (he had been the captain of a Massachusetts lobster boat in an earlier life) Introne. It was one of those days when I went out for what is called the "evening flight." (Waterfowl normally fly best, and are most susceptible to decoys, in the early mornings just after sunrise and in the late afternoons until dark.) We were in a fiberglass canoe, nicely painted in camouflage colors, that I had just bought, very cheaply, at a garage sale, and I was trying it out for the first time. I wanted to start using a canoe more than my aluminum boat with the outboard motor, because the narrower craft was easier to move across the hydrilla mats and around the rafts of water hyacinth, another invasive plant, originally from Brazil. The canoe was also more aesthetically pleasing, because it was silent and didn't produce any fumes, and it was a basic, primitive craft, which made it seem more "natural" and connected to earlier hunters and anglers, the Native Americans who had once lived on the shores of Lake Trafford and paddled their own canoes across these very same waters.

While my older canoe was quite stable, this new one proved to be very tippy, something I noticed as soon as we put it in the water at the launch ramp. For a moment, I thought that maybe I should call off the trip until I purchased the outrigger pontoons I had seen advertised in a magazine, which are put on either side of a canoe and make it virtually impossible to roll over. But Cap and I were eager to get out on the lake, and I decided to go, with the promise to myself that I would be extra careful so as not to capsize the unstable craft.

We had gotten a late start from the ramp on the eastern side of Trafford, and I knew that we didn't have the time to go all the way across the northern side of the lake to the shallow water in the pickerel-weed patch.

My improvised plan was simply to paddle out parallel to the northern shore until we flushed feeding waterfowl, stop and throw out some decoys, and hide down in the bottom of the canoe with camouflage see-through netting over us. Paddling out probably well over one hundred yards on a seemingly deserted lake, we came to what looked like the perfect spot. After winding our way in and out of a large raft of tightly packed hyacinth, we arrived in an area of open water where we flushed about fifty ducks of several species feeding on hydrilla. Quickly pushing the canoe into a gap in the hyacinth, I tossed out a dozen decoys, and from the way they pulled their anchor lines straight down, I could see that we were in a deep part of the lake where the water was well over our heads. Cap and I then got down in the canoe after covering ourselves with netting.

It was only after we were in position that I realized just how late it was. We could only legally hunt until sunset, and that time was fast approaching.

The ducks didn't return as I had hoped, probably because we were too exposed, and it was getting almost too late to shoot when I saw a ringneck high up and coming fast in our direction. I threw the gun up, and from my cramped position in the canoe, I swung on and past the duck, and fired. It was one of those memorable shots when the angle and the speed of the swing, as well as the lead and the follow-through, were all exactly right, and the ringneck folded up and came down with a splash.

It was then that it happened. So excited was I by the successful shot that I forgot the promise to myself to be extra careful in that unstable craft. Dramatically shifting my weight to the left in order to get more comfortable, I suddenly realized that the canoe was rolling over past the point of no return. Going into the water was quite a shock. It had been cold that January, and the water temperature was probably in the fifties. I felt stupid, but not yet frightened, because I knew it would take some time for hypothermia to set in, and we were, after all, not that far from shore.

Cap and I managed to hold on to our shotguns and were able to tie them through the trigger guards to the bow lines I used to secure the canoe to my car. When I fired at the ringneck, I had only that one shell in the gun, Cap's gun was empty, and our shell boxes had been on the seats and were now at the bottom of the lake. We had no way to fire off three shots, the long-established signal for someone in trouble.

After getting out of our waders, we tried desperately to turn the heavy fiberglass canoe over to bail out the water with our hands in order to get back in, but it was a futile effort. We then climbed up on the bottom of the overturned canoe, but discovered that it had only enough buoyant material under the seats to keep it floating, barely, on the surface. Unfortunately, we found that only one of us could lie on top before the craft began to sink. Because I had created this problem for us, I did not hesitate before deciding that Cap should be the one to rest on the canoe while I swam for help. Even with the aid of a floating boat cushion, I didn't think I could tread water next to the canoe for at least twelve hours, until the early morning of the following day when a hunter or angler *might* come out on the lake. The air temperature seemed to be dropping, and both Cap and I began to feel cold. So I set out for the northern shore, which was a lot closer than the launch ramp to the east. Once I made it into shallow water, I could wade along the swampy edge of the lake back to the ramp and get help.

I had gone only a short distance when I discovered that we were in real trouble. The floating mats of hydrilla were hard enough to swim through, but I was stopped dead in the water by the dense rafts of linked water hyacinth. As I write these words, I can once again feel that sickening feeling in my stomach when I tried to push the hyacinth apart to get through.

Blocked in my efforts to get to the closer northern shore, I tried to find the circuitous path we had taken in and around the hyacinth to arrive in the pocket of open water, which I hoped I could follow back to the launch ramp. But in the dark, I couldn't locate the path, if indeed it even still existed, since bunches of these plants tend to drift together if there is the slightest breeze.

I was quickly exhausting myself pushing against the edge of a hyacinth raft that might be an acre in size. What was particularly disconcerting was that many of the plants were over a foot out of the water, and they loomed over my head in the dark in a kind of menacing rebuke to any puny attempts I might make to move them. An additional fear factor was the possibility of being attacked from below by one of the many sizable alligators in the lake. While I had no fear of them when I was calmly wading, I now felt vulnerable splashing on the surface, making just the kind of commotion that might convince one of them that I was an injured animal, and an easy meal.

The whole time I was desperately trying to push the hyacinth plants apart to swim through them, I was shouting HELP with all my strength. As I have been told, in criticism, many times, I have a loud voice that carries a great distance. This would be one time when that attribute would come in very handy. I had finally given up trying to swim to shore and was about to turn back to the canoe and hope that Cap and I could survive all those hours in the cold water when I heard the sound of an outboard engine and then saw a spotlight shining on the water. Our saviors were coming!

They were two Cuban-American waterfowlers from Miami who had been hunting without success (that's why we hadn't heard any shooting earlier in the day) on the opposite side of the lake. Once Cap and I were pulled into their large boat, we retrieved our guns hanging from the canoe's bow lines, turned the canoe right side up and drained out the water, picked up the decoys, and headed in. After we got back to ramp and they gave us dry olive-drab t-shirts to put on (which Cap and I still have), the younger man told us the story of just how lucky we had been.

Still hoping for some shooting, the two hunters had stayed out on the lake much later than they had intended, and by the time they arrived back at the ramp, it was dark and no one was around. They assumed that they were the last ones off the lake. Even though there was one vehicle parked on the side of the road leading to the ramp, which happened to be mine, it wasn't obvious that it belonged to a hunter or fisherman out on Trafford. This was because there was no trailer with my car since I had transported the canoe on the roof, resting on boat cushions.

The waterfowlers had pulled up their boat and secured it to the trailer, packed up their gear, and were all set to leave. The younger of the two men, who I would guess was in his late teens, said that he and his friend had been talking the whole time, but now, as they sat in the vehicle, all was quiet when he thought he heard something just as he was closing the passenger side door. Even though the older man wanted to get going, his friend was adamant and told him to step out of the car, and listen. I don't think he ever heard me, but his teenage friend told us—and this touched me then and now, again, as I recall his words—that he considered himself a "good Catholic," and though he wasn't sure what it was he had heard out in the darkness, he *had* to see if someone needed help.

I know that sound carries well over water, and perhaps it was aided that night by a favorable breeze blowing towards the boat ramp, but it still seems miraculous to me that my shouts could have been so loud, and the young hunter's hearing so acute, that he could have heard anything over a distance of probably well over one hundred yards. What if we hadn't started out late and been able to go all the way across the lake to a deep-water spot near my special place in the northwestern corner, well out of earshot of even my teenage rescuer? And what if he had closed his car door, with the window up, between my intermittent shouts, a few moments earlier?

As in the case of all my misadventures in nature, most of which were the result of poor judgment, the incident on Lake Trafford did not lessen my love for the natural world or my desire to be actively out in it as much as possible. I simply treated the event as a learning experience. The following day I located, and purchased, a pair of the outrigger pontoons like the ones I had seen advertised in an outdoor magazine, and after mounting them across the middle of my canoe, I was out on Trafford again within a week. With the pontoons in place, it was now seemingly impossible to roll the canoe over, and I have used them with great success in all the years since.

While the Lake Trafford near-calamity didn't make me fear the water, it did change my attitude about invasive plants. For a long time, I had loathed invasive species of animals, like starlings and English (house) sparrows, because of the way in which they take over the habitats, especially the nesting sites, of native birds and dramatically reduce their populations, but I had little concern about invasives like hydrilla and hyacinth dominating, and eventually eliminating, native plant communities and all the wildlife that depends on them.

There is, however, nothing like having plants almost kill you to see them in a new light! Though I warily accepted the hydrilla for the rest of my time in Florida because of its food value for waterfowl, I came to hate hyacinth. To this day, whenever I see the plant, beautiful though it may be, floating on the surface of a canal in Florida or an artificial goldfish pond in Ohio, I think back to that dark night on Lake Trafford when it towered ominously over my head and blocked my efforts to swim to safety.

*When I moved to Florida in 1970*, I assumed that all of the outdoor activities that involved my direct involvement in nature, as distinct from more passive pursuits like birding and hiking, would be limited to fishing and hunting. But I was wrong.

The event that added another whole dimension to my orientation to the natural world was the reading of a little article in the January 1973 issue of *Muse News*, the publication of the Miami Museum of Science. Written by the unnamed members of a local archaeological society, the piece was entitled "The Salvage Excavation of a Tequesta Indian Site in the Kendall Area."

I was amazed by what the article contained. My whole life I had been interested in the pre-Columbian inhabitants of what became the United States, but I always thought that they would only be accessible in books or films. Even though I knew that "arrowheads" were sometimes picked up in ploughed fields, I assumed that one had to be an expert to make these discoveries, and in any case, it was only in a few selected places in the country, I thought, where one could find these vestiges of vanished cultures. The article in *Muse News* proved that all of these assumptions were wrong. The authors described how they were conducting a dig on a site rich with the artifacts used by early hunters and fishers only a few miles away from our apartment in South Miami!

What they had unearthed fascinated me. There were bone and shell tools, "ornaments," and hundreds of pottery sherds, some of which, they claimed, could be dated back at least seven centuries. (I later learned that the site itself was far older, with the deepest horizons possibly stretching back to 1000 B.C.E.) The article intrigued me not only because this ancient site was so close to where I lived, but also because the authors described it as only one of many nearby. The problem, however, was that these places were being destroyed at a rapid rate, and it was up to the "disciplined amateur" (as distinct from the indiscriminate "digger" who wants artifacts only to collect, trade, and sell) to help the professional archaeologists "accumulate as much information as is possible before progress destroys the many … sites in the area." After starting a systematic dig, based on cataloguing all of the artifacts in each three-inch level dug down from the surface, the amateur archeologists discovered on their fourth and last visit that their work had to stop because the place "had been bulldozed, thoroughly churned over and [made] useless for further scientific study." It may have now been useless to them, but I had to see for myself what a real, live pre-Columbian site looked like.

Even though the authors described its location in general terms, I thought that finding the site in one of the many clusters of trees and bushes in the agricultural fields of south Dade County might still be something of a challenge. Before the area was drained and "reclaimed" for farming in the 1920s, these islands of vegetation called hammocks stood on slightly elevated ground surrounded by the shallow waters of that great wetland, the Everglades. Because these "tree islands," as they are also called, were above the water, they were the natural centers of habitation in the Glades, the only places the Indians could keep their feet dry and their fires lit.

Within a day or two of reading the article in *Muse News*, I set out to find this wondrous place that would connect me to people who had hunted and fished in South Florida all those centuries before me. The best clue to the site's exact location was the presence of three large strangler fig trees (*Ficus aurea*). After unsuccessfully exploring two of the hammocks in the general area described in the article, I started into the southern end of a third tree island and pushed north through heavy brush until I saw the tops of big trees up ahead. Breaking out into the open, I was thrilled by what I saw. There, in front of the fig trees, was an obviously cleared place with what looked like pieces of clay pottery (sherds) scattered all around.

I had discovered my first "prehistoric" (the term archaeologists use for the time before recorded history) Indian site.

Getting down on my hands and knees for the closest possible inspection of the ground surface, I found that most of the sherds seemed to be pieces from the sides or bottoms of pots, but then I picked up one that was obviously from the rim. On the inside of the sherd was a round, indented place where the Indian woman (presumably the potters were women) had pushed in her thumb while the clay was still wet. Putting my own thumb into that same spot where she had placed hers perhaps seven hundred years ago was a strangely mystical experience, connecting me in an intimate way to the long ago world in which she lived.

That rim sherd was not the only exciting artifact I found that afternoon. In one area of the site, where the bulldozer had churned up some of the black midden soil and pushed it into a heap at the base of one of the ficus trees, I spotted something white poking through the dirt. Unearthing the rest of the object, I found that it was about four and a half inches long, up to two inches wide, three fourths of an inch thick, and made of some heavy shell-like material. In places there was a black crusty film on the surface, as well as a small piece of what appeared to be bone fused into the surface on one corner.

While the artifact looked something like a small, tapered axe, I really couldn't be sure what it was, but I knew I had found a treasure, a well-crafted object that was last held in a human hand when the Everglades all around my tree island was a pristine ecosystem, a "river of grass" flowing slowly out of Lake Okeechobee on its way south to Florida Bay and the Gulf of Mexico. All the wildlife was there then, in incredible abundance, the panthers and bears and hundreds of thousands of egrets, herons, and ibises. How I would have loved to have seen the Glades as they were then, long before the drainage and manipulation of the flow of water that has reduced the bird life by as much as 90 percent.

By the time I left the hammock in the late afternoon, I was a committed "avocational archaeologist," determined to find out everything I could about the world of the original human inhabitants of my new home in South Florida. The first thing I needed was to find someone who was knowledgeable about the region's prehistory, who could give me a crash course on the subject and who could also identify the mysterious shell artifact I had found on the site. After making some inquiries, I was directed to just the right person to help me, the Dade County Archaeologist, Robert Carr. That first meeting with him in his downtown Miami office was the beginning of a friendship that has lasted to the present day.

Bob told me that my treasure was what is called a "celt," a grooveless axe, and that it was made from the flaring lip of a queen conch (*Strombus gigas*). The black crusty coating on the celt probably came from the greasy ashes of a campfire and, similarly, the piece of bone adhering to the artifact was part of a meal. Because the blade was smashed in, it was hard to tell whether it had been used mainly as an adze for hollowing out dugout canoes or as an axe for cutting down small trees and for striking enemies. As Bob noted, the absence of hard igneous or metamorphic rock in South Florida meant that aboriginal people used heavy marine shells, particularly conchs and *Busycon* whelks, as a sturdy substitute for making tools.

In addition to the information I gleaned from Bob Carr during my many visits to his office, I now began subscribing to *The Florida Anthropologist*, which often contained relevant articles, and read every monograph that had ever been written on the subject of South Florida archaeology. I then applied what I had learned in my studies to the artifacts I was finding on the surface of dozens of pre-Columbian sites on both coasts of the state.

Other than the months of May and June, when I was tarpon fishing at Channel Two, and December and January, when I was duck hunting on Lake Trafford, I now spent most of my time outdoors escaping into a world that combined my love of nature and my fascination with pre-European history. Every exploration of these new special places—which could be as varied as the tiny remnant of a site in a just-cleared vacant lot in suburbia and a large, undamaged mound complex in the wilderness of the Ten Thousand Islands—had the potential for yielding up some previously unknown, or poorly understood, artifact that would help me to enter the lives, and maybe even the minds, of these extinct people. I use the word "extinct" advisedly, because unlike other parts of the country, where individuals can link their ancestry and cultural identity to some present-day tribe like the Cherokee and Navaho, there are no people alive today who belong to the Tequesta, Calusa, or any of the other South Florida tribes that were here when Ponce de León arrived in 1513. The well-known Seminoles are not indigenous inhabitants, having only begun their migrations into Florida in the eighteenth century.

The most dramatic evidence of the previous existence of the original Floridians is the high shell heaps and habitation mounds they left behind. Constantly under siege from private developers, these places should be cherished and preserved for future generations. But however much I liked seeing these sites, my archaeological focus was not on the tops of the small hills but on the ground, where my eyes hunted for the single artifact that could unlock the secrets of how its owner related to the world, both human and natural. After finding an object that had this potential, I applied the same skills I had learned in graduate school in analyzing written records to the unwritten "material culture"—the artifacts—of the pre-Columbians. In doing so, I was simply engaging in another form of historical research, with the same objective of adding to the body of knowledge by publishing my findings.

These analyses appeared in several articles in *The Florida Anthropologist*. My early work had to do with shell-tool use, but I later became determined to answer a question that has puzzled archaeologists since the late nineteenth century: what was the primary function of the shell and stone artifacts popularly known as "plummets," because of their resemblance to the small, oblong-shaped objects with a grooved knob at the top used to determine whether a wall, etc. is perfectly vertical, or "sinkers," because they also look like the lead weights anglers attach to their lines to get their baits down on the bottom?

After extensive research in both the archaeological literature and early historical accounts, as well as by a physical examination of many of these artifacts, some of which I found myself, I believe that I have answered the question. The great majority of plummets were pendant-charms that conveyed artistry, status, and power. It was my long experience in Florida

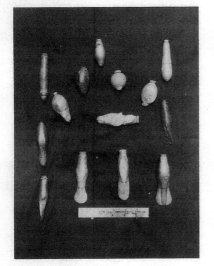

*The cover of* The Florida Anthropologist *with my lead article on the enigmatic pre-Columbian artifacts known as "plummets," some of which are illustrated.*

fishing that showed me that these shallow-grooved, often beautifully crafted objects were probably not created to catch powerful bottom fishes like big groupers and snappers.

I found the first of these wonderful artifacts that provide a window into the minds of Florida's first inhabitants on the remnant of a large pre-Columbian village site in a residential area at the southern end of Marco Island, on the state's southwestern coast. Delicately carved from a small, light-colored, limestone pebble with a "solution hole" on one side, it lay in the sandy soil kicked out of a gopher tortoise's tunnel by its then current occupant.

My most special of special archaeological places, the "Otter Site" was always a delight to explore as I crawled around under the cool shade of tall trees and through thick vegetation that hid me from cars and pedestrians passing nearby. It was as if I was a child again in my very first special place, the vacant lot near our home in Forest Hills Gardens. Now I was hunting for artifacts, rather than grasshoppers, but my feelings of anticipation and joy were the same. On each trip to the Otter Site, I began my reconnaissance by visiting the mouths of the tortoise burrows to see if they had provided me with any treasures. It was unethical for me to dig in these places, but I saw no harm in removing, studying, and finally donating to the Miami museum the artifacts brought up by my unwitting reptilian co-workers.

The presence of these interesting animals added much to my explorations of the site. Sometimes I could hear the tortoises coming home before I could see them through the thick vegetation, and I always crawled off to the side to allow them to reach the safety of their burrows. Like the bobwhite quail in the Bay Harbor Islands so many years before, the colony of tortoises rapidly declined as the house lots around the Otter Site were developed and the automobile traffic increased. Between habitat destruction and deaths on the roads from being run over, the welcome sound and sight of these animals became increasingly rare and finally disappeared completely. During my last visits, I kept going back to what had been active tunnels, hoping that perhaps a breeding pair might have somehow survived, but all I ever found were deserted, caved-in burrows.

Here was yet another example of why public ownership, and protection, of these special places is always better than private ownership and "development." From the mid-1970s on, I worked to save what was left of the Otter Site, but the credit for its preservation has to go to Bob Carr and his Archaeological and Historical Conservancy, an organization he created to protect as many of these irreplaceable sites as possible before rapacious capitalism swallows them up. I am delighted, of course, that future generations will be able to visit this special place and perhaps come away as fascinated with the people who once lived there as I have been. I only wish we could have saved the tortoises as well.

While the Otter Site may have been my favorite archaeological special place, there were many others across South Florida that I also found intriguing. Located in virtually every major ecosystem in the region—the Everglades, the Keys, Big Cypress Swamp, the Ten Thousand Islands, Lake Okeechobee, and the mangrove forests on both coasts—they provided me with many of the most enjoyable days of my life. But like some of my earlier experiences in fishing and hunting, these archaeological explorations could also be life threatening when I became careless.

One trip to the Florida Keys illustrates this point very well. I was on the western side of Key Largo, on a large site in the mangrove forest bordering Barnes Sound, not many miles from the Ocean Reef Club to the north where my family had fished with Tommy Gifford. The site was in a particularly interesting area because of the presence of large saltwater crocodiles, which I had encountered while wading around the northern edge of Barnes Sound looking for evidence of pre-Columbian habitation. Despite their reputation, I found them to be no more aggressive than their cousin, the alligator, at least when I was wading.

My frightening experience occurred as I was crawling around on my hands and knees looking straight down for artifacts within reach, rather than on the ground ahead of me. I suddenly had a cramp in my back and felt the need to straighten up slowly. As I raised my head, I looked right into the dark eyes of a huge diamondback rattlesnake. Well camouflaged and partly coiled in a dark, hollow pocket at the base of a big mangrove tree, its head was up in the air, facing me, well within striking distance of my chest, neck, and face.

It is quite an experience to realize instantly that in the next moment or two you are either going to be all right or receive a bite that will probably kill you. Andi had no idea where I was that day, the hike out to the road through heavy brush was about twenty-five minutes long, and I had seen rattlesnakes much smaller than this one being "milked" (where an agitated snake empties its amber-colored venom into a glass vial) at the Miami Serpentarium. I knew that the amount of venom a snake this large could put into me in a spot so close to my heart meant that I had little chance of making it back even to my car, much less to a hospital.

After the initial shock, which felt like a huge weight on my chest, left me, I moved with snail-like slowness, inch by inch, back the way I had crawled. When I initiated my backward travel, the snake moved its head a little toward me, and I thought for a second I was dead. But, of course, it never struck.

When I had crawled back a safe distance, I jumped up and wanted nothing more than to kill this creature that had terrorized me. Only then did the diamondback begin to rattle as it slithered out of its protected place at the base of the tree. For the first time, I could see just how big it was, well over six feet long and with a body nearly as thick as my arm. In my rage, I picked up a heavy water-logged chunk of wood and threw it down at the head of the moving snake just as it passed under the curved prop root of a mangrove tree, but the root broke the piece into two parts, and the rattler passed unscathed beneath it. This futile effort to kill the diamondback seemed to calm me down and bring me back to my senses. Why should I try to destroy the snake when it had allowed me to live? So, I simply turned away and walked out of the swamp, as the sound of the rattling grew ever fainter until I could hear it no more.

Over the years, I have sometimes thought about what would have happened if I hadn't gotten that sudden cramp in my back at that precise moment. Another foot or two of crawling would have pushed me right into the snake, which was cornered in its hollowed-out area up against the tree, and it would have had no way out except over me.

This adventure with the diamondback didn't lessen in the least my enthusiasm for archaeological exploration, though in the future I made sure to look ahead as well as down when I crawled over a site! Every outing satisfied, at least for a time, my need to escape into both nature and history. And because these first inhabitants of Florida were my fellow fishers and hunters, I felt a mystical bond with them that is hard to describe. There was, however, a melancholy aspect to it all. Not only was I visiting sites that were often under siege, and some in fact were destroyed between my visits, I was also trying to know long-dead human beings from an extinct world I could never fully enter.

But once I found archaeology and began to see with what anthropologist and naturalist Loren Eiseley called "the archaeological eye," there was no going back. As he wrote in *The Night Country* (1971):

> No one, I suppose, would believe that an archaeologist is a man who knows ... that from the surface of rubbish heaps the thin and ghostly essence of things human keeps rising through the centuries until the plaintive murmur of dead men and women may take precedence at times over the living voice. A man who has once looked with the archaeological eye will never see quite normally [again]. He will be

wounded by what other men call trifles. It is possible to refine the sense of time until an old shoe in the bunch grass or a pile of nineteenth-century beer bottles in an abandoned mining town tolls in one's head like a hall clock. This is the price one pays for learning to read time from surfaces other than an illuminated dial. It is the melancholy secret of the artifact, the humanly touched thing.

Now that my explorations of archaeological sites joined my earlier pursuits of fishing at Channel Two and hunting on Lake Trafford, I could escape into nature every month of the year. Because I never knew exactly what I would catch, bag, or collect on these trips, every one was an adventure. Still, there was something important missing in my life, and that uneasy feeling became more intense as I reached my mid-thirties. By that time, it was apparent that I would probably continue to do well as a teacher-scholar at the University of Miami, and therefore have a secure position at the institution for the next thirty years. My problem was that I wasn't convinced that all I wanted to do for the rest of my life was to live in South Florida and be a history professor.

It gradually became ever more clear to me that the missing something in my life was an unfulfilled desire to become a more active conservationist, both in the aesthetic and utilitarian senses of that term. I was as concerned with protecting natural areas where hunting wasn't allowed as I was with preserving, and even restoring, games species of wildlife that could be hunted. Increasingly, I had become frustrated by the apparent gulf between the theoretical world of the teacher-scholar and the outside society where most of the concrete environmental decisions are made. I wanted to do more than send letters on environmental issues to legislators, and teach and write about the contributions of earlier conservationists, and had decided, if accorded the chance, to give something back, in a permanent form, to the natural world that had given so much to me. This desire to do full-time conservation work was fueled, of course, by the writings of the sportsmen-conservationists who had come before me, especially George Bird Grinnell, Theodore Roosevelt, and Aldo Leopold.

After discovering Grinnell in 1967, when I made him and the early conservation movement the subjects of my doctoral dissertation, I read all of his crusading editorials in *Forest and Stream*, the weekly newspaper he had taken over while still in his early thirties, and they inspired me to emulate his efforts in behalf of nature. An example is "Their Last Refuge," which appeared in the issue of December 14, 1882, and called for an end to the market hunting of large mammals in Yellowstone National Park for their heads and hides. Grinnell wrote:

We have seen it [the West] when it was, except in isolated spots, an uninhabited wilderness; have seen the Indian and the game retreat before the white ... tide of immigration .... There is one spot left, a single rock about which this tide will break, and past which it will sweep, leaving it undefiled by the unsightly traces of civilization. Here in this Yellowstone Park the large game of the West may be preserved from extermination; here ... it may be seen by generations yet unborn. It is for the Nation to say whether these splendid species shall be so preserved, in this, their last refuge.

Grinnell's plea that we must work to ensure that wildlife in unspoiled places "may be seen by generations yet unborn" affected me deeply. That phrase, and the profound, unselfish ideology behind it, seemed to encapsulate all the reasons why I should become a full-time conservationist.

The second of my big three sportsmen-conservationists, Theodore Roosevelt, inspired me because of his administration's great achievements in setting aside millions of acres of land under public control that would have probably been lost otherwise to private exploitation. Those lands include his many national wildlife refuges, intended mainly for the protection of *non*game species. Roosevelt's attitude about extinction is revealed in an 1899 letter to the ornithologist Frank M. Chapman, which the latter recorded in his *Autobiography of a Bird-Lover* (1933):

How immensely it would add to our forests if the great Logcock [ivory-billed woodpecker] were still found among them! The destruction of the Wild Pigeon and the Carolina Paroquet [parakeet] has meant a loss as severe as if the Catskills [New York mountain range] or the Palisades [Hudson River cliffs] were taken away. When I hear of the destruction of a species, I feel just as if the works of some great writer had perished, as if we had lost all instead of only part of Polybius or Livy.

The last of my sportsmen-conservationist heroes was, of course, Aldo Leopold. As discussed earlier, I became familiar with his writings while still an undergraduate at Duke, even before I had a detailed knowledge of the conservation record of George Bird Grinnell or Theodore Roosevelt. While there are many passages in Leopold's writings that touched me, I found one that seemed to be speaking to me directly. It appeared not in his well-known *A Sand County Almanac*, but in *Game Management* (1933). Written as a textbook on how to increase the "crops" of game animals and birds for hunting by improving their habitats, the book also reminded its readers about their responsibilities for all wildlife. In a fully developed form of what I have called the code of the sportsman, Leopold applauded the coming of what he termed "the Rooseveltian era" and "the Crusader for conservation, ... who insisted that our conquest of nature carried with it a moral responsibility for the perpetuation of ... threatened forms of wildlife" and, by implication, the habitats upon which they depend. This acceptance of responsibility, Leopold believed, "constitutes one of the milestones in moral evolution."

By the late 1970s, I wanted very much to obey the moral imperative to become a full-time conservation activist given me by Grinnell, Roosevelt, and Leopold. The birth of our two children, Caren Dance in 1976 and Christopher John in 1978, heightened my desire to act soon, for I was worried now not only about the kind of natural world in which Andi and I would live, but also the one that the children would inherit after we were gone.

The arrival of our children affected me in another way as well. Try as I would to see them in a purely rational way, as simply the end result of a biological process, I found myself drawn ever closer to the belief that they were not only physical beings, with their bodies formed by evolution, but spiritual entities as well. The agnostic since childhood was turning toward the very unscientific view that these little human beings were gifts from God.

After Carrie and Chris entered our lives and revolutionized my thinking, several years passed before the kind of full-time conservation opportunity I was looking for finally arrived. In the spring of 1982 Milan ("Miley") Bull, an old friend and staff member of the Connecticut Audubon Society, called me to say that the executive director of the organization was leaving and that the board of directors wanted a replacement to start by the first of the year. I decided to apply for the position. Headquartered in Fairfield in the southwestern portion of the state, the society had first come to my attention in 1967 when I discovered the papers of George Bird Grinnell, then stored at its Birdcraft Museum. Founded in 1898, the organization was one of several surviving state Audubon associations that had remained independent of the more recently established National Audubon Society.

After being interviewed, I was almost surprised to be chosen over some other applicants, who, I thought, had far stronger hands-on environmental experience, especially administratively, than I had to offer. But in addition to the support of Miley Bull, whom I had first met in the late sixties when I was working in the Grinnell papers, I had that of the president of the society, Roland Clement, a distinguished environmental writer and activist who wanted an executive director with what he called "historical perspective."

The main fears I had about taking the position were all financial. Though the University of Miami would be willing to grant me a leave of absence for one year, if I decided to stay on beyond that time I would be giving up not only the lifetime security of a tenured full professorship, but also free college tuition for Carrie and Chris at any school in the country. This had been one of the great perks offered to new faculty members at Miami when I arrived in 1970. Despite these profound considerations, I felt I had to seize this opportunity. It seemed almost to be something I was destined to do. After all, I had discovered the Grinnell papers in the society's own Birdcraft Museum, and it was Grinnell, in 1886, who had founded the first Audubon society.

In addition to these connections to Grinnell, there was the strange incident in the hospital in Coral Gables soon after the birth of our daughter in July 1976. Andi had been kept there longer than usual because she had developed an infection after she gave birth that didn't respond at first to antibiotics. On one of my last visits with Andi and Carrie before we all went home, I walked up to the window that looked into the little nursery and was surprised to see a newborn baby girl named Grinnell lying next to baby Reiger, with only three or four other babies around them. When I visited Andi a short time later, I remember saying to her, "Wouldn't it be amazing if that baby was related to George Bird Grinnell?"

When I tracked down the grandmother of the baby, the only relative I could locate in the hospital, she told me that, yes, she believed that she and her grandchild were related to the "famous Grinnell family," both the Eastern Grinnells, like the "Indian expert," George Bird, as well as the Midwestern Grinnells, like the namesake of Grinnell College in Iowa. Our conversation was brief, because the woman had an imperious manner, and showed not the slightest interest in this incredible occurrence—that in a country of well over two hundred million people, her grandchild should be placed in a bassinet in the nursery of a small hospital right next to the firstborn child of a biographer of George Bird Grinnell. Because Grinnell married late in life and never had children, I knew that the connection could not be a direct one, but this incident seemed more than a mere coincidence, to be brushed off with that cliché about how "it's a small world." It seemed somehow like a sign that I had done well in trying to bring Grinnell's conservation achievements to light and that I should now follow his example in a more direct way.

On a less mystical level, I knew I had to take the position of executive director of the Connecticut Audubon Society so that I wouldn't have to wonder in later years about what would have happened if only I had accepted that offer back in 1982 to direct a statewide environmental organization just across the water from my cherished Long Island. Now, sink or swim, I would know the answer to that question. As always, Andi was fully supportive, and so, after twelve years as a history professor, I began my new life as a full-time conservationist on January 1, 1983.

From the start, I thought that Connecticut Audubon had great potential for doing good. Though a small organization—it had only about forty-four hundred members in 1982—the society already operated a modest legislative office in the capital city of Hartford that could be expanded into the central conduit of environmental action in the state. And with the administrative and educational center of the society located in Fairfield County, one of the most affluent sections of the country and the site of a large number of corporate headquarters, I believed that Audubon's efforts in educating the public about conservation could be financially supported and reach well beyond Connecticut. Finally, I liked the promise I had received from Robert Larsen, the chairman of the board of directors, that I would be given almost free rein, for up to five years, to take the society into the future. After my term was up, I hoped to be able to return to the academic world, satisfied that I had accomplished something of significance in the conservation of wildlife and habitat.

I had been hired to formulate and implement a five-year plan for Connecticut Audubon. With no personal experience to guide me, I necessarily drew upon my knowledge of figures in conservation history with proven records of success, particularly, of course, George Bird Grinnell, Theodore Roosevelt, and Aldo Leopold. The three men used different approaches when pursuing their respective goals, but what I took from each was integrated into a composite individual who, I thought, would help me meet the political and administrative challenges that lay ahead.

Grinnell, for example, appealed to me because he combined tenacity with the realization that a pragmatic, often economically oriented approach, is usually the most successful lobbying style, even if it means submerging one's true motives, which are often aesthetic and philosophical in nature. Though tenacious, even over a period of years, he preferred a low profile and a self-effacing demeanor. This unassuming manner was partly the consequence of a patrician upbringing. But I suspect he also knew that others will always want to take credit for your successes; if you let them do so, they become your allies and not your enemies.

I liked Roosevelt for his stubborn commitment to both utilitarian and aesthetic conservation and his willingness to use every means at his disposal to achieve concrete results. No other president has come close to

201

his administration's accomplishments on such a wide conservation front over such a large area: 148 million acres of timberland set aside and the establishment of five national parks, eighteen national monuments, and fifty-one national wildlife refuges.

As already noted, on a philosophical level I had embraced Leopold's land ethic long before I came to Connecticut Audubon. Later, when we sought to create a new mission statement for the society, I found myself constantly returning to his ideas about the necessity of maintaining—and when possible restoring—the ecological integrity of the natural world.

Let us now turn to some specific cases where my composite historical figure was utilized, and see how "he" helped me deal with the many challenges I faced. Not long after assuming my new post, I learned that the society's staff ornithologist, Miley Bull, had been doing basic research for several summers on Chimon Island, in Long Island Sound off of Norwalk, and had discovered that a far greater number of herons, egrets, and ibises nested there than had previously been thought, making it the most important breeding site for these species between New Jersey and Massachusetts. I also learned that representatives of the state chapter of The Nature Conservancy, led by Ken Olson, had contacted the island's owner about the possibility of selling the property to them.

When I transmitted this information to the executive committee of the society's board, I found both a resentment toward the conservancy for trying to "take over our research project" and a suspicion of its motives, especially since the conservancy and Connecticut Audubon were supposedly competing for members and financial support from the same sources. A final concern was that the society receive its fair share of the publicity if the island was preserved. The breeding colonies of long-legged wading birds were almost lost in the discussion. It was a revealing and rather depressing experience to learn how a volunteer board of directors could so completely misunderstand an issue.

At this point, I could have taken the safest tack, which was to avoid the entire subject of Chimon Island and its occupants. But my composite historical figure would not let me. I knew from him that a Grinnell, Roosevelt, or Leopold would see this situation for what it was: a window of opportunity through which I *had* to climb, the parochialism of the board of directors notwithstanding. I also knew from Grinnell's experience how important it is to work harmoniously with other environmental groups and bury your differences, if any, at least until victory is won. Education, too, was the key. Grinnell had his newspaper, *Forest and Stream*, and Roosevelt had his "bully pulpit," but I had *Connecticut Audubon* magazine, the newsletters that went out of Connecticut Audubon's Hartford office, and a certain amount of access to the media. All of these vehicles of communication were employed to help create an atmosphere receptive to the concept of a national wildlife refuge comprising not only Chimon Island but two other bird-rich islands and Milford Point, a barrier beach protecting a large, ecologically rich salt marsh at the mouth of the Housatonic, one of the three largest rivers in the state.

Using Grinnell's example, I emphasized the practical results of saving the three islands and the barrier beach from proposed condominium development: an enhancement of the local residents' property values; the chance for the public to use the beach at one end of Chimon Island; the maintenance of bird-watching, sport-fishing, and waterfowl-hunting opportunities in the large salt marsh behind Milford Point; and the preservation of scenic backdrops for the boaters and sailors who make Long Island Sound one of the most popular recreational bodies of water in the world.

I reminded the members of the society that as Auduboners, this was one environmental campaign they *had* to enter. When Grinnell founded the Audubon Society in 1886, his major concern was protection of *non*game birds, especially the herons, egrets, and terns that were being systematically slaughtered by commercial hunters for plumes and feathers to adorn women's hats. Some of these species had not yet built back their populations to safe levels. Thus, the Auduboners of the 1980s would be engaged in a crusade that seemed to have the sanctity of history behind it.

But none of these arguments would have worked unless we had the biological facts to back them up. Miley Bull compiled the recorded observations that proved an ecological interconnection between all four units of the proposed refuge. For example, the glossy ibises and several species of herons and egrets from Chimon Island and the roseate and common (*Sterna hirundo*) tern species that nested on Falkner Island off Guilford all fed around Milford Point at the mouth of the Housatonic River, and the terns used it as a staging area for migration. Finally, the point was also crucial as a nesting site for the threatened piping plover.

In putting this information together, I recalled Grinnell's admonition that one should never go beyond the limits of his or her expertise when giving testimony. In my own congressional testimony before members of the House of Representatives, I followed his example to good effect by stressing only the biological facts. As I was told by congressmen at the time, that testimony was particularly important in keeping Milford Point in the refuge legislation. Some homeowners in the area had been

*Sitting on Miley Bull's duck boat in December 1975, with decoys, black ducks, and my shotgun on the deck in front of me. We are on the west bank of the Housatonic River, across from the Wheeler marsh where, during a duck hunt the year before, I heard the alarming news about the plan to build condominiums on Milford Point.*

*A view of the Wheeler marsh, looking west from the observation tower of the Connecticut Audubon Coastal Center on Milford Point.*

*On July 29, 1985, with Congressman Stewart McKinney, who led the effort in Congress to establish the national wildlife refuge along the Connecticut coast later named for him. We are at the dedication ceremony of Falkner Island, the last unit to be added in the original refuge legislation.*

concerned that public ownership would lead to trespassing on their properties and representatives of the federal government had been worried that easy accessibility to the point would make this unit of the refuge hard to manage.

With a groundswell of public sentiment behind the project, with the entire congressional delegation of Connecticut in support, with The Nature Conservancy raising the necessary funds to buy the individual land parcels to secure them until they could be sold to the United States Fish and Wildlife Service, and with the passage of the federal enabling legislation providing the funds to buy the parcels, the Connecticut Coastal National Wildlife Refuge became a reality in 1984. To honor the Republican who had led the fight in Congress to preserve these lands, the name was changed in 1987 to the Stewart B. McKinney National Wildlife Refuge.

Everyone in the political and environmental fields in Connecticut seemed to feel good about this victory, made all the sweeter because of the location of the refuge in the middle of one of the most congested commuter corridors in the nation and because it came at a time when the administration of Ronald Reagan had supposedly frozen expenditures for conservation projects. Connecticut's political leaders saw as never before that conservation was good politics, and the harmonious working relationship that my composite historical figure had encouraged me to seek with them continued throughout my entire five-year term at Connecticut Audubon.

One result of their new enthusiasm was that greater attention was now being paid to Long Island Sound, that fertile arm of the sea that millions of people in Connecticut and New York had taken for granted. When the federal government launched a new multi-million-dollar study of several major bodies of water along the Atlantic and Pacific coasts, influential Connecticut Republicans made sure that funding for a study of Long Island Sound was included.

As soon as the project was off the ground, I arranged to have Connecticut Audubon made a member of its steering committee. After a number of meetings had taken place, the committee helped to decide what scientific inquiries were to be made in the sound and which scientists were to do them. But the study's worthy aims of testing the health of Long Island Sound and devising treatments for its problems did not seem to interest the public, even residents of towns right on the shore.

If environmental history teaches us anything, it is that a project will not succeed *simply* because it is worthwhile. Grinnell, Senator George Vest of Missouri, and the sportsmen-conservationists of the Boone and Crockett

Club fought for years to have Yellowstone National Park—established on paper in 1872—adequately protected from vandals, loggers, and poachers, but they only succeeded in 1894 when a notorious commercial hunter appeared in the park and began to kill the last of the wild American bison to sell their heads and hides to taxidermists. Seizing the opportunity provided by the poacher's capture, Grinnell blew a bugle of alarm in his *Forest and Stream*, complete with pathetic photographs of slaughtered buffalo in the snow. Enough of the public was outraged that the Yellowstone Park Protection Act passed almost immediately.

Quite simply, I told the steering committee of the Long Island Sound Study that if the project was to be funded adequately well into the future, the public would have to be convinced that what scientists were discovering was of some immediate and dramatic benefit. One well-publicized success story early on would have important political consequences. As it turned out, such an issue was readily available. The same Connecticut Audubon ornithologist, Miley Bull, who had provided much of the basic data for Chimon Island, had, a number of years earlier, done a preliminary study of lead poisoning in waterfowl, mainly black ducks, in the 840-acre salt marsh protected by Milford Point. Now, in the mid-1980s, black ducks were a species whose population had dropped substantially since the 1950s. Now, too, Milford Point was part of a national wildlife refuge, and the federal government had announced that a nation-wide ban on the use of lead shot in waterfowl hunting would take effect in 1991.

In his earlier, unfinished study, Miley had examined the gizzards of ducks bagged by sport hunters in the Charles E. Wheeler Wildlife Management Area behind Milford Point and had found that a significant number of birds had ingested lead pellets. Waterfowl instinctively pick up tiny particles like spent shot because they help their gizzards grind up food. What was interesting about the recovered lead pellets was that many of them were smaller than those customarily used by duck hunters; they were, in fact, the size of shot used in skeet and trap shooting at clay pigeons. Across the mouth of the Housatonic River, opposite the national wildlife refuge at the Milford Point barrier beach and the state-owned salt marsh that Milford Point protects, is, or was, one of the largest skeet-and-trap-shooting ranges in America. Run by the Remington Arms Company, a subsidiary of DuPont, and in operation for over sixty years, most of the range's target houses faced the open water of the Housatonic estuary, and the total accumulation of lead was obviously very great.

An employee at the Remington range told me that up to a million clay pigeons were being propelled out over the water each year, and as a former member of a skeet team, I knew already that the average skeet load holds about an ounce of shot. Thus, as much as a million ounces, over sixty-two thousand pounds, or thirty-one tons of lead were being shot into the Housatonic estuary every year, and this had been going on for decades! How could such a huge discharge of a toxic substance go uncontested? Why was the unfinished, but highly suggestive, study done by Connecticut Audubon's ornithologist hidden away and apparently known only to him and to me?

The reasons were not hard to find. Simply, neither the society nor the Connecticut Department of Environmental Protection (which was also involved in the original study) had, at that time, wanted to anger the Remington Arms Company, a financial supporter of Connecticut Audubon and an industry in a state whose history and economy have been closely tied to the making of firearms and ammunition.

Given the built-in time limits of my tenure at Connecticut Audubon, I felt that I could afford to take on Remington, if necessary, even though I still hoped for accommodation. In any case, I knew that *none* of my three historical models would have retreated from a fight if it were absolutely necessary.

At the next meeting of the steering committee of the Long Island Sound Study, I brought up the issue and explained that Connecticut Audubon's ornithologist hypothesized that the smaller skeet-and-trap-sized pellets that he had found in the gizzards of black ducks were coming from the shallows around the Remington range, picked up there at night when black ducks do much of their feeding. But whether or not the ducks were being lead-poisoned near Remington really was not the essential point, I argued, for lead is a highly toxic element and its deposition, even in small quantities, had to stop. And why shouldn't Remington be required to use nontoxic steel shot for skeet and trap, especially when hunters in the public duck-hunting area across the river had been using it for years? Here was a quick way to prove to the public that the people involved in the Long Island Sound Study were doing more than just talking to each other, that the study had some relevance for the so-called "real world," the occupants of which included the hunters and anglers who were consuming game taken over a huge toxic waste dump.

Not more than a week later, I received a telephone call from Jim Murphy, a scientist in the Connecticut Department of Environmental Protection who had learned of my comments at the meeting and wanted to know more. After a lengthy conversation, he promised to recommend to the commissioner of the Department of Environmental Protection, Stanley Pac, that he order Remington to cease using lead in favor of nontoxic steel shot.

This seemed to both of us to be a good compromise approach, because it would allow the range to stay open. He was, however, especially concerned that Connecticut Audubon would support the state in what was sure to be a major political fight. Luckily, we were aided by circumstance: the commissioner, like myself, was not going to remain in office much longer. He was, in fact, soon to retire, and he could order a cessation of lead-shot use without having to bear the brunt of the coming controversy.

Much to our delight, that is exactly what he did. His order to Remington to stop discharging lead into the water around its range by December 31, 1986 was followed by a tide of protest from company employees, local businesses, and shooting-sports enthusiasts all over the country; the latter group believed that nontoxic steel shot would not perform as well ballistically as lead and would, over time, damage their gun barrels, requiring them to buy new ones every few years. They also argued that the rules of skeet and trap would have to be changed to accommodate the new ballistic realities imposed by steel shot. But what seemed to anger critics most was their belief that Connecticut Audubon's involvement in the state order was the result of anti-gun and anti-hunter sentiment.

In an on-site meeting, all the parties involved discussed the commissioner's order and what it meant for the future of the Remington range. With the pragmatic approach of Grinnell and Roosevelt always in mind, I argued that Remington would not lose economically—at least in the long run—by converting its shotgun-shell making machines from lead to steel shot. By doing it now, the company would anticipate the future and appear environmentally concerned to the public at large. Lead had been removed from paint and gasoline; it was only a matter of time, I predicted, before the ban on the use of lead shot in waterfowl hunting would be extended to upland hunting and target shooting as well.

Many present did not believe that lead poisoning in waterfowl was really a problem, and members of a hunter-oriented association attacked Connecticut Audubon for originating this issue simply as a way of disparaging hunters. I assured them that the literature on lead poisoning in waterfowl was conclusive, going back at least to 1894, when Grinnell discussed the subject in detail in the February 10 issue of his *Forest and Stream*.

As for the charge that Connecticut Audubon was anti-hunter, I came prepared with a copy of my own book on the central role of hunters and anglers in early conservation, and a clear memory of Grinnell's retort to Westerners who mocked him in the 1880s for his efforts on behalf of Yellowstone wildlife by calling him an Eastern "tenderfoot" who had no personal experience with the West and its "inexhaustible" big game. To silence these critics, all he had to say was that he had ridden with George Armstrong Custer on his 1874 Black Hills expedition, had explored and hunted the Yellowstone region in 1875, and had ranched in western Nebraska with the likes of "Buffalo Bill" Cody and scout Luther North.

Though my life had been *far* less exciting than Grinnell's, my response to the sportsmen at the meeting was based on his example. Not only were Miley Bull and I not anti-hunting, I asserted, but we had, in fact, been ardent sportsmen since childhood, and in that regard, we followed squarely in the tradition of the founders of the Audubon movement. Furthermore, our deep affection for the Housatonic River estuary came from many dawns spent in duck blinds right across the river from the Remington range. These revelations seemed to disarm the sportsmen completely. If we were charter members of the shooting-sports fraternity, then how could our arguments be based on knee-jerk hostility—perhaps there was something of substance in what we had to say.

In the end, the commissioner's order stayed in effect. DuPont, which owned Remington, closed down operation of the range rather than become involved in the creation—or so it claimed—of an entirely new game of skeet-and-trap shooting. A scientific study was then conducted of black ducks feeding around the range that found greatly elevated levels of lead in their blood, thereby vindicating the preliminary report done by Miley Bull years before.

After I left Connecticut Audubon, DuPont was held legally responsible for creating a toxic waste dump in the waters off its Remington Gun Club and required to begin an investigation of how best to go about the herculean task of extracting the lead from the estuary. Finally, the clean-up effort began. It can only take place for part of the year, from August until freeze-up, so as not to disturb the threatened piping plovers that might be nesting on the beach nearby. By early 2011, an incredible eight hundred tons of the poisonous pellets had been removed!

While there are still pockets of lead in the sediments, Miley Bull, who is monitoring the clean-up for the society, is confident that these will be reduced eventually to acceptable levels as shown by blood tests conducted on ducks taken in the area. When that happens and the Connecticut Department of Environmental Protection is able to declare the estuary lead-free, it is hoped that the buildings at the former Remington range will be converted into a visitor center for the McKinney National Wildlife Refuge, which now includes a number of additional units up and down the Connecticut coast.

*Looking west across the mouth of the Housatonic River toward the former site of the Remington shooting range.*

Connecticut Audubon had played a key role in ending decades of lead pollution and setting the stage for the clean-up that followed. In getting the state to recognize its responsibility to stop this toxic deposition, the society also helped to establish a powerful historical and legal precedent affecting all other American shooting ranges, especially those over water. They should either convert to nontoxic shot or be shut down. In addition, the well-publicized effort to make the Housatonic estuary healthy again brought attention to the fragility of the ecosystems of Long Island Sound.

*Though the society had done much* to preserve the natural state of Milford Point on the eastern shore of the Housatonic by eliminating the threat of condominium development and by stopping the massive lead deposition from the Remington range on the western bank, I felt that there was one more project we had to undertake to complete our mission of protecting the estuary and the abundant wildlife that used it. Connecticut Audubon needed to have a coastal center on the shore of Long Island Sound for doing educational programs, conducting research, and leading birding trips, while, at the same time, continually monitoring the ecological health of the adjacent 840-acre salt marsh behind Milford Point.

My aim was to acquire from the state of Connecticut the fifty-year, renewable lease, then held by a local bird club not connected to Connecticut Audubon, of a small parcel of land at the base of Milford Point, just to the east of the boundary line of the national wildlife refuge. On this property were two derelict buildings that Miley Bull, who first came up with the idea, thought we could retrofit and turn into a coastal center that the society sorely needed to round out its holdings.

From the beginning, the project received much opposition both in and out of Connecticut Audubon. While a couple of key board members

*With Miley Bull, congratulating each other on the opening of the Connecticut Audubon Coastal Center on October 19, 1995.*

thought the plan had potential, others didn't like the fact that the society would be raising what might be a great deal of money to restore the buildings and still not own the land on which they stood. Opposition within Connecticut Audubon was, however, nothing compared to the protests by the New Haven Bird Club, the group that held the lease, and their local allies. Understandably, they railed against the big, wealthy outsiders who thought they could simply snap their fingers and take over "their" property.

The negotiations with the bird club and between the society and the state took months of often stressful effort on my part. But with Miley's help, I eventually persuaded the bird club that they would be welcomed at our new center, and the society's board of directors began, cautiously, to accept the plan. The state, too, came around to the realization that their property would be cared for better under our management than that of the smaller, poorly funded organization. Particularly important in bringing about that welcome conclusion was the deputy commissioner of the Department of Environmental Protection, Dennis DeCarli.

Finally, in 1986, the fifty-year renewable lease, which all the parties involved assumed would be a lease in perpetuity, was transferred to Connecticut Audubon. Now, with the state property securely in our hands, I could begin the fund-raising campaign. It would be a long drawn-out process, with a number of serious setbacks along the way, including an order by the Federal Emergency Management Agency to demolish the buildings Connecticut Audubon was retrofitting, because they would not be high enough off the ground to be safe in times of coastal flooding. An alternative plan had to be developed and the money raised for a new, elevated, state-of-the-art facility, which didn't open until several years after I returned to academe.

But when I was invited back for the grand opening in 1995, I knew immediately that the Connecticut Audubon Coastal Center at Milford Point was everything that Miley Bull and I had hoped it would be. Overlooking Long Island Sound on the south and the great Wheeler salt marsh on the north, and with the Milford Point unit of the McKinney National Wildlife Refuge just to the west, the center quickly became a mecca for birders and other nature lovers from all along the northeastern Atlantic coast.

*My enthusiasm for launching the effort* that finally resulted in a coastal center for the society stemmed not only from a desire to monitor and permanently protect the Housatonic estuary, but also from my wish to make Connecticut Audubon a true leader in science-based environmental education. This was not the case when I became executive director in 1983.

The central problem in what I considered the miseducation of young people in the many classes conducted by the society's "teacher-naturalists" was the "wildlife-care-and-rehabilitation program." Some staff and board members seemed to feel that the program was not only educational, but a form of wildlife conservation and good public relations as well. Individual animals and birds were being "saved" and supposedly returned to the wild, while children and their parents were being made happy by this "service" to Connecticut Audubon's members. Regardless of the alleged benefits of the program, how could the staff turn away a teary-eyed child clutching a shoe box containing a "baby" bird or mammal?

Here was a real administrative dilemma. Given my study of the conservation movement, I knew immediately that this was not the kind of program the society should have. My composite historical example understood the meaning of priorities; apparently, the supporters of Connecticut Audubon's so-called rehabilitation program did not. Each year, as the state was losing twelve hundred to fifteen hundred acres of inland wetlands, the society was spending many thousands of dollars on staff salaries, food, medicines, and other supplies to care for species that were, for the most part, either invasive or overabundant. Typical of the most commonly cared-for birds and mammals were pigeons, starlings, English (house) sparrows, raccoons, and squirrels.

Furthermore, there was no way to know if the wildlife cared for and released was actually surviving. Most studies indicate that a large percentage of such animals do not survive, especially those that are very young when taken from the wild. All my efforts to have raccoons collared to test their survival rate were blocked by the executive committee of the board because of fears that animals raiding garbage cans would be traced back to the society, creating a public-relations problem.

Even a modest effort to reduce the types or numbers of wildlife was strongly resisted, because the philosophy behind the program was theologian Albert Schweitzer's concept of "reverence for life." Of course, nature has no such reverence, and until recently at least, the mainstream history of the Audubon movement likewise contained very little of this philosophical orientation. From Grinnell to Donal C. O'Brien, Jr., longtime chairman of the board of directors of National Audubon, many Audubon leaders have been sportsmen. Neither the national organization nor any of the half-dozen state associations have ever had a mission statement anything like Schweitzer's; indeed, they have always accepted, at least officially, the lawful use of wildlife, including hunting.

Though the reverence-for-life concept of Connecticut Audubon's wildlife-care-and-rehabilitation program had, in recent years, become the unofficial mission statement for the society in the minds of some of the staff and board, the older motto over the front door of the headquarters building in Fairfield still read: "Helping the People of Connecticut Appreciate and Conserve Our Natural Resources." Given the frequently stated anti-hunting views of those who supported the reverence-for-life ideal, it is rather ironic that the society's motto was conceived by Jack Douglas Mitchell, a former public-relations executive of the Remington Arms Company and a nationally known writer on hunting. Obviously, in drawing up the mission-statement portion of the five-year plan, I had to try to reconcile differences among wildlife enthusiasts in the state, whether hunters or anti-hunters, whether existing or potential members of Connecticut Audubon.

As with the other problems I faced as executive director, my background as an environmental historian taught me that I did not have to "reinvent the wheel." The ecologically derived land ethic of Aldo Leopold, not the moral philosophy of medical missionary Albert Schweitzer, was the model on which the society should base its goals and plans. This meant that Connecticut Audubon should strive not to care for alien species like starlings and mute swans but should, instead, endeavor to preserve—and restore when possible—the ecological integrity of Connecticut's natural world. Just as Leopold and his family worked successfully to restore the ecological health of a used-up farm in Wisconsin, the society should also work to bring back the native plants and animals and eliminate, whenever possible, the invasives, the "living pollutants" as I called them, that were competing with, and in many cases threatening, the indigenous species that had long adapted to life on this continent.

A mission statement emphasizing the interrelatedness of life forms and their natural environments would cover just about every issue Connecticut

Audubon was likely to face in the future. It would automatically establish priorities. Present and potential members would see that a major goal of the society was preserving threatened species and their ecosystems. We would not duplicate the efforts of humane societies and groups like Friends of Animals by caring for individual mammals and birds. Because it would stress conservation, rather than morality, hunting would be a relevant issue only when the "harvesting" of wildlife posed a proven hazard to entire species. Finally, such a mission statement would have the advantage of emphasizing the urgency of the ecological crisis. Connecticut Audubon did not have either the time or the money, I asserted, to care for injured pigeons and squirrels in a state that had one of the highest rates of environmental destruction in the country.

As can be imagined, my efforts to abolish the wildlife-care-and-rehabilitation program, which had been entrenched for years, were not met with universal acclamation. The twenty staff members and the executive committee of the board divided over the issue, with me in the middle, and I sometimes wondered if I was going to survive my allotted five years.

The worst time came when the director of the program, who was also the head teacher-naturalist, rallied her allies on the staff to write letters to the executive committee demanding my resignation. In response, a board member sympathetic to her views conducted a kind of hearing with all the staff present at the Birdcraft Museum while I waited alone for a verdict on my future in an adjacent room, the same place I had discovered the Grinnell papers in 1967. After more than an hour of discussion, the board member entered the room to tell me that the staff was split over whether or not I had acted in a dictatorial manner in wanting to adopt a new mission statement and phase out the animal-care program. Consequently, he had decided to take the matter to the full executive committee and let them decide my fate.

I will never forget that terrible meeting, held ominously in the office of the society's attorney and presided over by the president, my immediate boss, Stephen Kellert. A professor at the Yale School of Forestry & Environmental Studies, with a Ph.D. in biology, he was well known at the time for his surveys of the attitudes of Americans regarding their interaction with the natural world. I had personally recruited Kellert for the position of president, and after a number of conversations with him, I thought we were on the same page when it came to the animal-care program, which he contemptuously referred to as "our zoo."

At the head of a large rectangular table around which the executive committee and I were seated, Kellert began the proceedings with the following words: "John, I have been asked to call this meeting because some members of the board of directors have lost faith in your leadership abilities." Wow! I remember feeling like I had just been punched in the stomach. Still, I had hope, because surely my friend, the president, with his background as a Yale ecologist, would support me by telling the others about our mutually agreed-upon decision to phase out the animal program over time, which was the reason for the protest by its director and the teacher-naturalists under her.

Kellert, however, said nothing. At first, there was a long, awkward silence, but then one of the board members began attacking me for undercutting the educational mission of Connecticut Audubon by trying to do away with a program that had done so much good for the state's wildlife and made the members of the society feel good that Connecticut Audubon was helping injured and orphaned birds and mammals. Others then piled on, and one individual even suggested that I might be immoral, or at least amoral, in my feelings about wildlife! Though I tried to defend myself, nothing I said seemed to have any effect.

The whole time I was going through this ordeal, I kept thinking about my visit to the Fairfield post office only a couple of months earlier, when I mailed my resignation to the University of Miami's history department. The chair had given me an extra six months to make up my mind, and when the deadline arrived in mid-1984, I knew I had to stay at Connecticut Audubon because there were several worthy projects still to complete, and if I had returned to Coral Gables, I would have felt that I had failed to take full advantage of this unique opportunity to do good work in environmental education and conservation.

Now, when it looked as if I could be fired right on the spot, I saw myself standing again in front of the mail slot at the post office with the resignation letter in my hand. Holding the envelope on one end, I slid it back and forth several times through the opening before I finally let go, and said good-bye to the security of tenure and free college tuition for both of our children. As I was being assailed that night in the attorney's office, I thought about what a fool I had been, and I would have given almost anything to have had my fingers around that envelope again—only this time I would have come to my senses at the last moment, pulled the letter out, and torn it up into a dozen tiny pieces.

Just when I thought all was lost, the chairman of the board of directors, Bob Larsen, began to speak. When Bob talked, everyone listened. He was (and I presume still is) an impressive individual, with a no-nonsense, quiet authority about him. The son of Roy Larsen, who had been at the center of the rise of *Time* magazine as a publishing giant, Bob was a multimillionaire whose financial support of Connecticut Audubon had been key to its success. To the seeming disappointment of some around the table, Bob said that he thought that this trouble I was having with some staff members would pass, because I had learned from it that I must try harder to accommodate the views of everyone. Furthermore, he stated his belief that I was trying my best and that he, for one, had not lost confidence in me.

His brief comments were enough to save me, and the meeting broke up soon afterwards. I don't think Bob cared particularly for the animal program, and I'm sure that his business sense made him like the idea of saving money by phasing it out. But more than anything else, he proved that he was a man of his word. Unless I did something so egregious that I really had to be fired immediately, I would have my promised five-year term to devise, and implement, a mission plan for Connecticut Audubon. Still, I had been traumatized by the hearing at the Birdcraft Museum and the later meeting in the attorney's office, and I never felt entirely secure in my position again.

Despite some continuing hostility toward me from a few staff and board members, I would eventually be successful in terminating the care-and-rehabilitation program after its director left the society. Instead of the six hundred or more mammals and birds Connecticut Audubon used to care for in an average year, the society now maintains only a small number of indigenous animals representing the various biological categories for use in children's classes. These include some native species of injured or captive-bred hawks, owls, and falcons, most of which are in decline and are, therefore, worthy of special treatment.

At last, many thousands of dollars were being saved each year that could be put toward "conservation, education, and research," the three words I added to the society's logo and to the inside cover of every issue of *Connecticut Audubon* magazine. In addition, the society's teacher-naturalists were no longer miseducating young people, however unconsciously, with the idea that caring for individual mammals and birds has much to do with understanding ecology or why entire ecosystems must be preserved. The mission of Connecticut Audubon would now be science based, after the example of Aldo Leopold, not morality based, after the model of Albert Schweitzer.

*In looking back over my five years* in Connecticut, it is gratifying to think about what was accomplished. Besides those issues already discussed, the society had played an important role in several statewide initiatives, including the creation of a nongame wildlife-conservation program, the funding of open-space preservation, the passage of a recycling act, and the abolishment of tolls on Interstate 95. Before the toll booths were eliminated, the concentration of air pollution around them had been a major concern, as was the number of fatal accidents resulting from their interference with traffic flow.

These efforts had been coordinated through Connecticut Audubon's Environmental Center in the capital city of Hartford. By the time my tenure ended in 1988, the society had developed a high profile as a leader in environmental affairs, just as I had hoped it would when I began as executive director in 1983. Much of the credit for that result should go to Joey Corcoran, whom I hired to be director of environmental affairs.

Other achievements were the development of the relatively new Connecticut Audubon Holland Brook Center near the Connecticut River south of Hartford into a flourishing facility, the addition of new sanctuaries to the society's holdings, and a huge increase in Connecticut Audubon membership. One reason, I believe, for that expansion was that the society now provided many more opportunities for members to go on field trips.

With that old slogan in mind that we should "think globally but act locally," I had inaugurated a greatly expanded field-trip program to familiarize members with environmental problems not only in distant locations in North America but on other continents as well. Because birding was always a major component of these adventures, our ornithologist Miley Bull led many of them, though I, too, acted as the guide on trips to pre-Columbian Maya sites in Mexico that were rich in both history and bird life, as well as one to Alaska, where we traveled to such rarely visited places as Point Barrow, at the end of land in North America, and the Pribilof Islands far out in the Bering Sea.

I always felt it was a great privilege to be able to go to these remote areas where I could interact with the indigenous people, like the present-day Maya, Inupiat, and Aleut, as well as see new species of wildlife. This was never more true than on a trip I co-led in 1986 with Miley to Kenya, where we were able to visit with the Masai in the Masai-Mara National Reserve and the Samburu in the Samburu Game Reserves in the Northern Frontier Province. But the focus of the trip was, of course, on the diversity and abundance of wildlife. Finally getting to the vast, unfenced plains of East Africa and seeing the Great Migration, which totaled about three-hundred thousand zebra and a staggering one-and-a-half million wildebeest, was the fulfillment of a dream I had had since boyhood. Countless thousands of both species were in the valley of the Mara River when we arrived that summer.

Because they have a humped back, buffalo-like horns, a long, dark mane, a dull grayish brown body that appears black at a distance when seen against the tawny-colored grass of the plains, wildebeest, though much smaller, reminded me of the North American bison. This resemblance was particularly striking on one of our first "game drives," after we had stopped our four-wheel-drive vehicle on a ridge above the Mara and looked down toward the river. Up and down the ridge as far as I could see, there were long lines of hundreds of wildebeest trudging along in single file over deeply eroded paths that had been used for centuries. They were all heading down to the Mara to drink and possibly to cross over and join their innumerable brethren already on the other side.

The scene I was witnessing looked just like an illustration I remembered seeing in George Bird Grinnell's stirring tribute to the bison, "The Last of the Buffalo," an essay published in the September 1892 issue of *Scribner's Magazine*. Called "Going to Water," the drawing shows long lines of bison walking in single file along deeply worn trails down to a river somewhere in the American West when the species still numbered in the millions. It was a thrilling, somehow mystical, experience to know that I was looking at a scene that could have been very similar to one observed by Grinnell in the unspoiled West of the 1870s. What a privilege it was to have this opportunity, not only because the wildebeest migration was the greatest movement of large mammals left on earth, but because I was well aware that its days were probably numbered, just as they had been for the buffalo when Grinnell saw the huge herds shortly before they—as he put it in his essay—"passed into history."

That wonderful morning on the ridge above the Mara River always came back to me whenever I visited Connecticut Audubon's Birdcraft Museum, because of what I discovered there. One day, soon after I became executive director, I was standing in one of the rooms of the museum when it suddenly dawned on me that the large skulls I was looking at, mounted high on a wall in a rather obscure location, had to be the same two buffalo skulls, from a bull and a cow, that Grinnell described in his famous essay.

I knew that it was through his friend, John P. Holman, that the society had acquired Grinnell's papers and bird specimens, both study skins and full mounts, and so it was obvious that these two skulls, which I made sure were, indeed, those of bison, were those Grinnell memorialized in his famous eulogy to the vanished multitudes. He had picked them up from the prairie after the buffalo were all gone and kept them, one on either side of his fireplace, "as mementoes of the past, to dream over, and in such reverie to see again the swelling hosts which yesterday covered the plains, and to-day are but a dream."

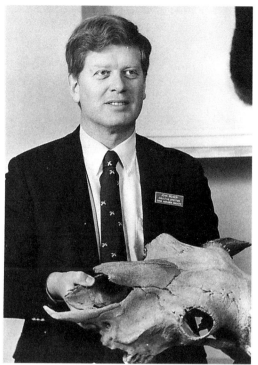

*As executive director of the Connecticut Audubon Society, I am holding one of two bison skulls collected by George Bird Grinnell about the time he created the original Audubon Society in 1886 and kept "as mementoes of ... the swelling hosts which yesterday covered the plains, and to-day are but a dream."*

My trips to faraway places like the Mara Valley of Kenya and the state of Chiapas in Mexico were, of course, highlights of my time at Connecticut Audubon. Though I had established the foreign field-trip program to educate its participants about environmental issues around the world and, hopefully, to make them more committed to conservation efforts both at home and abroad, I had to explain the new policy to the board of directors. While some on the executive committee never embraced the program, most of them accepted it because it was financially self-sustaining and because it might encourage some participants to make large donations.

It was fundraising, however, that was my one conspicuous failure at Connecticut Audubon. Several directors of development came and went during my tenure, but neither they nor I proved to be as effective as we should have been in obtaining grants or attracting major donors. My deficiencies in this area came, I suppose, from the fact that I never took this aspect of my job *nearly* as seriously as the work in education and conservation. And of all the issues in which I had a part, the most satisfying was the preservation of the mouth of the Housatonic, which, along with the Connecticut and Thames, is one of the three major river systems in the state.

As we have seen, it was largely through the efforts of the society that the outer portion of Milford Point had been added to the McKinney National Wildlife Refuge and the larger Wheeler salt marsh behind it protected by the Connecticut Audubon lease of the state property at the base of the point and by the soon-to-be-built coastal center. Across the river, on the western shore, the society had also initiated the successful campaign to stop, and later clean up, the massive deposition of one of the most toxic substances known to humankind.

*I think I was so gratified* by these achievements not only because they were the kind of concrete contributions in conservation I had hoped I could make before taking the position at Connecticut Audubon, but also because our efforts were all interconnected with the Housatonic estuary, a very special place of mine since the early 1970s, when Miley Bull, who had grown up in the area, began acting as my guide on many fishing and hunting trips to the mouth of the river during summer and Christmas vacations. Of these outings, I remember most the waterfowling adventures off the jetty jutting into Long Island Sound on the eastern side of the main channel of the Housatonic and in the Wheeler marsh, where we hunted from his grassed-up, traditional wooden duck boat, over old, beautifully carved cork and wooden decoys, and with his never-failing black Labrador making the retrieves.

Given our role in helping to protect the estuary in the following decade, there was one trip to the Wheeler marsh in the 1970s that I now recall with a real sense of pride. It wasn't because we had shot well and bagged our limits of black ducks and mallards, but rather because of a conversation Miley and I had about the future of Milford Point. As we crouched down behind the blind in his duck boat and looked south over the decoys in the direction of the point, he happened to mention that some developers wanted to build multi-story condominiums on the outer portion of this sandy peninsula extending out into the river.

I distinctly remember getting angry, because I knew that these tall buildings would be a form of visual pollution impinging on the natural beauty of the area. In addition, the structures would interfere with what I could already see were the customary flight paths of waterfowl and waders in and out of the marsh, and the condominium owners would not only disturb birds feeding or nesting on the beach in the warm months, but their permanent presence would inevitably produce pollution runoff that would impact the wetlands. While I was upset about the condominium proposal, I felt impotent to do anything about it. After all, this was Connecticut, and I lived over thirteen hundred miles away in South Florida.

On that morning in December 1974 in Miley's duck boat, I could never have imagined that only a decade later I would be living in nearby Fairfield and have the opportunity, as head of a statewide environmental organization, to play a key role in stopping, once and for all, this awful plan. In some strange way, it seemed almost as if this favorable outcome had been fated to occur as it did. But whether it was destiny or simply coincidence, my part in the protection of this beautiful and vibrant salt marsh was something of which I will always be proud.

*Though the Wheeler marsh would remain* a special place for waterfowling during my five years at Connecticut Audubon, it would not be my only duck-hunting retreat. One of the great things about being just across the water from my old homeland of Long Island was that I could make frequent hunting trips back to my most special of all special places, Jones Inlet and the nearby channel, bay, and marsh on the South Shore of Long Island, near the village of Point Lookout. On some occasions, I went with friends, but most of the time I went alone, trailering my fourteen-foot aluminum boat and 9-horse outboard motor down through southern Connecticut and New York State, into the borough of the Bronx in New York City, over the East River, and across Long Island to the launch ramp on Reynolds Channel just west of Point Lookout.

As soon as I launched the boat and headed out onto the water, I felt exhilarated and carefree. At least for these hours spent hunting, all of the stress and worry of my high-pressure position evaporated. I had a number of favorite locations where I could hide my boat, erect my portable blind, and set out my brant decoys. The spot chosen could be the end of a marsh island poking out into Reynolds Channel, the mouth of a creek running through one of those islands, or a jetty along Point Lookout Beach where I had hunted in the late sixties. It all depended on the direction of the wind, the flow of the tide, and the sighting of brant flocks in the distance.

Once I arrived at the selected location, going over the side of the boat in my chest waders and becoming one with the watery world around me was always a highlight of the trip. As I waded through the clear, knee-deep water to arrange the decoys in what I hoped would be an effective pattern for attracting waterfowl, I experienced the same feeling of keen anticipation I had known for almost thirty years, all the way back to my first duck hunting on Lake Okeechobee. After placing the decoys and making sure they rode properly on the water and were at the right distance from where I would be shooting, I entered the blind, sat down on a folding stool, and waited. Now I was in heaven, alone with the wind, tide, and brant. These little sea geese, my favorite waterfowl and main quarry, were always present in large numbers, their flocks moving up and down Reynolds Channel as the tide either covered or exposed their feeding grounds. Sometimes they decoyed well, and sometimes they didn't, but I never tired of seeing these graceful, fast-flying waterfowl or listening to their wild calls as they passed by.

Because I enjoyed these hunts so much, I always regretted having to return to the boat ramp for the trip back to Fairfield. That feeling soon passed, however, because I believed I was accomplishing something significant at Connecticut Audubon, and after Bob Larsen defended me during the controversy over the animal-care program, I thought I had at least a minimally secure position at the society for the duration of the promised five-year term. But during my last waterfowl season before the end of that term, in December 1987, I experienced more than a feeling of simple regret when I returned to the launch ramp. I now had a sense of foreboding about what would happen the next month, the five-year anniversary of my coming to Connecticut.

While I always knew that the day of reckoning would probably come in early 1988, I had pushed that likelihood to the back of my mind as I went about working in a hectic schedule that often included six-day weeks. It seems obvious to me now that I should have begun an academic job search at the start of my fourth year with the society, but I was afraid that if the executive committee of the board discovered that fact, some of its members who didn't like me could put pressure on Bob Larsen to end my employment before the five-year deadline; they might argue that since I wanted out anyway, why not hurry me along?

Though I didn't know what the future would bring, I hoped that any career after Connecticut Audubon would include college teaching and the chance to research and write. Otherwise, I was sure that my long-term mental health would suffer greatly. I had, in fact, never lost my love for the old life of a history professor, even as I engaged in helping to achieve what I believe were some significant conservation accomplishments. During my years with the society, I managed to keep my hand in as a historian by lecturing on environmental history at Yale, Fairfield University, and the University of Connecticut, teaching my "Ecology and the American Experience" course at Wesleyan, and overseeing the publication of new paperback editions of my two books by the University of Oklahoma Press.

In the time I was at Connecticut Audubon, I think I also knew that in the future I would probably continue to work toward bringing George Bird Grinnell more into the light for his central role in the early conservation movement. As part of that effort, I made sure that the large collection of

Grinnell's papers I had discovered at the Birdcraft Museum in 1967 would not be lost to posterity. Soon after becoming executive director in 1983, I learned that a few years earlier, a board member had, on his own initiative, taken all thirty-eight letterbooks of copied outgoing letters to the curb, to be taken to the city dump. Only the timely intervention of a staff member had saved the papers. As executive director, I arranged for the transfer in 1984 of the entire collection to Yale.

Given my enduring interest in Grinnell and the history of conservation and my desire to return to the academic world in a tight job market, I waited for the end of my term with a great deal of apprehension. I was exhausted after my five years with the society and longed to be back in the less stressful world of the university. I believed that I had accomplished, or at least set on a firm foundation, all of my major projects, and it was definitely time to go. But the big question was: what would the executive committee do? Would they want me to stay on indefinitely, give me an extension of several months to find other employment, or cut me off immediately, with the demand that I and the family vacate the society-owned house we lived in next door to the Fairfield Center? Since neither Andi, a registered nurse, nor I had any family money and lived paycheck to paycheck, this possibility caused me tremendous anxiety.

Once 1988 arrived, I didn't have long to wait for the board's decision. On the morning of the first Friday after the New Year's Day holiday, I received a phone call at the Fairfield Center requesting that I meet with several members of the executive committee at a local restaurant later that day. I knew, of course, that a late Friday afternoon meeting meant that I would not be given an indefinite renewal of my contract; people in business seem to prefer doing their unpleasant tasks at the end of the week, so that their employee will go home rather than return to the workplace to complain about the alleged injustice that has just befallen him or her.

When I walked into the restaurant's main dining room, feeling like a condemned man about to have his last meal, I saw that in addition to Bob Larsen, there were only two other members of the executive committee seated at a small, round table. One was a food company executive and the other a retired dentist, who had formerly been a friend and ally but who had turned hostile after the controversy regarding the animal-care program.

On the table in front of my seat was a document drawn up by the society's attorney that I was to sign before leaving the restaurant. The bottom line was that I had to tender my resignation, effective April 15, though I would supposedly act as a consultant to Connecticut Audubon for another year after that. (This provision was inserted into the document as a kind of bogus face-saving device they thought I needed.) The family and I would be allowed to stay in the society's house until the end of the school year so that the lives of Carrie and Chris would not be disrupted more than necessary. And finally, my secretary would be instructed to give me every assistance in my efforts to find new employment.

All things considered, it was a very generous severance package. Still, I was hurt, because none of the three men had anything at all positive to say about my tenure at Connecticut Audubon. It was almost as if they had been chafing at the bit for a long time to get rid of me, and the only thing that had stopped them up to that point was Bob Larsen's promise that I would have my five years.

After I signed the document, one of the board members scooped it up, and then all three of them hurried out of the restaurant, leaving me alone at the table "to finish your meal," as one of them put it. Only then, did the full shock of what had just happened sweep over me.

As I drove back to our house, I wondered how I could tell our children that they would soon have to leave their friends and this beautiful area of Connecticut that they had come to love. Carrie and Chris were home when I got there, and they took the news better than I expected, probably because Andi maintained a supportive and upbeat demeanor. Like the children, Andi, too, was surprised by what had happened. Though she knew my term was ending that month, I think she assumed that everything would be fine because I would be given an indefinite extension.

*From as early as 1969,* when I engaged in my first academic job search, I had been aware of just how difficult it was to obtain a tenure-track position at a college or university. By 1988, from what I could tell, the employment situation hadn't gotten much better. In fact, for me personally, it had probably gotten worse. Now in my mid-forties, I was older than some search committees seemed to want for their entry-level assistant professors. And because of the surprising provincialism of at least one other search committee, my administrative experience as the chief executive officer of a statewide environmental organization counted for nothing when it came to my application for a chair position. I was told later that a key member of that committee had rejected my application outright, because I had become an "environmentalist" and was no longer a "historian"!

As the weeks rolled by with no good prospects in sight, I became increasingly desperate and pursued every opportunity I came across. As long as it was within the forty-eight states, I applied for it. I was afraid that if I didn't obtain a teaching or chair position by September of 1988, another whole academic year would then come and go, and I would never make it back at all. I was now learning more about individuals with tenure who had given it up for a time to direct a foundation, serve in government, or pursue some other worthy end, and who later found that when they tried to return to their former lives as teacher-scholars, all avenues had been closed to them. Would I end up like these poor souls and never again be able to practice my profession?

All through this terrible time, I was helped tremendously by several friends who continued to write letter after letter on my behalf. Besides my former professors at Northwestern, George Fredrickson and Bob Wiebe, this little group included Dick Bartlett, who knew my scholarship and had written a very favorable review of *American Sportsmen*, and Bob Zaller, a friend from the University of Miami days who could speak to my teaching and collegiality. I will always be grateful to them for sticking by me.

Finally, I was able to have two interviews for chair positions, one for the University of North Florida and the other for Northern Arizona University. In both cases, I flubbed them. In one I was far too passive, asking few if any questions, and in the other, I went to the opposite extreme, and probably came across as an aggressive know-it-all. After I had time to think about my "performances," I realized that I wouldn't have hired me! Perhaps, I subconsciously wanted to avoid, if at all possible, having to become a chair, even if it was at a university where I could do some teaching along with my administrative duties. Though I would seize any opportunity, what I really wanted was to be a full-time teacher-scholar again and escape completely the stresses that always go along with the duties of an administrator.

With the arrival of spring, the announcements of openings steadily decreased. There had not been many to begin with, and they were now approaching the point of nonexistence.

Then one day I saw what I knew was probably going to be my last chance for an interview for a position starting in the fall of 1988. The opening was for an entry-level assistant professor of history at one of the regional campuses of Ohio University, founded in 1804, the oldest college west of the Allegheny Mountains and north of the Ohio River. Located in Chillicothe, a town of twenty-three thousand in south-central Ohio in one of the state's Appalachian counties, the school is sixty miles west of the main campus in Athens. A nonresidential campus with about one thousand students in 1988, Ohio University-Chillicothe had a relatively small number of "Group 1" (tenure-track) faculty members, the great majority of faculty being annual contract or adjunct instructors. Most of the history courses were, in fact, taught by a single tenured professor, who had decided to retire early and move out of state.

For this one last chance, I pulled out all the stops and urged my little group of faithful letter-writers to send yet one more recommendation and if possible, to please follow it up with a verbal communication. All complied with enthusiasm, and I was delighted to receive the hoped-for phone call offering me an interview.

After leaving the airport in the capital city of Columbus, about forty-five miles to the north of Chillicothe, I drove south in my rental car through a relatively flat region of farms, small towns, and occasional industrial zones. On approaching Chillicothe, I found it fringed by hills and its skyline dominated by the giant smokestack of the Mead Corporation's paper mill. The nearly one-hundred-acre campus of O.U.C., however, is in a pleasant suburban part of town, on top of well-wooded Carlisle Hill.

My interview seemed to go well, and I was surprised, and impressed, by the members of the search committee. Though I expected them to have Ph.D.s, I thought they might all be local Ohioans. Instead, they were a male economist originally from Iran, a female English professor originally from India, and another English professor, a male, who grew up in Illinois but whose family was of Peruvian Hispanic and South-American Indian descent. I was surprised by their diverse backgrounds, and I now felt sure that if I got the job, I would have cosmopolitan colleagues with whom I could have some interesting conversations.

After my return to Connecticut, I was hopeful but by no means confident. When the end of the school year arrived, which had been the original deadline given me by the Connecticut Audubon executive committee for vacating their house and there was still no word from Chillicothe, I became increasingly worried, and depressed. Then, a few days after my June 10th birthday, I received the phone call for which I had hoped. It was O.U.C. Dean Delbert Meyer, who stated: "The Affirmative Action Office of Ohio University has authorized me to make you the offer of a tenure-track assistant professorship at Ohio University-Chillicothe." I had made it back in—I would be able to practice my profession again.

# CHAPTER EIGHT

# Back in Academia and Providing Historical Models for Today's Sportsmen (and Sportswomen)-Conservationists:

## *Mainly Appalachian Ohio, 1988-2012*

After living in affluent places like Spring Lake on the "Jersey Shore," where Andi grew up, and Coral Gables and Fairfield, moving to Appalachia, where poverty was so evident and widespread, was something of a culture shock for the both of us. We adapted quickly, however, to our new environment. Because the per capita income of people living in the Chillicothe area was well below that of communities in which we had lived before, our modest salaries as an entry-level assistant professor and an R.N. working in a nursing home allowed us to make the down payment on a home we could never have afforded in those other places. The house we chose was on a one-acre lot in town (where the public schools were supposedly better than out in the country) and within a ten-minute walk of O.U.C.

Now with our own home, we had a feeling of security and permanence that we had lacked when we lived in the Connecticut Audubon house, with the implicit five-year timetable for vacating the building hanging over our heads. Though Carrie and Chris have grown up and moved out long ago, Andi and I still live there today. Not only did our new home in Chillicothe meet our needs on the inside, it met mine on the outside as well. I now had my own big backyard that I could let grow wild into a lush oasis for wildlife. And after a little searching, I located a nursery that supplied my old favorites, the quick-growing London plane tree, and had two planted right outside my bedroom window, where I could see them every morning when I woke up and experience the same sense of stability and connectedness to the natural world I had felt as a boy back in Forest Hills.

In addition to the more secure future I believed we now had in Chillicothe, I also found the surrounding hill country a fascinating new environment to explore. Particularly appealing were the sycamore-bordered creeks beneath high ridges that contained that great battler, the smallmouth bass, as well as the flathead catfish (*Pylodictis olivaris*), a species that can reach a weight of more than fifty pounds! There is something really exciting about catching a big fish in a small body of water, particularly if it is done on rod and reel rather than with the heavy trotlines used by most fishers in this area. For years, I was unsuccessful in this quest until I became friends with Ben Eberts, an expert fisherman and hunter, who guided me to some catfish weighing up to thirty-five pounds. And there were, of course, the proverbial "ones that got away" that probably weighed much more.

Hunting, too, in my new home of southern Ohio could be exciting, and aesthetically pleasing as well, because of the beauty of the surroundings. Sitting against a big oak on a spring morning, with shafts of sunlight just starting to penetrate down to the forest floor, and watching the hen turkey decoy out in front of us just as the old gobbler Ben has been calling suddenly comes into view and begins to strut, is an unforgettable experience. Whether I shoot well and bag the turkey or miss it entirely, which is surprisingly easy to do, we have outwitted our wary quarry and actively bonded with nature in a way that perhaps only a hunter can fully understand.

Though the Scioto River running through Chillicothe is one of the biggest streams, other than the Ohio, in the state, it is not directly on one of the four major flyways for migrating waterfowl. Nevertheless, the river valley and surrounding streams and swamps do attract a fair number of ducks and geese, and I found several special places for waterfowl hunting with decoys that I have returned to year after year.

Still, I never lost my love for brant hunting around Jones Inlet on Long Island, and I went back many times from Ohio to this most special of special places. In more recent years, I also hunted for brant and black ducks with my friend Phil Andersen, a professional guide, in the marshes across from Atlantic City, New Jersey, and for eiders with another friend and guide, Chris Whitton, on the South Shore of Massachusetts.

*After coming to O.U.C.* and getting to know the chair of the history department on the main campus, Bruce Steiner, I discovered that he had played a crucial role in accepting me for consideration for an entry-level position despite my two books, then in paperback from a university press, and my background as a full professor at the University of Miami. His reasoning seemed to be that if I was desperate enough to go after a position where the department could get me for about half of what a senior person would make (my salary was $26,000), then why not do so. If Bruce had been less flexible and had demanded that O.U.C. stay within the original criteria laid out in the announcement for the opening, I might never have been able to resume my career as a university teacher-scholar. Once again, I had been lucky in having the right person in the right place at the right time.

It is hard to exaggerate the joy I felt when I walked into my first class at O.U.C. in September 1988. I was back doing what I was meant to be doing, "work" that has never seemed like work at all. Though I was proud of having taken the gamble of going to Connecticut Audubon and doing something concrete about my conservation ethic, rather than simply talking and writing about it, I knew very well that if I had failed to get back into college teaching, I would have lost the gamble by being forced into employment I disliked or even hated simply to survive financially. If that had been my fate, I never would have forgiven myself for leaving the University of Miami.

I especially enjoyed teaching my environmental history course again, which I added to the permanent Ohio University curriculum under its new title of "American Environmental History." Now, with my experience as an "environmental professional," I think I brought a new dimension to the course that had been lacking when I taught it at the University of Miami. "Ohio History," a new course I began teaching from the first year I was at O.U.C., has also been a fascinating subject for me, particularly the long and complex Native-American history of the state, from Paleo-Indians hunting megafauna to nineteenth-century warriors fighting to keep their lands. Regrettably, however, I have never found the archaeology of the region to be as interesting as that of South Florida, because there are so few sites that bear any resemblance to their original appearance, at least before being reconstructed, unlike many in the Everglades and Ten Thousand Islands.

Because of the five years away from my academic career when I went to Connecticut Audubon, I wanted to return to my previous status as quickly as possible after arriving at O.U.C. in 1988. By 1991, I had received tenure and been promoted to associate professor, and three years later, I was back to full professor rank.

After coming to Chillicothe, I continued to participate in "eco-travel" programs like the one I inaugurated at Connecticut Audubon. I was enthralled by the national parks of Costa Rica and exotic species like the three-toed sloth and what is perhaps the most spectacular bird in the New World, the resplendent quetzal. The male is a vivid emerald and golden green with a red belly and an extremely long green tail. I spent at least an hour watching several of these breathtaking birds among huge forest trees just outside the famous Monteverde Cloud Forest Reserve.

I failed, however, to see the other best-known occupant of the Monteverde area, the golden toad. These small, brilliantly colored amphibians hadn't been spotted for quite a while by the time I visited the reserve in 1991, and the naturalist at the visitor center told me he thought they "were all gone," even though the species was not officially designated as extinct until a few years later.

At first, I simply refused to believe the naturalist. He must be mistaken, because my nature guide, published only the year before, stated that I would be able to see the toads, and they must still be alive, and nearby, because there were huge photographs of them all around the visitor center! After my initial shock, when it finally became obvious that this local wildlife expert knew what he was talking about, I became profoundly depressed. This was my first, direct experience with extinction. It was one thing to read about the process, which has been speeded up a thousand times or more by human activity, and quite another to be confronted by it here and now.

I remember slumping down in a chair in the visitor center, trying to recall the exact words of ornithologist Charles William Beebe, who pondered the true meaning of extinction in his book, *The Bird, Its Form and Function*, published in 1906. His poignant statement about evolution and the finality of a species' end affected me so deeply when I discovered it in 1973 that I had the quotation printed out, framed, and hung up in our living room. Beebe wrote:

> The beauty and genius of a work of art may be reconceived though its first material expression be destroyed; a vanished harmony may yet again inspire the composer; but when the last individual of a race of living things breathes no more, another heaven and another earth must pass before such a one can be again.

There are several possible explanations for why the golden toad became extinct, and at least two of them have to do with human activity. Air-borne pesticides and acid rain are two of the suspects, but whatever the cause, or causes, of its demise, amphibians around the world seem to be vanishing at a faster rate than any other class of vertebrates.

Another trip that fulfilled a lifelong dream was my 1993 visit to the flooded forest of the Upper Amazon Basin of eastern Ecuador with an entomologist from the main campus of Ohio University, Bill Romoser. Traveling up the Cuyabeno River in our large dugout canoes to the tiny village of the Siona-Secoya Indians was like being transported back into another time, especially when we turned a bend in the river and saw their palm-thatch covered, open-sided houses, raised up off the ground on platforms, that must be very similar to the dwellings of the pre-Columbian Indians of South Florida whom I had studied so intensely.

It was exciting, of course, to see exotic birds like the blue and yellow macaw and primitive hoatzin, several species of monkeys, and the endangered Amazon River dolphin (*Inia geoffrensis*), with its pink and white body and long narrow "beak." But the highlight of the trip was sitting in a tiny, overloaded, dugout canoe, with no more than three inches of freeboard, with Bill and our Indian woman guide, the chief angler of the village, fishing for piranha.

We were after the most dangerous species of this family, the red-bellied variety, and our "fishing outfits" consisted simply of a trimmed branch with one end of a cord tied to its tip and the other end to a long-stemmed steel hook baited with a piece of fish. After stopping in two potential deep pockets in the flooded forest, without success, the guide entered a third, just off the main channel, and thrashed the water next to the canoe with a palm branch to simulate an animal or bird that had fallen into the water and was struggling to get to shore. In probably no more than twenty seconds, a school of piranha was all around the canoe, and we were catching them as fast as we could get a bait into the water. Because of their famous teeth, the Indian woman took them off the hook *very carefully*. That night I had some for dinner and found them quite tasty, and I kept the jaws of one as a trophy from that memorable afternoon in the flooded forest along the banks of the Cuyabeno.

While the trips to Costa Rica and Ecuador were wonderful experiences, the most exciting eco-travel I did after coming to O.U.C. consisted of two return safaris to the Masai Mara-Serengeti ecosystem of Kenya and Tanzania. On one of those adventures, in Kenya in 1997, I was thrilled beyond words to witness the iconic event in the Great Migration when hundreds of wildebeest and zebra jumped into the Mara River and swam the gauntlet while crocodiles came from below and pulled them under. After the herd had crossed, I spotted a drowned zebra downstream being rolled over and over by a croc as it went about dismembering the animal.

All of these opportunities to enter the natural world in these supposedly pristine places in Costa Rica, Ecuador, Kenya, and Tanzania reconfirmed my view that nature everywhere on the planet is fragile and under siege by human beings. In Costa Rica, there was the extinction of the golden toad; in Ecuador, there was the presence of the multinational oil corporations in the Amazon region, which had already done great ecological damage; and in Kenya and Tanzania, there was the threat to the Great Migration posed by the destruction of the forests at the headwaters of the Mara River in Kenya, and the plan to build a major commercial highway across the migration path of the wildebeest and zebra in Tanzania. The firsthand knowledge I gained from visiting these endangered places became part of my American Environmental History course. As a result, I believe my students have been given a wider perspective on the worldwide environmental crisis.

Despite a heavy teaching load, I found time to engage in my other love, scholarship. Of my published work, I am most proud of the second, much more thorough, 1999 article in *The Florida Anthropologist* analyzing the enigmatic artifacts called "plummets," and the third, revised and expanded, 2001 edition of *American Sportsmen and the Origins of Conservation.*

It was at one of the conferences of the American Society for Environmental History that historian Char Miller urged Warren Slesinger, the acquisitions editor of Oregon State University Press, to consider publishing a new edition of *American Sportsmen*, which the University of Oklahoma Press had recently taken out of print. Char was one of a number of scholars across the country who had used the book in their environmental studies classes. When Oregon State consulted Hal Rothman, editor of *Environmental History*, he generously supported the idea, praising the book as "one of the seminal works in conservation history."

I would now be presented with an opportunity that few scholars ever have, a chance to make many improvements in the work. Rather than simply reprinting the book, with perhaps a new introduction, the Press's editors allowed me to create what was essentially a new work, with new pagination and two new chapters, and with additions and revisions throughout. One example is the greater development of the discussion on angling and fish conservation in the third chapter, "Conservation Begins with Wildlife." Another is the use of longer captions for many of the ninety-two illustrations in the book, providing better documentation for ideas presented in the text.

What was particularly exciting for me was the chance to reinforce my thesis on the importance of sportsmen in originating conservation by tracing the antecedents of their organized efforts back into the early years of the American Republic. The third edition's new first chapter, "Precursors of Conservation: American Sportsmen Before the Civil War," is now the longest in the book. One more issue the editors wanted me to address was whether or not the code of the sportsman and the sportsman-conservationist ideal continued to have an influence after 1901, when the main time period covered by the book ends. In order to answer that question I provided a new epilogue on Aldo Leopold, the best-known exponent of this ideal that continues to inspire recreational fishers and hunters right up to the present day.

Because of all the added material in the 2001 third edition that greatly reinforced my thesis on the central role of sport anglers and hunters in the making of conservation, *American Sportsmen and the Origins of Conservation* was reviewed along with new books in both *Environmental History* and the *Journal of Sport History*, the two main journals in my subject matter, and received highly complimentary evaluations. Besides those reviewers, other scholars seemed to be favorably impressed by the new expanded edition. Eminent historian Douglas Brinkley used the book as a major source in the researching and writing of his 2009 epic biography, *The Wilderness Warrior: Theodore Roosevelt and the Crusade for America*, as did Ken Burns and Dayton Duncan in their six-part television documentary, *The National Parks: America's Best Idea*, which aired in 2009. It was a moving experience for me to see George Bird Grinnell finally get his due as a pivotal figure in the making of early conservation. Even the title of Episode Two of the Burns-Duncan documentary came from an 1882 editorial by Grinnell in *Forest and Stream*, "Their Last Refuge," cited earlier in the present work, which I used to begin the fifth chapter of the new edition of *American Sportsmen*.

Despite the generally positive response of scholars to the book, there are still historians who have trouble accepting my interpretation, probably because they abhor the whole idea of hunting. As a former editor of *Environmental History*, Mark Cioc, recently asserted, *all* bird hunters are nothing more than "slaughterers," and those in the past who became conservationists did so only because they "were all penitent butchers."[17] In fact, as I document in *American Sportsmen*, at least two of the five individuals Cioc cites as penitent former hunters, William Temple Hornaday and George Bird Grinnell, never gave up hunting, despite what he would like to believe. As in the case of other scholars, who have argued erroneously that Aldo Leopold stopped this recreation once he saw the wrongness of it,[18] Cioc's treatment of hunting tells us more about his own sentiments than it does about the historical figures he is discussing.

Over the years, these attacks by some historians on recreational hunters and on me personally for my thesis—one scholar referred to me in print as a member of a "despised minority"[19]—have become increasingly irrelevant. For one thing, I have long since realized that trying to make clear to the committed anti-hunter how one can be both a sportsman or sportswoman and a conservationist is a waste of time. As Robert McCabe, Aldo Leopold's hunting partner, observed, "To explain the respect and reverence that a hunter feels toward his quarry is like trying to describe the color blue to a person born blind."[20]

The main reason, however, that I am not concerned about the opinions of those historians who find my thesis ethically troubling, or even downright immoral, is that very few of them seem to have any impact on those who are actively engaged in what counts most to me: the real-world, day-to-day work of conservation. To my surprise, and delight, it is those dedicated men and women in the state and federal wildlife agencies, the natural resource management programs of universities, and nongovernmental organizations like the National Wildlife Federation, Theodore Roosevelt Conservation Partnership, Boone and Crockett Club, Wildlife Management Institute, Ducks Unlimited, and National Wild Turkey Federation who have found *American Sportsmen* to be an important guide in understanding the values and dedication of those who preceded them in the struggle to conserve wildlife and habitat for—as George Bird Grinnell put it—"generations yet unborn."

It is gratifying beyond words to know that the lives of the early sportsmen-conservationists, as described in my book, have helped inspire many sport hunters and anglers in the present to even greater efforts on behalf of the natural world. The opinions about my work of people like Greg Petrich, Alaskan conservation activist and director of the Northern Sportsmen's Network, John Hitchcock of United Waterfowlers-Florida, Robert Model of the Boone and Crockett Club, and Richard McCabe of the Wildlife Management Institute, who happens to be the son of Aldo Leopold's hunting partner, mean infinitely more to me than the ideology of that group of historians who will always see recreational hunting, and increasingly fishing as well, as vile activities that one day, hopefully, will no longer exist.

I have been especially fortunate in getting to know Dick McCabe, who invited me to deliver the keynote address, "Lessons from History: The Conservation Legacy of Theodore Roosevelt," before the 67th North American Wildlife and Natural Resources Conference in Dallas in April 2002. A few years later, because of "information on Grinnell, mainly from or derived from your [my] work,"[21] Dick honored me again by arranging to have the Wildlife Management Institute's highest award given to an

*Delivering the keynote address before the 67th North American Wildlife and Natural Resources Conference on April 4, 2002. From left to right are Steve Williams, Director of the U.S. Fish and Wildlife Service; Bob McDowell, President of the International Association of Fish and Wildlife Agencies; John Woodley, Jr., from the Department of Defense (who spoke on "Conserving America's Training Lands"); and Rollin Sparrowe, President of the Wildlife Management Institute.*

*Receiving a recognition plaque from the Boone and Crockett Club for "Furthering the Conservation of Wildlife and Natural Resources in North America" on December 11, 2003 at the National Press Club in Washington, D.C., before delivering an address on the club's important place in the history of conservation. Standing on the left is Bob Model, president of the club, and on the right is George Bettas, its executive director.*

individual, the "Distinguished Service Award," renamed the "George Bird Grinnell Memorial Award for Distinguished Service to Natural Resource Conservation." In praising John Cooper, the 2010 recipient, for his work in wildlife habitat protection and restoration, the president of the institute, Steve Williams, observed, "We have no doubt that George Bird, himself, would have commended our selection of John for his stellar career to date." How wonderful that Grinnell and his vision of conservation—that it must include both aesthetic and utilitarian components and be based on a continuous, apolitical, and scientifically based approach—have been enshrined as both a model and an inspiration for active conservationists, both in today's world and the one to come.

*Back in 1975, when I published* the first edition of *American Sportsmen*, I never imagined that I would have the opportunity to know, however briefly, Dick McCabe's father, Robert McCabe, the student, disciple, and hunting partner of Aldo Leopold. The last photograph, taken by Bob, in all of the editions of my book shows Aldo examining a woodcock after a hunt they made together in the autumn of 1946, and the caption reads: "His [Aldo's] land ethic represents the highest development of the environmental responsibility inherent in the code of the sportsman." It was an exciting experience to be able to meet and interview Bob in September 1992, and discover that he confirmed that the caption I chose for his photograph of Aldo accurately reflects the central role played by fishing and hunting, particularly the latter, in the evolution of Leopold's thinking about the natural world and humankind's place in it.

At the end of the interview, Bob invited me out to Madison, Wisconsin, where he was a retired professor of wildlife ecology at the University of Wisconsin in the same department where he had obtained his master's and doctoral degrees in wildlife management under Leopold. As a fellow hunter, Bob knew that I would love to visit the special places where he and Aldo had spent so many cherished days afield in pursuit of woodcock, ruffed grouse, and pheasant. And he hoped that I would come out in the fall, so that I could be with him while he was hunting, in order that I could more fully appreciate what it must have been like to have accompanied the two men and Flick, Aldo's German short-haired pointer, on their hunts.

My problem was that the autumn hunting season is the busiest period at a university, and I put off calling up Bob until the spring of 1995 to arrange for a trip later that year. But there would be no time together with him in his and Aldo's special places, for his wife Marie told me that he had died only a short time before. It is hard to exaggerate how angry I was with myself for not immediately seizing this once-in-a-lifetime opportunity

*Bob McCabe, Aldo Leopold, and Flick, Aldo's German short-haired pointer, after a successful woodcock hunt in 1946. The tags hanging from the birds recorded field data like sex and weight.*

when it was presented to me, particularly when Marie told me about how much Bob was looking forward to going with me to the two hunters' old haunts.

Knowing how disappointed I must have been, Marie, in her great generosity, said that even though she couldn't take me to where Bob and Aldo had hunted, she could do the next best thing and arrange for a visit with the two of us and Nina Leopold Bradley, Aldo's eldest daughter, to the "Shack" property made famous in *A Sand County Almanac*. Because I knew that Bob and Aldo must have done at least some hunting there and because I had long wanted to make a pilgrimage to Aldo's most special of special places, I jumped at her offer. The warmth of Marie and Nina, as they took Andi and me around the Leopold retreat on June 20, 1995, will always be remembered.

Even before going out to the Shack, I was moved deeply when I visited Marie in her home, and she showed me a well-worn, 1975 first edition of *American Sportsmen* that Bob had held in high esteem. Of all the people in the world I would have wanted to like my book, none was as important as Aldo Leopold's hunting partner. It made me think that Aldo, too, would

*Andi, Nina Leopold Bradley, and Marie McCabe in front of Aldo Leopold's "Shack" on June 20, 1995.*

*With Marie McCabe inside the Shack on June 20, 1995.*

have judged the work a worthy contribution, and that thought made me very happy.

During our visit with Nina and Marie to the Shack, we talked about the supposed inconsistency of America's greatest nature philosopher being an avid hunter to the end. I was interested to hear what Aldo's daughter thought about this subject, which invariably comes up in any discussion of how his famous land ethic originated. During our discussion, Nina revealed a deep understanding of how hunting often leads to the development of a system of moral values regarding the species pursued that includes the need to preserve the ecosystems on which they depend. She illustrated that understanding the same year when she published "How Hunting Affected Aldo Leopold's Thinking and His Commitment to a Land Ethic."[22] According to Nina, "To him [Leopold], hunting was an expression of love for the natural world; you might even say it initiated a kind of bonding with the land." His "enjoyment of the hunt led to his later pioneering efforts in wilderness protection and toward an ethical approach to land use."

On the drive home from Wisconsin, I thought a lot about the irony of the crusade by animal-rights advocates to "save" all "sensate beings," often including even invasive species, and to put a stop to recreational hunting and fishing once and for all. If that time ever comes, we, and the natural world, will be in far greater trouble than we are today. Human beings only want to protect what they know and love, and it is the indifference to nature on the part of an increasing number of young people who have little or no experience in it that I find so worrisome. While many can enter the natural world and grow to love it without engaging in hunting or fishing, millions of other Americans require the more active involvement with nature that those activities provide.

The enlightened leadership of the Sierra Club, not an organization usually thought of as connected in any way to sport hunting and fishing, has come to realize that all nature lovers, regardless of their orientation to the natural world, must unite if we are to have a chance of hampering, let alone defeating, those on the far right of the political spectrum who possess an insatiable desire to exploit nature for immediate financial gain by deregulating industries, repealing environmental laws, and privatizing public lands. As a result of this growing sense of urgency on the part of the Sierra Club, the organization created a website in July 2007 called Sierra Sportsmen Network and honored me as the first interviewee.

According to a recent statement by the club, the network "is a countrywide, thousands-strong group of conservation-minded anglers and hunters." And the organization is not simply for adults. As the club's chairman, Carl Pope, stated when the website was announced, "We're investing in the future by actively helping [to] get more of our kids away from television and video games and into the outdoors for camping, fishing and hunting trips." What a worthy goal, one that George Bird Grinnell, Theodore Roosevelt, and Aldo Leopold would have heartily approved.

There are some positive developments, therefore, in the fight for conservation as we go on to face the growing challenges of habitat and whole ecosystem destruction by humans, invasive plants and animals, and climate change. The struggle may be intensifying, but it has been a part of the American Progressive worldview since the latter part of the nineteenth century, and I am proud to have played a role, however small, both as an activist and historian, in aiding a cause for which I have long felt a deep passion.

*After a wild turkey hunt near Lake Rupert in southern Ohio on April 25, 2007. The restoration of this species by sport hunters and their biologist allies is one of the great success stories in wildlife conservation. This was the photograph used for the interview in July 2007 on the new Sierra Club website, Sierra Sportsmen Network.*

# Epilogue:
## Reflections on a Fortunate Life

In recent years, as I approached the final stage of my life, I have found myself longing to return to the special places of my youth, like the canal between the lakes at Flushing Meadows-Corona Park near our home in New York, the beaver pond and the waters around the sunken log at the northern end of Long Lake in Maine, and the woodlot east of the Lawrenceville campus in New Jersey.

On a visit to the canal where I had spent so many wonderful days along its banks, I discovered nothing that resembled the ecologically rich waterway of the 1950s. Highways had been built over and alongside it, and all kinds of garbage, including large tarpaulins, shopping carts, and steel drums, filled it right to the surface. It had become a lifeless scene of desolation.

The beginning of a visit to Long Lake also started out badly when I looked for my beaver pond and found only a tiny remnant of what had been a good-sized body of water. According to the local historical society, the road around the northern end of Long Lake had been expanded in the 1960s, and apparently, a new highway had been built right over the top of my special place. Because I knew that the dams holding back water in beaver ponds are often washed out, and subsequently abandoned, I didn't expect to find my little world of the 1950s to be just as I had left it, but I was depressed to see how "progress" had diminished its former beauty and ecological richness.

It was now on to the second site I wanted to visit along the northern shore of Long Lake. While I was certain that the log had rotted away after all these years, I hoped to find the tiny public park intact and the large flat rock on which I had stood whenever I fished in that very special place. Happily, the park was just where I remembered it, and I was full of anticipation as I entered it from the road. Would the shoreline be unchanged, and would I find my fishing platform, the rock, still in its place at the water's edge?

As I approached the lake, I suddenly spied something I couldn't believe I was seeing. There it was, the end of the underwater log lapping the surface of the lake, looking just like it did when I had first seen it nearly half a century before. Only its position was different, for it now seemed to be farther offshore. How could such a thing be possible? Why had the log not rotted away?

It was only after I returned home to Ohio that I was able to research the question and learn that the lake water was probably cold enough to have impeded the organisms that cause wood to decay. Whatever the reason for its survival, this precious natural object from my childhood was still where I had first seen it in the summer of 1957, and I wondered if, at that very moment, there was another big pickerel lurking beneath it.

My fishing platform, the large flat rock, was also just where I had left it, and as I stood on it, looking out at the log, unexpected emotions welled up in me. The last time I was on this spot, I was a boy, with, as they say, "my whole life ahead of me." Now, I was a man in my sixties, in the last stage of that life. Had I used the intervening years well? Was I as good a man as I could have been, as a family member, friend, husband, father, teacher, conservationist, and historian? Perhaps it was because I wasn't sure of the answer to that question, or maybe it was just because I longed for my lost youth; whatever the cause, I suddenly found that the view of the log and the lake beyond had been obscured by the tears in my eyes.

As poignant as my visit was to the northern shore of Long Lake, there would be one other journey to my old special places that would surpass even that experience for the deep emotions the trip aroused in me. It was my return to Lawrenceville and the spiritual retreats east of the campus, in particular the beech woods in my favorite woodlot.

The pilgrimage began on the afternoon of Saturday, August 7, 2010, when I met Steve Laubach, a Ph.D. student in environmental history at the University of Wisconsin and a former master of biology and environmental studies at Lawrenceville. It was Steve's recent article in *The Leopold Outlook*, a publication of the Aldo Leopold Foundation, that was the catalyst for our rendezvous. By the time I read Steve's article, I knew about the incredible coincidence that Aldo had attended Lawrenceville. I was also aware of the equally amazing fact that of the five Circle Houses at the school that could have been his residence, he had lived in my own Kennedy House.

What I didn't know before reading the piece was that Aldo's correspondence contained detailed information on his own special places east of the campus, including a favorite woodlot of his that sounded like mine, as well as on his single room in Kennedy *and its location*. In my two years in the house, I had two different single rooms on separate floors; could it be that one of them was Aldo's?!

As Steve and I approached the outside of Kennedy House, I could see that it looked pretty much the same as it had in the 1950s. Even the name REIGER that my brother George had cut into the brick, with his graduation year of 1956 (after which I later scratched in my own year of 1961), was still plainly visible. I was pleased to find that the interior had also changed very little. Although the main staircase to the upper floors had been closed off, the rooms still had their windows in the same place and the original wooden molding around the doors. They were as I remembered them.

Quickly, I located the single rooms I had occupied on the second and third floors during my third- and fourth-form years, their present numbers being 204 and 311. Standing for a time in each one, I could see myself once again sitting on the bed putting together fishing tackle I would need for the next afternoon and counting out the shotgun shells I had after a crow hunt. Strangely, I remember absolutely nothing about any of the intense studying I must have done in those rooms.

Though the numbering system had changed over the years, Steve and I used Aldo's quite specific description of the location of his third-floor room to determine that it is the present 306, just around the corner and down a short hallway from my own 311. Being a talkative individual, I know that I spent a great deal of time discussing all kinds of topics with housemates who lived around me, and standing in Aldo's room, I wondered about the content of those numerous conversations. Some of them undoubtedly had to do with the same subjects that were close to his heart fifty years before, hunting, fishing, and a desire to preserve the natural world we loved so much. But the most stirring moment I experienced in Aldo's room was my sudden vision of him sitting at his desk, composing the letter to his mother (but undoubtedly also intended to be read by his sportsman-conservationist father) that I had cited in "Aldo Leopold and the Continuing Tradition of the Sportsman-Conservationist Ideal," the epilogue for the 2001 third edition of *American Sportsmen*. It was penned on March 21, 1904, and the seventeen-year-old Aldo assured his parents that "when my turn comes to have something to say and do against it [the hunting, and sale, of waterfowl in the spring] and other related matters, I am sure that nothing in my power will be lacking to the good cause."[23]

Going to Kennedy and finding Aldo's room, and mine, much as they had been when we lived in them, will always be a special memory, but the trip was only a prologue to the main event, the grand "tramp" (a favorite word of Aldo's) the next day when I returned to the special places he and I had shared as teenagers. Because of the foresight of Lawrenceville's administration in purchasing the land east of the campus to preserve as a buffer zone against future residential or commercial development and as an outdoor laboratory for students' biological studies, I hoped to find the Shipetaukin creeks, muskrat marsh, farm pond, and beech woodlot more or less as I remembered them. I was to be disappointed only in the sense that though the land had been preserved, much of it had been engulfed by an almost impenetrable tangle of invasive plants, particularly multiflora rose. I was, nevertheless, able to locate my old haunts, including my main objective, the woodlot with the ancient beech trees.

My desire to return once more to this spiritual retreat of my youth had been fueled by reading a copy of one of Aldo's letters that Steve had sent me. Writing to his mother on January 22, 1905, he described what seemed to be his most cherished special place east of the campus:

> In passing through the tract of woods down along the lower
> Shipitaquin [sic], I found four grey squirrels in one tree, and could
> have killed any or all of them during any one of the twenty minutes
> which I spent watching their antics. [He was hunting crows with his
> shotgun.] Before this I did not know … there were four squirrels in that
> whole tract, with which I am well acquainted. I call it "The Woods of
> Eerie Gloom" on account of the prevalence of beech in its boundaries,
> and have more than once gone out of my way to pass through it at
> dusk and feel the magic of the beeches. Even in the daytime there is a
> vague dimness and mystery about the beechwoods, which would be
> second only to the mystery of the pine-glooms, were they not entirely
> dissimilar. Many poets and writers have written about the pines, and
> some have succeeded, but I have never read of the "beeches in winter."

Given its location, and Aldo's description, "The Woods of Eerie Gloom" had to be *my* woodlot, the most precious of my special places at Lawrenceville. I had written down my memories of this shaded sacred grove and the great beech trees that had uplifted me in spirit before I read Aldo's letter. Now I knew that he, too, had been spiritually moved by that same woodland, and like me, had gone out of his way on return trips to campus "to pass through it at dusk and feel the magic of the beeches."

*One of the old beech trees, with Steve Laubach standing beside it, in "The Woods of Eerie Gloom," the special place Aldo Leopold and I cherished when we were at Lawrenceville.*

When I entered those woods again with Steve on that August afternoon, I experienced an indescribable surge of delight. Impulsively, I reached my arms as far as I could around one of the biggest beeches, and wondered if Aldo, like me, had sat beneath that very tree, looking for a crow flying over in range or simply watching the natural world go by. Though I had felt a strong bond with Aldo Leopold as a fellow sportsman-conservationist long before I returned to Lawrenceville, the discovery that he and I had lived down the hall from each other in Kennedy House and had chosen the same beech woods as our most cherished special place seemed to make our interconnectedness wonderfully providential in nature.

After leaving Lawrenceville and heading home to Ohio, I reflected on how lucky (or blessed) I had been to have had first Aldo Leopold and later George Bird Grinnell and Theodore Roosevelt to inspire me to keep the natural world at the center of my existence, both as a conservationist and a historian. I also thought about how fortunate I have been to have had key individuals in exactly the right spot at precisely the right moment to move me forward in the direction I wanted to go.

There was Robert Durden at Duke, who inspired me to be a college history teacher and showed me the way to begin that journey; John Mahon at the University of Florida, who took a chance and allowed me to enter the M.A. program even though I had not gone through the prescribed process for admission; William Baringer, also at the University of Florida, who did everything in his power to enable me to finish my thesis and obtain my degree in one year; Richard Leopold at Northwestern, who saved my career when I was on the verge of being forced out of the Ph.D. program; Charlton Tebeau at the University of Miami, who decided that I was the right person in a large field of candidates to replace him after his retirement; Roland Clement, president of the Connecticut Audubon Society, who thought that the organization needed a conservation historian to be their new executive director; Robert Larsen, the chairman of the society's board of directors, who made me the promise of a five-year term, a promise that he kept even though there were others on both the staff and board who wanted me out long before; Bruce Steiner, chair of the history department of Ohio University, who interceded in the search for the Chillicothe-campus historian to make sure that I would be given favorable consideration despite being "overqualified" for the position; historians Char Miller and Hal Rothman, who urged Oregon State University Press to publish a new edition of *American Sportsmen and the Origins of Conservation*, which gave me the opportunity to provide much new documentation for my thesis on how American conservation began, which in turn brought the book to a far larger audience than had seen it before; and Pamela Kraft, my colleague and friend of many years at O.U.C., who has been my research assistant, editor, and typist, and without whom I could never have finished this work or several others before it. If any of these people had not been there for me, it is difficult to see how I would have succeeded, regardless of any abilities I might possess.

Besides those individuals who have been critically important in my career, Andi, Carrie, and Chris have always supported me and given over their love, without reservations, in a way I never experienced with my parents or brothers. Indeed, one of the great sources of happiness in my life is that our children cherish each other and demonstrate none of the traits of unrelenting competitiveness and one-upmanship that have plagued my relationship with my brothers to the present day.

But despite the tension I have always felt when interacting with the males of my original family, I know very well how lucky I was to be included in their fishing and hunting adventures, which not only enhanced my love for the natural world but also gave me the experience to understand the subculture of anglers and hunters, both in the past and the present, and how their avocations engendered a commitment to conservation. As we have seen, my own intimate involvement in these sports primed me for the teachings of Leopold, Grinnell, and Roosevelt, whom I emulated in my efforts to become a complete sportsman-conservationist.

While neither Carrie nor Chris has ever shown much interest in hunting, both like fishing and are knowledgeable about, and committed to, preserving the natural world. What is particularly gratifying to their parents is that they are dedicated to public service, as shown by their career paths. Carrie is an elementary school teacher and Chris a clinical psychologist working with schools to provide a more harmonious environment for all involved.

In looking back from the vantage point of a man nearly seventy years old, it is extraordinary to think about everything I have been privileged to see and do. I found a calling, the teaching and writing of history, with a focus on environmental history, and a cause, wildlife conservation, and managed to combine them for my life's work. Along the way, I have had innumerable adventures in special places, from the vacant lot near our home in Forest Hills where I crawled through the tall grass hunting for grasshoppers and other insects, to the hillside behind Lake Rupert in southern Ohio where I waited for the approaching gobbler to finally show himself.

Through all the years, the one constant in my life has been the joy I have experienced from being an active participant in the natural world. By escaping into nature, I have been given the spiritual renewal we all seek, but many of us never find.

1. Where there is any chance of confusion over a species' identification, I have provided the scientific name.
2. Gifford Pinchot, *Just Fishing Talk* (New York and Harrisburg, Pennsylvania: Telegraph Press, 1936), 163-64, cited in John F. Reiger, *"Gifford Pinchot with Rod and Reel"/"Trading Places: From Historian to Environmental Activist"—Two Essays in Conservation History* (Milford, Pennsylvania: Grey Towers Press, 1994), 10-11.
3. Aldo Leopold, *Round River: From the Journals of Aldo Leopold.* Edited by Luna B. Leopold (Minocqua, Wisconsin: NorthWord Press, 1991), 186. First published in 1953.
4. *Ibid.,* 245.
5. Samuel R. Slaymaker II, *Five Miles Away: The Story of the Lawrenceville School* (Princeton, New Jersey: Princeton University Press, 1985), 216.
6. In later years the Corps of Engineers tried to undo some of the damage it had done earlier by restoring the marshes, and it has been fairly successful in this effort.
7. Richard H. Pough, *Audubon Water Bird Guide: Water, Game and Large Land Birds* (Garden City, New York: Doubleday & Company, 1951), 206.
8. Frank C. Bellrose, *Ducks, Geese & Swans of North America* (Harrisburg, Pennsylvania: Stackpole Books, 1976), 40.
9. Albert Fein, *Frederick Law Olmsted and the American Environmental Tradition* (New York: George Braziller, 1972), 168.
10. Joy Schaverien, "Boarding School: The Trauma of the 'Privileged' Child," *Journal of Analytical Psychology*, Vol. 49 (2004), 684.
11. *Ibid.,* 686.
12. I am grateful to Thomas L. Altherr and Wiley C. Prewitt, Jr., for bringing this important phrase, and concept, from Faulkner to my attention.
13. Curt Meine, *Aldo Leopold: His Life and Work* (Madison: University of Wisconsin Press, 1988), 526.
14. Robert A. McCabe, *Aldo Leopold: The Professor* (Madison, Wisconsin: Rusty Rock Press, 1987), 124.
15. Pough, *Audubon Water Bird Guide*, 105.
16. McCabe, *Aldo Leopold*, 124.

17. Mark Cioc, *The Game of Conservation: International Treaties to Protect the World's Migratory Animals* (Athens: Ohio University Press, 2009), 63 and 65.

18. John F. Reiger, *American Sportsmen and the Origins of Conservation*. Third, revised and expanded, edition (Corvallis: Oregon State University Press, 2001), 194-95.

19. Thomas R. Dunlap, "Sport Hunting and Conservation, 1880-1920," *Environmental Review*, Vol. 12 (Spring, 1988), 58. For my response, see "John F. Reiger's Commentary on Thomas R. Dunlap's Article, 'Sport Hunting and Conservation, 1880-1920'," *ibid.* (Fall, 1988), 94-96.

20. McCabe, *Aldo Leopold*, 124.

21. Richard E. McCabe to Reiger, e-mail of June 29, 2006.

22. *Proceedings of the Fourth Annual Governor's Symposium on North America's Hunting Heritage* (Minnetonka, Minnesota: Wildlife Forever, 1995), 10-13.

23. On page 191 of *American Sportsmen and the Origins of Conservation* (2001), I incorrectly stated that Aldo addressed this letter to his father.

# Author's Selected Bibliography

BOOKS

*American Sportsmen and the Origins of Conservation.* Third, revised and expanded, edition. Corvallis: Oregon State University Press, 2001. Earlier editions with different publishers in 1975 and 1986.

*"Gifford Pinchot with Rod and Reel"/"Trading Places: From Historian to Environmental Activist"—Two Essays in Conservation History.* Milford, Pennsylvania: Grey Towers Press, 1994.

Editor and commentator. *The Passing of the Great West: Selected Papers of George Bird Grinnell.* Norman: University of Oklahoma Press, 1985. Earlier editions with different publishers in 1972 and 1976.

ARTICLES IN PROFESSIONAL JOURNALS

"Pathbreaking Conservationist: George Bird Grinnell (1849-1938)," *Forest History Today*, Spring/Fall, 2005 (published in Fall 2006), 16-19.

"Lessons from History: The Conservation Legacy of Theodore Roosevelt," *Theodore Roosevelt Association Journal*, Vol. XXV (2003), 10-15.

"Artistry, Status, and Power: How 'Plummet'-Pendants Probably Functioned in Pre-Columbian Florida—and Beyond," *The Florida Anthropologist*, Vol. 52 (December 1999), 227-40.

"Academic Historians and Hunting: A Call for More and Better Scholarship" (coauthored with Thomas L. Altherr), *Environmental History Review*, Vol. 19 (Fall 1995), 39-56.

"'Part of My Life ... Part of My Identity': Hunting, Fishing, and the Development of Jimmy Carter's Conservation Ethic," *Journal of Sport History*, Vol. 20 (Spring 1993), 43-47.

"'Plummets'—An Analysis of a Mysterious Florida Artifact," *The Florida Anthropologist*, Vol. 43 (December 1990), 227-39.

"John F. Reiger's Commentary on Thomas R. Dunlap's Article, 'Sport Hunting and Conservation, 1880-1920,'" *Environmental History Review*, Vol. 12 (Fall 1988), 94-96.

Editor, "With Grinnell and Custer in the Black Hills," *Discovery: The Magazine of the Yale Peabody Museum of Natural History*, Vol. 20 (1987), 16-21.

"An Analysis of Four Types of Shell Artifacts from South Florida," *The Florida Anthropologist*, Vol. 34 (March 1981), 4-20.

"*Strombus* Celt Caches in Southeast Florida" (coauthored with Robert S. Carr), *The Florida Anthropologist*, Vol. 33 (June 1980), 66-74.

"The Making of Aboriginal Shell Tools: Clues from South Florida," *The Florida Anthropologist*, Vol. 32 (December 1979), 130-38.

"A Dedication to the Memory of George Bird Grinnell, 1849-1938," *Arizona and the West*, Vol. 21 (Spring 1979), 1-4.

"Florida After Secession: Abandonment by the Confederacy and Its Consequences," *Florida Historical Quarterly*, Vol. 50 (October 1971), 128-42.

"Deprivation, Disaffection and Desertion in Confederate Florida," *Florida Historical Quarterly*, Vol. 48 (January 1970), 279-98.

"Secession of Florida from the Union—A Minority Decision?" *Florida Historical Quarterly*, Vol. 46 (April 1968), 358-68.

OTHER PUBLICATIONS

"Interview with Dr. John Reiger, Sportsman, Conservationist, and Author," by Jon Schwedler of the Sierra Sportsmen Network (July 2007), http://www.sierraclub.org/sierrasportsmen/

"An Inspiration to Us All: The Boone and Crockett Club's Place in the History of American Conservation," *Fair Chase*, Vol. 19 (Fall 2004), 50-57. An abridged version of an address delivered to the Boone and Crockett Club at the National Press Club in Washington, D.C., on December 11, 2003.

"The Merging of Sport, Art, and Conservation in Late Nineteenth-Century America," in William V. Mealy and Peter Friederici, editors, *Value in American Wildlife Art: Proceedings of the 1992 Forum* (Jamestown, New York: Roger Tory Peterson Institute of Natural History, 1992), 44-51.

"Wildlife, Conservation, and the First Forest Reserve," in Harold K. Steen, editor, *The Origins of the National Forests* (Durham, North Carolina: Forest History Society, 1992), 106-21.

"The Sportsman Factor in Early Conservation," in Roderick Frazier Nash, editor, *American Environmentalism: Readings in Conservation History* (New York: McGraw-Hill Publishing Company, 1990), 52-58.

ACKNOWLEDGMENTS

*During the several years of working* on this autobiography, I have, of course, received the help of many individuals. First and foremost is Mary Elizabeth Braun, who not only proposed the idea for the project, but kept after me until it was completed. She also selected two anonymous reviewers, whose criticisms proved invaluable in revising the original manuscript. Mary's colleagues at the Press, Jo Alexander, Tom Booth, and Micki Reaman, later provided expert guidance throughout the publication process.

Ohio University, too, was supportive. In addition to some reductions in my regular teaching load, I received a summer research grant and a sabbatical for the entire 2010-2011 academic year. My colleague at O.U.C., Denny Fowler, gave me crucial assistance during the final preparation of the manuscript.

There are a number of people with whom I checked the accuracy of my remembrances, or whose thinking about conservation helped clarify my own, who are not already cited in the text, notes, or bibliography. They are Bill Lane, Bob Passantino, Phil Jordan, Ned Allen, Jacqueline Haun, Zoe Vybiral-Bauske, Amy McDonald, E. Carter Burrus, Jr., Dick Vaughan, Chris Madson, Worth Mathewson, Mary Zeiss Stange, Jim Posewitz, Paul Schullery, Hugh Grinnell, Neil Hammerschlag, and Dave Golowenski.

I am particularly grateful to the Aldo Leopold Foundation of Baraboo, Wisconsin for the use of Leopold's Lawrenceville letters, which were transcribed by the school's students under the supervision of Kevin Mattingly and Steve Laubach, with funding from Edmund Stanley. Kevin, who is now dean of faculty, also provided generous financial support for Steve's and my 2010 return trip to Lawrenceville.

Whit Streicher did the excellent photographic reproduction for the book, often enhancing the pictures beyond what I thought was possible. I am indebted to Polly Burroughs, the great-niece of George Bird Grinnell, for her gift of the photograph of an elderly Grinnell in his duck blind, and to the late Bob McCabe for permission to reproduce the picture of him and Aldo Leopold in Bob's book, *Aldo Leopold: The Professor*, published in 1987.

Finally, I would like to thank Grey Towers Press for permission to reprint excerpts from my little book, *"Gifford Pinchot with Rod and Reel"/"Trading Places: From Historian to Environmental Activist"—Two Essays in Conservation History*, published in 1994.